# CONSUMPTION, POVERTY AND INEQUALITY

# CONSUMPTION, POVERTY AND INEQUALITY

*By*

**Dr. Prasant Sarangi**
*Lecturer*
*School of Management*
*Apeejay Institute of Technology*
*1, Institutional Area*
*Greater Noida*
*(Uttar Pradesh)*
*&*
**Dr. Bijaya Kumar Panda**
*Reader*
*P.G. Dept. of Economics*
*Berhampur University*
*Bhanja Bihar*
*Berhampur–760 007*
*(Orissa)*

**DISCOVERY PUBLISHING HOUSE PVT. LTD.**
**NEW DELHI-110 002**

First Published - 2008

Reprinted - 2016

ISBN: 978-81-8356-264-5



**Consumption, Poverty and Inequality**

*Published by:*

DISCOVERY PUBLISHING HOUSE PVT. LTD.
4383/4B, Ansari Road, Darya Ganj
New Delhi-110 002 (India)
*Phone*: +91-11-23279245, 43596064-65
*Fax*: +91-11-23253475
*E-mail*: discoverypublishinghouse@gmail.com
sales@discoverypublishinggroup.com
*web*: www.discoverypublishinggroup.com

*Printed at:*
Infinity Imaging Systems
Delhi

# PREFACE

There is renewed interest all over the world on the studies of Poverty, Inequality and Household Consumption pattern. This interest has arisen from the growing realisation in both developing and developed countries that fruits of rapid economic growth achieved, have not reached the poor and the vulnerable sections of the society and to some extent, growth has ever accentuated their problems. In India, eradication of poverty and reduction of economic inequality have been among the important objectives of each of our Five Year Plans and the Draft Fifth Plan goes even further in this direction. But as compared to the rhetoric of the plan documents and public policy pronouncements, concrete achievements not have been realised. So it is pertinent to look at these issues in right direction.

Poverty as a concept is closely related to inequality. Given the average income level, a high level of inequality reflected by the usual measures will tend to be associated with a higher level of poverty. Furthermore, the so-called 'Poverty Line' may some times be drawn in the light of the socially accepted 'minimal' standard of living, and the latter can be influenced by the average income level, so that poverty measures, thus, defined, may catch an aspect of relative *inequality* as well.

Household budgets have often been studied for a variety of purposes such as constructing cost of living indices, demand forecasting, analysing consumption and demand patterns, measuring absolute poverty, disparity in the level of living etc. Demand analysis is based on both time series and cross-section data on average per capita quantity consumption/average per capita income or total expenditure and prices. Cross-section household data are generally used for constructing cost of living indices and Engel curve analysis, which reflects the consumption pattern and the living standards of the households. Cross-section data are also used for measuring the level of poverty and disparities in the level of living. Finally, the continuing cross section or panel data on household budget are helpful in studying dynamic aspects of consumer behaviour. The scope of the study is limited to cross-section and time-series analysis of household budget data of six quinquennial rounds conducted by the National Sample Survey Organisation (NSSO) during the period from 1972-73 to 1999-00 using appropriate models for ascertaining the magnitude of income inequality and the level of incidence of poverty and the consumption pattern of the state vis-a-vis the country.

It is hard to limit the horizon of the study of household consumption as there are numerous factors, viz. the economic status, family size and its composition, occupational structure, level of education, social attitude, climatic and regional factors, religious beliefs, social customs etc. which influence household consumption and also the magnitude of inequality in living standards and the level of incidence of poverty among different section of the population. These factors are reflected with sub-factors categorising into quantitative and qualitative factors. India being a nation of great complexity, it seems impossible to study household consumption taking into account all its dimensions. We confine our attempts only to few important dimensions that are absolutely essential. The present study *'Consumption, Poverty and Inequality'* covers household consumption of four different occupation groups in the rural sector of Orissa for fourteen broad food items and non-food items groups using eleven different functional form of Engel curves within its scope.

The composition of a household always influences its level of living. Two households with the same income/total expenditure level and family size but differing in their composition may not necessarily be in the same level of economic welfare. So, the present study seeks to incorporate household composition in the analysis of household consumption, measurement of absolute poverty and economic disparities estimating specific and overall unit consumer scales using the unit record data of 600 households collected by the NSSO during its 55$^{th}$ round (1999-00) for the state.

A popular way of looking at the level of living of the people in the country is to look at the state of inequality in the distribution of income and the level of poverty by analysing their consumption pattern. One of the major curiosities in the Indian economy is to define and estimate a poverty line and to determine the percentage of people below it. There are number of methods to estimate poverty line and number of indices to measure the magnitude of inequality and incidence of poverty. The scope of the study is limited to some popular and widely used traditional, modern (non-ethical) and the recently developed ethical measures of poverty and to some positive and normative measure of inequality for estimating the disparity in the living standard of the people in the state.

The study is organised into seven chapters. Chapter-I is the introduction. It deals with the overall methodology of the study, objective and scope of the study, data and models used, the hypotheses formulated for testing in the study. Chapter-II provides a brief review of studies on household consumption pattern, inequality in living standards and different aspects of poverty. The procedure of estimating unit consumer (adult equivalence) scales both 'specific' and 'overall' is examined and estimated in Chapter-III. Chapter-IV reveals the household consumption pattern of different food and non-food item group in the state vis-a-vis the country. Chapter-V deals with the measurement and interpretation of different inequality measures both in per capita and per unit terms in the rural areas of the state and the level of inequality in the country whereas Chapter-VI is devoted for the estimation of poverty indices both in per capita and per unit terms to ascertain the incidence, depth and severity of poverty. Finally, Chapter-VII is the summary of the findings of the study.

**Authors**

# CONTENTS

# 1

# INTRODUCTION

## 1.1 Introduction

The linkages between economic growth, poverty, inequality and employment are complex and crucial for policy formulation especially in developing countries. The evidence across developing countries indicates that rapid and sustained economic growth is the quickest and most effective way of reducing poverty and inequality. This is because, on average, growth of income of the poor has been found to be very similar to the growth of mean income. However, there is substantial variation around the average income, indicating that the same growth in mean income has more or less yield in term of reduction poverty and inequality. This simply means that growth can be more or less pro-poor. The East Asian countries have been among the most successful in achieving sustained pro-poor growth through a combination of outward-looking, labour-intensive industrialisation, initially egalitarian income distributions, fiscal prudence, broad-based and effective human development policies and flexible labour markets. In these countries, rapid employment growth in manufacturing has been a powerful transmission mechanism between economic growth and reduction poverty and inequality. The employment intensity and poverty reducing potency of economic growth has been weaker in South Asian and Latin American countries. This is due to a less pro-poor pattern past growth in Latin American countries and a more unequal distribution of income in South Asian countries (Khan, 2001; Islam, 2004 and World Bank, 2006).[1]

To understand the impact of economic growth on poverty, it is also important to know the trends of inequality and the inequality effect which has the tendency to destabilise the positive effect of economic growth. If economic growth is accompanied by a decline in inequality, poor benefit more than the non-poor. This situation is described in the literature as 'pro-poor growth' (Kakwani and Perina, 2000). Even when inequality rises, observed poverty may still decline. In this case growth effect dominates the inequality effect i.e. the extent of fall in poverty due to growth is larger than the rise in poverty due to rise in inequality. Growth effect which dominates over the inequality effect caused poverty to decline during eighties and nineties (Brahmamurthy and Mitra, 2003). In India inequality was rising till 1978 and then it decreased in the year 1983. After the economic reforms, these fluctuations became more intensive. The rural inequality started declining while the urban inequality started rising during nineties (Deaton and Dreze, 2002).

Poverty and Inequality were the major issues that figured importantly in policy debate during nineties when several developing countries launched the policy of Liberalisation, Privatisation and Structural reforms. The experience of many of the Latin American and African countries where poverty and inequality have sharpened due to the programme of Globalisation, which weighed heavily on the mind of the Indian planners. There were serious apprehensions that India might experience similar trends in poverty and inequality after adopting the New Economic Policy since 1991. As the country had more than thirty-five per cent of the population below poverty line during nineties, and for the rural area in particular the situation was even worse, further deterioration of the situation would create serious social tension and threaten democratic structure of the country.

Poverty is a feeling of deprivation. Deprivation may be absolute or relative. Thus, there arises the notion of absolute and relative poverty. Poverty is a relative measure because a person would be regarded as poor with reference to the society in which he lives. The relative poverty refers to a man's relative deprivation in the society. He may be above a minimum standard of living but below the level of standard of living of many others in the society

(Meade, 1972). But in a low-income society, the relative definition would not hold because even a person having a medium level of income may be living in semi-starvation conditions. This suggests that when there is existence of poverty among the masses then the issue needs to be studied from an absolute angle. For studying the incidence of poverty in the developing countries, it is imperative to estimate an absolute poverty line.[2]

The World Bank defines poverty as the inability of people to attain a minimum standard of living. This definition gives rise to three pertinent questions: i) how do we measure standard of living ii) what is meant by minimum standard of living iii) how can we express the extent of poverty in a single measure. The most obvious measure of living standard is an individual's real income or expenditure. The same level of real income or expenditure in different countries or different regions of a country, however, may be associated with different level of nutrition, life expectancy, infant mortality, and so on. Measure of living standard based on per capita income, therefore, should be supplemented by other measures that include these variables. The United Nations Development Programme (UNDP) has estimated a human poverty index taking into account some of the above factors. The other way to identify the poor from the non-poor is to provide a minimum acceptable level of consumption. There are two main ways of setting a consumption poverty line to measure poverty and make comparison across countries: (i) the purchasing-power parity rate popularly known as PPP method and (ii) the food energy method. The World Bank estimated the revised International poverty line in 1999 at $392.88 per person per annum or $ 30.42 per person per month or $1.08 per person per day in 1993 PPP rates.[3] The food energy method of setting a consumption poverty line is one way of dealing with this problem by fixing a minimum internationally agreed calorie intake line, and converting consumption bundles into calorie intakes using the nutritional value of consumption of food items with zero nutritional value to the consumption of non-food items. The problem with these methods is that the consumers in different countries may choose different combination of food, which requires different income to meet nutritional requirements. Commodities, which are regarded as optional extras in some countries, may be necessities in others.

India has a plural society with people of different religion, caste, social and economic groups. Social and economic factors are the important determinants of standard of living and needs to be important ingredients in policy mechanism to reduce poverty. Unbalanced economic development among the social classes and across regions leads to tensions and conflicts in society (UNDP, 2004). The socio-economic and regional indicator which provides a macro level scenario of standard of living of different sections of the society and across different regions of the state/country, therefore assumes great significance. Hence, the identification of the poor and measurement of poverty among the social classes and across regions has received considerable attention. Generally, poverty refers to a state of existence in which the overall needs of the individuals are not satisfied due to lack of enough purchasing power. In order to measure the proportion of poor below the poverty line, the state of poverty is to be clearly specified. Then, the poverty line signifies the minimum level or a level to satisfy minimum biological as well as educational, cultural, social, regional and other needs.

Regional as well as social inequality and poverty are the most important problems facing our country since its independence. Right from the advent of Indian Planning, the Centre as well as the State Government has implemented a good number of developmental and anti-poverty schemes with the avowed objectives of reducing poverty, and regional and social inequalities in the country so that the benefits of economic growth would be fairly distributed over the regions and among different sections of the society. But, unfortunately all these developmental measures could not yield desired results. While there has been some reduction of poverty, the social class inequalities and regional imbalances perpetuated between and within the States, which causes serious concern to planners and statesmen.

The debate on poverty trend in rural India during nineties is inconclusive. There is wide variation in the incidence of poverty among the states. Some states are extremely poor and their macro economic performance is not comparable with the relatively rich states. The inter-state disparity in rural per capita consumption expenditure has widened during the post-reform period. Also there is variation in the changes in incidence of rural poverty among the states. The interdependence of state level per capita consumption expenditure growth and poverty is not very clear. Growth is not evenly distributed within the states. Some states have experienced higher rural inequality than the others. The state level trend of rural-urban disparity and rural-urban polarization is showing no relation with the trend of poverty. The interdependence of rural poverty and rural development in the states of India needs further examination during the period of globalisation.

The incidence of poverty is higher in rural areas than the urban areas. It would be important to discuss the rural-urban disparity during nineties. The rural-urban inequality in income and consumption expenditure exists in India since independence and even before that. During nineties this disparity has been sharpened after the new economic policy was adopted. The rural economy doesn't show any impressive growth in comparison to the urban economy during this period. In the rural areas of some poorer states, there has been virtually no increase in per capita expenditure between 1993-94 and 1999-2000 (Deaton and Dreze, 2002)[4]. Hence, there is disparity in incidence of poverty in rural and urban areas. The differences in inequality, poverty and mean per capita consumption expenditure are rising over the period 1993-94 to 1999-00 (Jha, 2000). The disparity has not only widened in income and consumption expenditure but also reflected in social sector development (Pradhan, Roy, Saluja and Venkataram, 2000). Orissa was having highest poverty ratio during 1983 and Bihar was in second rank. In 1993-94, the reduction of poverty ratio in Orissa was higher than that of Bihar which pulls Orissa down to the second position and Bihar went up to rank of highest poverty ratio in 1993-94. Again in 1999-2000 the reduction of rural poverty in Orissa became very slow and now Orissa is having the highest poverty ratio in rural areas. Punjab and Haryana are the two rich states in India having lowest rural poverty ratio among the major states in India. There is a huge gap between Punjab and Orissa in rural poverty ratio. In this scenario, the present study is an attempt to explore the pattern of consumption; the magnitude of inequality in the standard of living; and the level of incidence, depth and severity of poverty in India and its constituent major states in general and in the state of Orissa in particular.

Orissa located on the East Coast of India is a backward state characterized by persistent poverty, underemployment, low per capita income, inadequate development of socio-economic infrastructure, and recurrent natural calamities which have ravaged the state over the last four decades. The State Gross National Product (SGNP) at constant prices (1993-94) of Orissa increased from Rs. 8,536.22 crore in 1993-94 to Rs. 28,685.68 crore in 2003-04 registering an annual growth rate of 4.46 per cent over the period which is much below the national growth rate. The state comprises of 36.08 million people which accounts for 3.58 per cent of the population of the country. Nearly 87 per cent of its population live in rural areas and depend mostly on agriculture for their livelihood. Agriculture and its allied sector continued to be the main stay of the state economy with a contribution of about 25.97 per cent of the state domestic product during 2003-04 at 1993-94 prices. The decennial growth rate of population of the state during 1991-2001 was 16.25 per cent as against 20.06 per cent in the previous decade. This decline in the growth rate of population in the state may be attributed to the rise in the literacy rate, effective dissemination of the masses about the benefits of small family and partly high IMR. The density of population was 203 persons per square km in 1991 which increased to 236 per square km in 2001. The urban population increased from 13.4 in 1991 per cent to 14.99 per cent in 2001. On the literacy front, the achievements have been remarkable. It has been noticed that the literacy rate increased from 49.09 per cent in 1991 to 63.1 per cent in 2001 as against the increase from 52.10 per cent to 64.8 per cent at the national level. The male and female literacy rates were 63.1 per cent and 34.7 per cent in 1991, which increased to 75.3 per cent and 50.5 per cent respectively in 2001.

## 1.2 Scope of the Study

Household budgets have often been studied for a variety of purposes such as constructing cost of living indices, demand forecasting, analysing consumption and demand patterns, measuring absolute poverty, disparity in the level of living etc. Demand analysis is based on both time series and cross-section data on average per capita quantity consumption/average per capita income or total expenditure and prices. Cross-section household data are generally used for constructing cost of living indices and Engel curve analysis, which reflects the consumption pattern and the living standards of the households. Cross-section data are also used for measuring the level of poverty and disparities in the level of living. Finally, the continuing cross section or panel data on household budget are helpful in studying dynamic aspects of consumer behaviour. The scope of the study is limited to cross-section and time-series analysis of household budget data of six quinquennial rounds conducted by the National Sample Survey Organisation (NSSO) during the period from 1972-73 to 1999-00 using appropriate models for ascertaining the magnitude of income inequality; the level of incidence of poverty and the consumption pattern of the state vis-a-vis the country.

It is hard to limit the horizon of the study of household consumption as there are numerous factors, viz. the economic status, family size and its composition, occupational structure, educational standards, social attitude, climatic and regional factors, religious beliefs, social customs, etc., which influence household consumption and also the magnitude of inequality in living standards and the level of incidence of poverty on different section of the population. These factors are reflected with sub-factors categorising into quantitative and qualitative factors. India being a nation of great complexity, it seems impossible to study household consumption taking into account all its dimensions. We confine our attempts only to few important dimensions that are absolutely essential. The present study covers household consumption of four different occupation groups of the rural sector of the state for fourteen broad food items and non-food items groups using five different two and three parameter functional form of Engel curves within its scope.

The composition of a household always influences its level of living. Two households with the same income/total expenditure level and family size but differing in their composition may not necessarily be in the same level of economic welfare. So, the present study seeks to incorporate household composition in the analysis of household consumption, measurement of absolute poverty and economic disparities using the unit record data of 600 households collected by the NSSO during its 55$^{th}$ round (1999-00) for the state.

A popular way of looking at the level of living of the people in the country is to look at the state of inequality in the distribution of income and the level of poverty by analysing their consumption pattern. One of the major curiosities in the Indian economy is to define and estimate a poverty line and to determine the percentage of people below it. There are number of methods to estimate poverty line and number of indices to measure the magnitude of inequality and incidence of poverty. The scope of the study is limited to some popular and widely used traditional, modern (non-ethical) and the recently developed ethical measures of poverty and to some positive and normative measure of inequality to estimate the incidence of poverty and magnitude of inequality in the state.

## 1.3 Objectives of the Study

The present study is an attempt to take into account some vital aspects of consumption pattern, inequality in the living standards and the level of poverty in the state as well as in the country particularly in the rural areas. The objectives of the study are as follows:

1. To estimate the Engel ratio and elasticities and to explore the extent of inter-sectoral and inter-occupational variations in household consumption pattern of the state using the Dummy Variable Interaction Method (DVIM).
2. To classify fourteen broad item groups as necessity, luxury and inferior on the basis of Engel elasticities estimated at mean level of specific item expenditure and total consumption expenditure from the most suitable functional form of Engel curves.
3. To incorporate household size and its composition in the measurement of inter-sectoral and inter-occupational variations in the consumption pattern, magnitude of inequality and absolute poverty in the rural areas of the state.
4. To measure the inequalities in the living standards among different occupation groups in the rural areas

of the state, some widely used positive and normative inequality are estimated separately in per capita and per unit adult equivalence scale for each occupation group.

5. There are two distinct methods for the specification of the poverty line: the direct method and the indirect method. The direct method specifying the poverty line with an adequate intake of calories and nutrients. The indirect or income or expenditure method which specify the poverty line with the ability to meet the basic needs. In this study, the cost of calorie function proposed by Greer and Thorbecke, 1986 (which is an indirect method) is used for the estimation of the poverty lines separately for each occupation both in per capita and per unit terms (taking into account the nutritional requirements of households differing in age and sex).

6. To ascertain the magnitude, incidence, intensity and the severity of poverty among different occupation groups in the rural areas of the state, a number of ratios and indices are estimated separately in per capita and per unit terms for each occupation group. The widely used poverty measures estimated in the study include the traditional measures, modern non-ethical measures like Sen index, FGT index and Takayama index and ethical measures like Clark, Hemming and Ulph (CHU) and the Pyatt indices.[5]

## 1.4 Methodology

This section provides a brief description of NSS sample design for collection of data on household expenditure. It also includes the data, models, software used and hypothesis formulated and to be tested in the study.

### *1.4.1 Data*

The study is based on both published and unpublished household survey data on consumption expenditure collected by the NSSO during its quinquennial surveys on consumption expenditure. The sampling design for the selection of households is a two-stage stratified, the first stage unit of selection being the sample villages and the second stage units are the households. Sample villages are selected by circular systematic sampling according to probability proportional to population in the form of two independent interpenetrating sub-samples of equal size. Then, the households are selected systematically using specified intervals and random start.

During 55th round, 296 sample villages and 88 urban blocks were selected for the survey in Orissa covering 3535 rural and 1040 urban households of the state. The unpublished unit record data for the study has been collected from the NSS inquiry schedule 1.0 for 600 rural households covering 60 sample villages which include at least two sample villages from each stratum scattered over the three NSS regions (viz., Coastal, Northern and Southern) of the state surveyed during 55th round. The households are then grouped into four occupation categories viz., (i) salary and regular wage earners households (type-A), (ii) small business and trader households (type-B), (iii) cultivators households (type-C), (iv) agriculture and other labour households (type-D) (Table-1.1).

**Table—1.1**

**Details of occupational categories**

| | | | |
|---|---|---|---|
| I. | Salary and wage earner household (type-A) | 1. | Professional, technical and related workers. |
| | | 2. | Administrative, executive and managerial workers |
| | | 3. | Clerical and related workers |
| II. | Small business and trader household (type-B) | 1. | Shopkeepers, traders and hawkers, retail traders and small merchants. |
| III. | Cultivator household (type-C) | 1. | Cultivators owing land more than 2.5 hectares. |
| IV. | Agriculture and other labour household (type-D) | 1. | Small cultivators, carpenters, shoemakers, brick-layers, construction workers, goldsmith, blacksmith, spinner, weaver, dyers, animal rearers, tailors, fisherman, hunter, logger related workers; service workers, production and related workers; Transport equipment operators; and all other workers. |

### 1.4.2 *Models*

For Engel curve analysis in Chapter-IV, we have used six two-parameter Engel function viz. Linear (L), Double-log (DL), Semi-log (SL), Exponential (EX), Log-inverse (LI) and Hyperbolic (HYP) and five three-parameter Engel functions viz., Parabolic (P), Log-parabolic (LP), Log-log inverse (LLI), Log-quadratic (LQ) and Semi-log-inverse (SLI). Both the dependent and independent variables of the Engel functions are measured in per capita terms ignoring household composition and the possibility of economies of scale due to variation in household size. To investigate inter-sectoral and inter-occupational variations of household consumption, the Dummy Variable Iteration Model (DVIM) has been used to test different hypotheses of inter-sectoral and inter-occupational homogeneity. The parameters of the Engel functions are estimated by the method of Weighted Least Squares (WLS) using grouped NSS data of 55$^{th}$ round (1999-2000).

For estimating the specific and income unit consumer scales in chapter-IIII, the most popular Singh and Nagar's model (1973), a modified and refined version of Prais and Houthakker's model, has been estimated from unit record data of 600 rural households of Orissa. The unit consumer scales for six different age-sex categories are estimated separately for each occupation group by the well-known iterative procedure proposed by Singh and Nagar. In this model all the eleven Engel functions mentioned above are tried and a most suitable form for each item group is chosen at each stage of iterative procedure.

To measure the inequalities in the living standards among different occupation groups in the rural areas of the state, we have used some positive measures like coefficient of variation, squared coefficient of variation, log-variance, Theil's entropy and second measure, relative mean deviation and the most important normative measure of Atkinson's inequality index for different values of the inequality aversion parameter. We have used the cost of calorie function proposed by Greer and Thorbecke (1986 for the estimation of the poverty lines separately for each occupation group both in per capita and per unit terms taking into account the nutritional requirements of households differing in age and sex. To ascertain the magnitude, incidence, intensity and the severity of poverty among different occupation groups in the rural areas of the state, the traditional measures like head count ratio, poverty intensity ratio and poverty gap index; some modern (non-ethical) indices like Sen index, FGT index and Takayama index; and the recent ethical measures like Atkinson; Clark, Hemming and Ulph (CHU) and Pyatt indices are estimated separately in per capita and per unit terms for each occupation group.

### *1.4.3 Computer Software*

For estimating the parameters of two-parameter and three-parameter Engel functions and the different 'F' statistics of the Dummy Variable Iteration Model, we have used an econometric software-Limdep version-7. For estimating the specific and income unit consumer scales, inequality indices and poverty indices, we have developed programs through a statistical package—SPSS and an integrated spread sheet package—Lotus Smartsuite version-9.

### *1.4.4 Hypothesis*

The following hypotheses are formulated for testing in the present study:

1. No unique Engel curve suffices for the complete range of consumer goods in the rural and urban sector of the state. Urban elasticities are lower than rural elasticities for food items and the reverse is the case for non-food items.

2. The Engel elasticities are less than unity for food items and greater than unity for non-food items in both the sectors.

3. There are significant inter-sectoral and inter-occupational variations in the consumption pattern of different items of consumption.

4. The specific and income unit consumer scales for different food and non-food item groups vary across different age-sex groups within each occupation type. These unit consumer scales are generally high for adult males and low for children between the age group of (0-4).

5. The magnitude of income/expenditure inequality is relatively more for type-A occupation and relatively less for type-D occupation households.
6. Most of the inequality measures have relatively higher values in per unit expenditure than per capita expenditure terms for different types of occupation households in the rural areas of the state.
7. The incidence, depth and severity of poverty are relatively higher for the type-D occupation and relatively lower for type-A occupation in the rural areas of the state.
8. The incidence, depth and severity of poverty are relatively higher in per unit expenditure than in per capita expenditure terms for different types of occupation households in the rural areas of the state.

## 1.5 Organisation of the Study

The study is structured into seven chapters. Chapter-I is the introduction. It deals with the overall methodology, objective and scope of the study, data and models used, the hypotheses formulated for testing in the study. Chapter-II provides a brief review of studies on household consumption pattern, inequality in living standards and different aspects of poverty. The procedure of estimating unit consumer (adult equivalence) scales both 'specific' and 'overall' is examined and estimated in Chapter-III. Chapter-IV describes the household consumption pattern of different food and non-food item group in the state vis-a-vis the country. Chapter-V deals with the measurement and interpretation of different inequality measures both in per capita and per unit terms in the rural areas of the state and the level of inequality in the country whereas Chapter-VI is devoted for the estimation of poverty indices both in per capita and per unit terms to ascertain the incidence, depth and severity of poverty. Finally, Chapter-VII is the summary of the findings of the study.

## REFERENCES

1. Good Recent Surveys on Linkage Between Economic Growth, Poverty, Inequality and Employment are World Bank Development Report, 2006. Also Refer Khan, 2001 and Islam, 2004.

2. Rowntree (1901), Orshansky (1965), Watt (1967), Planning Commission (1981), Greer and Thorbecke (1984), Paul (1989) and Other Researchers have Suggested Different Methods of Estimating the Absolute Poverty Line.
3. The Details of Its Derivation and Other Related Issues See Mac Donald, L and Bradford Smith, K: Purchasing Power Parity and the International Development Targets, DFID Internal Paper, 2001. Also See Dubey and Crook (2001) who have Looked at Much More Details on this Issue and Its Implications on Poverty Incidence Across the States.
4. See for Details Deaton and Dreze, 2002.
5. See for Detail Clerk, S. R. Hemming and D. Ulph (1981): 'On Indices for the Measurement of Poverty', *Economic Journal*, Vol. 91 and also Pyatt, G. (1987): 'Measuring Welfare, Poverty and Inequality', *Economic Journal*, Vol. 97.

# 2

# SURVEY OF LITERATURE ON CONSUMPTION, INEQUALITY AND POVERTY

## 2.1 Introduction

Development policies of the Government are increasingly judged not merely by their success in achieving a rapid expansion of aggregate output but also in terms of how the fruits of development are distinguished between different classes and regions. It is in this context that a proper understanding of the nature and extent of inequalities, the manner in which they change, and the specific factors underlying these phenomena assume practical importance. Over the years a considerable body of quantitative information on inequalities in living standards has been accumulated. The most important source is the National Sample Survey (NSS), which provides data on average per capita consumption and its distribution in rural and urban areas by states. It also provides valuable information on various aspects of economic activity which have a bearing on the distribution of income, consumption, poverty and inequality.

Consumption expenditure of the people is an important indicator of the level of living. The study of consumption expenditure can be analyzed from the empirical studies of consumer behaviour. Empirical studies of consumer behaviour have been undertaken to test various theoretical postulates and to quantify the extent of response of the consumers to change in economic factors such as income, prices, stock of wealth, extent of monetisation and so on; socio-demographic factors such as household size and composition, occupation, social class, community etc.; other factors such as the level of education and age of the head of the households, race, region, physical and climatic conditions, cultural factors etc., Apart from the above studies, the analysis on consumer behaviour has great significance in the formulation of planning programmes for achieving economic development, eradication of poverty, reducing inequality and bringing about equitable distribution of income and wealth.

The plan of exposition of this chapter is as follows: section-2.1 introduces the chapter followed by brief review of studies on household consumption expenditure in section-2.2. Various studies on inequality are presented in section-2.3 whereas section-2.4 narrates a brief survey on different aspects of poverty and empirical estimations of poverty indices. Finally, section-2.5 concludes the chapter.

## 2.2 Survey of Literature on Consumption

Empirical studies on consumer behaviour started in India in the fifties in connection with the formulation of India's second five-year plan. Since then a large number of studies have been carried out mostly on the basis of National Sample Survey (NSS) budget data. However, initially demand projections for individual items of consumption were carried out on the basis of Engel Curves, making many simplified assumptions. With the availability of more and more extensive budget data from NSS, the researchers were induced to study the effect of the total consumer expenditure on consumption pattern of different items of consumption. Gradually, methodological questions that arose in the context of demand projections from Engel Curves attracted researchers to examine the effects of factors other than consumer expenditure on household consumption pattern. In this context, a brief review of the Indian studies on consumption pattern, level of inequality and poverty in India is presented in this chapter.

There is a growing body of literature available on theoretical and empirical studies on consumer behaviour. However, the present study belongs to the category of empirical studies of household expenditure based on econometric analysis. Consumption expenditure of the people is an important indicator of the level of living. During the eighteenth and nineteenth centuries the empirical approach to consumer behaviour had made little progress in the measurement of demand functions despite its early and promising beginning worldwide. An outstanding contribution was made for the first time by Ernst Engel who formulated the famous empirical law of food consumption based on Belgian family budget in 1857, thus, opening the sphere of household budget data for research to many others during subsequent years.

However, in the late nineteenth century the fusion of the theoretical and empirical approaches in the writing of Marshall was perhaps the catalyst which encouraged the empirical studies on consumer behaviour. In the early twentieth century, Benini (1907) used multiple regression analysis to estimate demand functions for coffee in Italy. Pigou (1910) suggested an indirect method of deriving price elasticities from family budget data, which he illustrated by an analysis on expenditure on food and clothing. Lehfeldt (1914) estimated the elasticity of demand for wheat in England under the direct inspiration of Marshall. But the serious progress in the econometric study of demand was achieved with Moore (1929), who through a number of studies 1914 to 1929 dealing with the problem of shifting of supply and demand curves and of short-run and long-run positions of market equilibrium. During the 1930s modern sampling theory began to make its contribution to measurement problems. Frisch (1934) and Snedecor (1938) suggested more of the specific pathological problems of economic time-series, notably that of multicollinearity. At the same time the development of Slutsky model of consumer preference by Allen and Hicks (1934) and the work of Allen and Bowley (1935) on the analysis of British family budgets were the first major analysis of cross-section data based on a theoretical model.

By 1939, most of the strengths and weaknesses of the classical demand analysis had been proved and most of the techniques still in use had been discovered. Schultz (1938) had done a great deal of empirical analysis on the field of demand analysis. However, works of Wold (1952) and Stone (1953) can be regarded as a consolidation of the theoretical and empirical work on static demand models in the first half of the 20th century. Samuelson (1938) introduced the theory of revealed preference; Houtthakker (1950) and Samuelson (1950) worked on the derivation of conditions under which demand functions may lead back to preference mapping, that is, long-standing consistency or integrability problem. On the empirical side, the study of Stone (1953) on the treatment of the special problems associated with the durables and the application of the more sophisticated computational and econometric techniques, the works Praise and Houtthakker (1955) on the analysis of family budgets, and the study of Houtthakker and Taylor (1966) on dealing with a wider range of commodities in USA and upgrading of the Stone's methodology were note worthy.

Aguir and Hurst (2003) of the University of Chicago have examined the direct link between expenditures, time spent on home production and actual consumption by using the data set of the Continuing Survey of Food Intake of Individuals (CSFII), conducted by the US Department of Agriculture. The data is distinguished empirically between food expenditure and food consumption. The analysis indicates that consumption in a household is stable, both absolutely and relatively to expenditure, during anticipated or transitory shocks to income, except for the poorest households. Regarding the utility level they did not arrive at any conclusion due to the problem of maximization i.e., a person with higher wage can achieve greater utility. For food consumption, they found that any decline in total consumption due to temporary or anticipated fluctuations in income occurs along dimensions other than food because food is generally considered to be the necessary item of consumption.

### *2.2.1 Choice of the Functional Form of Engel Curves*

Engel curve analysis has been an important tool in understanding the dynamics of household welfare. In the absence of satisfactory income data, per capita total consumer expenditure 'x' is used as the explanatory variable of the Engel curves. The term 'Engel curve' is generally used to express the relationship between the expenditure on or consumption of an item and household income. The Engel curves have been estimated thorough appropriate weighted least squares procedures. In some cases, fractile group-wise averages of per capita item and total consumer expenditure are available and the ordinary least squares method is followed, since the weights in this case are same for all fractile groups. The 'Engel law' may be regarded as providing approximate guidelines in the theory of consumer behaviour. Since, its simplest form involves income/total consumer expenditure as the only explanatory variable, it may be regarded as the partial relationship subsuming the effects of all other variables under the error term. Even though the matter of choice of appropriate functional form of the Engel curve is a matter of strategic importance, yet it also depends more on the personal judgment, of course it is governed by certain economic-theoretical as well as statistical criteria.

In a large number of studies, the suitability of alternative forms of Engel curves for different items of consumption have been examined. These studies consider such forms as linear (L); double-log (DL); semi-log (SL); exponential (EX); hyperbolic (HYP); log-inverse (LI); parabolic (P); log-parabolic (LP); log quadratic (LQ); log-log-inverse (LLI) and semi-log-inverse (SLI). The choice of the algebraic form is crucial as the estimated Engel elasticity and the marginal propensity to consumer (for any item) often vary considerably from one form of Engel curve to another.[1] The criterion employed for choosing the best fitting functional form have generally been the coefficient of determination ($R^2$), the adjusted coefficient of determination, $\overline{R}^2$ the squared correlation coefficient between observed and the predicated item expenditure, $R_y^2$ other distance measures and the randomness of regression residuals measured by DW statistic or run test.

A number of study in India has examined the suitability of alternative form of Engel curves for individual items.[2] Roy and Laha (1960) fitted straight lines by inspection to the graphs showing log $y_i$ against log $x_i$ and found the graphs to be sensibly linear. Roy and Dhar (1960) showed that the Tornquist forms were somewhat superior to the double-logarithmic form in many cases especially for luxury items, when judged by the residual sum of squares. But the elasticities given by DL Engel curve was closer to the elasticity at the mean of x given by the best fitting Tornquist curve. Sinha's study based on extensive NSS budget data for rural and urban India, revealed the overall superiority of log-log-inverse form over other forms, viz., linear, semi-log, dougle-log, log-inverse and hyperbolic when judged by $R^2$ and $\overline{R}^2$ and the Durbin-Watson (DW) statistic for the residuals. Maitra, Bhattacharya and Maitra, and Singh also observe the superiority of LLI Engel curve.

Maitra (1969) examined state-level NSS data on the consumption of food-grain items in rural areas. He compared the hyperbolic, semi-log, log-inverse, double-log and log-log inverse forms; of them the SL and LLI, particularly the latter, gave the most satisfactory fit. Bhattacharya and Maitra carried out an extensive analysis using NSS grouped data of fourteen different rounds for rural and urban India for a number of item groups. In this analysis, four functional forms, viz., HYP, SL, DL and LLI were compared on the basis of $R^2$, $R_y^2$ and the DW statistic. The results showed that LLI was most satisfactory form in majority of cases.

Singh (1969, 1973), compared $R^2$ and $\overline{R}^2$ for ten algebraic forms in the course of an investigation of the effects of household composition on consumption patterns. The three-parameter forms, viz., P, LLI, SLI and LP were generally found to be satisfactory. It should, however, be mentioned that the sample size were quite small in his study.

Gupta (1968a, 1968b) tried eight functional forms to region-wise data on food-grains and clothing for rural and urban India from NSS rounds 11[th] and 12[th] and choose the LI form for food-grains and DL form for clothing for inter-regional comparisons. But, presumably, he disfavored the three-parameter forms on account of their complexity. He tried an interesting technique for choosing a curve-type. He examined the scattered diagram showing region-wise elasticities against the corresponding mean expenditures and tried to choose the curve-type with similar variations in elasticity along the fitted curve.

Jain and Tendulkar (1973) tried five two-parameter forms, viz., L, SL, DL, LI and HYP in a study of occupational differences in consumption pattern based on 19th round NSS data for rural and urban India. They used the distance criteria, i.e., for any item they calculated the functional form-wise sum of squares of deviations of observed and predicted item expenditure weighted by estimated population in different levels of per capita total expenditure and choose that form for which the distance measure turned out to be the smallest. Their results indicate that SL appeared to be the best for many necessary items while DL proved to be the best for luxuries. Jain (1972) showed that the indirect add-log system of Engel curves gave better predictions on the whole than those given by DL, SL, HYP, EX, LI and L.

Coondoo (1975) tried four two-parameter forms, viz., L, DL, SL and LI and a three-parameter form, LLI, in the study of occupational difference in consumption for fifteen items groups based on 18th round NSS data for rural India. In this analysis the functional forms were compared on the basis of $R^2$ and $R_y^2$ . The result showed that L and LLI were the satisfactory forms in majority of cases.

Rao, Raj and Singh (1982) examined the consumption pattern in different income brackets along with the Engel and income elasticities for some food and non-food items in Vijayawada town of Andhra Pradesh. The data on quantities and expenditure on ten broad groups of items are collected from a sample of 230 households randomly drawn from six selected localities of the town. They tried three two-parameter Engel functions, viz., L, DL and SL and observed the suitability of linear form (L) for milk and milk products and meat, fish and egg; semi-log (SL) form for cereals, sugar and jaggery and the double-log (DL) form for pulses, vegetables, fruits and chilli, fats and oils, all food items and all non-food items on the basis of $R^2$. Further, they have shown that the income elasticities for these items are less than unity.

Mukhopadhyay (1987), while examining the variation in the inter-state consumption pattern of item-wise cash expenditure on three broad item groups namely, cereals and cereal substitutes, all food and all non-food items, used two functional forms DL, and LLI and found the superiority of LLI form on the basis of $R^2$ and $\bar{R}^2$. He used the 18th round state-wise NSS data for the purpose.

### 2.2.2 *Effects of Household Composition on Consumption Pattern*

Household composition depends on the distribution of the numbers of the household over age, sex categories. All these factors and also the inter-relationships among the members are accepted as important in the decision-making process within the households. Chowdhury (1967) has obtained surprisingly reasonable estimates of the specific unit consumer scales for cereals through a crude approach. He assumed that the Engel elasticity for cereals to be zero and thus, expressed total household consumption of cereals as a homogeneous linear function of the household composition vector (the elements being the number of persons in six different age-sex groups). The relative magnitudes of the estimated regression coefficients provided the estimate of the specific unit consumer scale for cereals. National Sample Survey 4th round data for each of the six population zones of Rural India were used in this investigation. The same procedure had been adopted earlier by Chakravarti and Bandyopadhyay (1953) and Roy and Dhar (1960).

Contribution made by Singh (1969, 1973) and Singh and Nagar (1973) can be considered as extension of Praise and Houthakker's (1955, chapter-9) well-known iterative procedure of estimating unit consumer scales. This procedure was actually applied to NSS 15th round data for 381 sample households in rural western Uttar Pradesh. Separate estimates of unit consumer scales were obtained for four occupational groups. Household members were classified into four age-sex groups. Twelve food and eight non-food items were considered. The estimated unit consumer scales were not satisfactory. The negative estimates of the weights $(w_i)$s in some cases may appear quite strange since they have been estimated under the non-negative restrictions.

In a study of considerable methodological interest, Coondoo (1973, 1975) re-examined the well-known conclusions of Forsyth (1960) regarding the analytical impossibility of separating the specific and overall effects of a change in household size and composition on the household consumption pattern. The solution of the problem suggested by Barten (1964) was reviewed and it was shown that Barten's procedure for solving the Forsyth's problem had inadvertently assumed one set of specific coefficients to be zero. Coondoo, however, succeeded in extending Barten's procedure so that the problem could be solved, in general, if all the specific coefficients were assumed to be invariant with respect to changes in income. The procedure was illustrated with respect to a specific situation where the Engel elasticities met the adding-up criterion and it was shown that in these situations all the scale coefficients could be uniquely determined without making any additional assumptions. Iterative methods of estimation were also suggested.

Paul (1985) has analysed the effect of household composition on consumption of different items on the basis of continuous equivalent scales, and Jain and Patel (1990) estimated (discrete) adult equivalent scales of milk and milk products using NSS data.

Panda (1996) in his study has considered 150 rural and 120 urban households purposively selected from different stratum of Orissa drawn in the 43rd round of the N.S.S.O. He has estimated the specific unit consumer scale for eight food and six non-food item groups. He has classified household members into five different groups on the basis of age and sex. The major findings are that the household size affects household consumption and the extent of this effect varies between commodities and between sectors (rural and urban). The Engel elasticities and household size elasticities tend to move in opposite direction in both the sectors of the state. As regards to the magnitude of economics of scale in the expenditure pattern for the items considered in the study, it is found that there exists a considerable diseconomies of scale for rice and other cereals in the rural sector and economies of scale for these items in the urban sector.

Pradhan and Panda (2000) estimated the unit consumer scale using Sing and Nagar's (1972) iterative procedure by choosing the most suitable functional form of Engel curves for fourteen food and non-food items in the rural and urban areas of Orissa. As regards the magnitude of economics of scale in the expenditure pattern for the above mentioned items, their results indicates that there exists a considerable diseconomies of scale for rice and other cereals in the rural sector and economies of scale for these items in the urban sector. However, for milk and milk products, clothing and miscellaneous items, there exists considerable diseconomies of scale in both the sectors of the state. On the other hand, the significance of economies of scale is observed for fuel and light in both the sectors, diseconomies of scale for edible oil in the rural sector, and economies of scale for other food items in the urban sector.

Sarangi (2004) has estimated the specific and income adult equivalent scale for nine broad food items and five non-food items for the rural sector of Orissa using the iterative procedure of Singh and Nagar (1973) which is an extension of the well-known Praise and Houthakker's iterative procedure (1955). These specific and unit adult equivalent consumer scales are used to estimate the poverty line in per unit terms for the state. The estimated results reveal that the scale for adult males is the highest for most of the food items except milk and milk products, salt and spices, fuel and light and clothing than that of the adult females except the agricultural labourer occupation households (type-D). For milk and milk products, the scale is the highest and for other food items the scale is found to be the lowest for children (0-4 years).

### 2.2.3 *Occupational Variation in the Pattern of Consumer Expenditure*

The socio-occupational factors have been known to be important determinants of the consumer expenditure pattern. There are some important studies that examined the variation in household consumer expenditure pattern among different occupational groups.[3]

Ganguly (1960) compared the expenditure pattern of rural households having different types of agricultural occupation, viz., farmers and cultivators, agricultural labours and other households in Uttar Pradesh utilizing 7$^{th}$ round NSS data (October-1953-March 1954). In this study occupation-wise Engel curves for five food items were compared subjectively through graphs. He did not employ and rigorous statistical procedure to confirm his subjective conclusions. His findings show considerable inter-occupational variation in the consumption pattern of all the items considered in the study.

Singh's study, based on ungrouped consumer expenditure data for the rural and urban sectors of Western Uttar Pradesh obtained from the 15th round of NSS (July 1959-June 1960) and considered four broad occupation groups, viz., (i) semi-professionals, clericals, shopkeepers and big cultivators, (ii) cultivators, (iii) skilled and semi-skilled workers and (iv) unskilled, unemployed and unclassified workers. Expenditure pattern of these occupation groups were compared on the basis of Engel elasticities of twelve food and nine non-food items. This study has some limitations. First, the magnitudes of the estimated elasticities raise suspicion. Indeed, one may question the reliability of these estimates in view of the fact that in most cases the sample size was quite small. Finally, the conclusions about occupational differences in consumption pattern were not examined through statistical tests (Bhattacharya, 1978).

Jain and Tendulkar's study is elegant and satisfactory in many respects which used all India estimates of per capita expenditure cross-classified by levels of per capita monthly total consumer expenditure and occupation separately for rural and urban India, obtained from 19th round of NSS (July 1964-June 1965). For comparing expenditure pattern of different occupation groups in respect of specific item of expenditures, the authors insisted that in a sector the item-specific Engel curves must have the same functional form across occupation groups. Out of the fitted six two parameter forms of Engel curves, viz., linear, semi-log, double-log, log-inverse, hyperbolic and exponential, for each item in each sector using all occupation expenditure data, the best fitting for is the one for which the weighted sum of squares of difference between observed and predicted item expenditures turned out to be the minimum, the weights being the estimated population in individual per capita total expenditure classes in the sector. In subsequent analysis, dummy variable model was applied to test the homogeneity of the occupation-wise Engel curves for all item expenditure in each sector.

Coondoo, Mukherjee and Rao (1974, 1979) and Coondoo (1975) compared the consumption pattern of four occupation groups, namely (i) cultivators, (ii) agricultural labourers, (iii) other agricultural occupation and (iv) non-agricultural occupation of rural India based on the data available from the special tabulation of 18[th] round of NSS. They considered fifteen different food and non-food item groups in their study. For comparing the consumption patterns of different groups in respect of specific item expenditures, they fitted four two-parameter Engel curves, viz, linear, double-log, semi-log and log-inverse and the three-parameter log-log inverse form and selected the best fit form as the one which yield maximum $R^2$ and $R_y^2$ for most of the item-occupation combinations. They found that LLI yielded maximum $R^2$ and $R_y^2$ for most of the item occupation combination. Further, they applied the covariance analysis method to test the homogeneity to the occupation-wise Engel curves for each item groups. They also examined cash and kind components of item expenditure separately for each occupation. The results of the test indicated considerable inter-occupational heterogeneity of expenditure patterns across occupation groups in rural India. Specifically, the analysis based on total expenditure (both cash and kind expenditures) on different items suggest that while cultivators and agricultural labours have by and large distinct consumption pattern, household having other agricultural and non-agricultural occupations and more or less similar. They also observed that cultivators have a cash expenditure pattern different from those of agricultural labourers as well as households with non-agricultural activities.

## 2.3 A Survey of Literature on Inequality

The relationship between the distribution of income and the process of development is one of the oldest subjects of economic enquiry. The classical economic theory accorded it a central position in analysing the dynamics of economic systems, and while this pre-eminence was somewhat obscured in the heyday of neoclassical theory, in recent years the concept has again came to occupy the center place of development economics.

During the decades of 1950's and 1960's 'development' has been associated with high rates of growth in aggregates and per capita incomes. Hence, in those times, exclusive emphasis was laid on raising the aggregate rates of growth of domestic product. This tendency was, however, reinforced by international aid agencies which set growth targets and devices 'performance' indicators on the basis of which assistance was allocated. This focus on aggregate growth rates was prompted by the belief that rapid industrialization and structural transformation would spread the benefits of growth across the various strata of society eventually by 'trickle down' process. It was then assumed that 'reduction of absolute poverty' could only be tackled after a certain level of GNP has been reached. First, the cake had to be produced and made bigger before it could be equally distributed, because once high income levels were attained, the income distribution would exert its leveling effect with greater ease through rapid percolation. Hence, the occurrence of greater inequality in the earlier states of development was postulated as a necessary precondition for rapid growth in the various influential growth models. This initial trade off between the objectives of rapid growth and income distribution was viewed as a transitional cost of successful development before their eventually complementary was securely established.[4]

For the first time, Kuznets classified a number of conceptual issues involved in inter-spatial and inter-temporal comparisons of income distribution and provided tentative answers about the impact of charges in income distribution in the process of development. On a discussion on historical trends in income distribution, Kuznets pointed out that a marked feature of economic growth was a shift from the traditional agricultural sector to the non-agricultural sector to be accompanied by an increase in inequality. He examined the shift in terms of inter-sectoral differences, in average incomes, distribution of income within each sector and the migration of workforce from agriculture to the non-agricultural sector. The tendency of income distribution worsen in the earlier phases of development is accounted for by two reasons. The higher per capita incomes in the non-agricultural sector grow faster than in the agricultural sector and the inequality of incomes in the former is greater than in the latter and grow faster. He pointed out the various factors instrumental in widening the inequalities and argued that the greater proportional accumulations of assets by the rich than the poor and the urbanisation associated with development tend to concentrate distribution over time with reversal coming only later as low income groups gain political influence. He concluded that there probably was 'a long swing in the inequality characterising the secular income structure widening in the early phases of growth when the transition from the pre-industrial to the industrial civilisation was rapid, becoming stabilized for a while, and then narrowing in the latter phases'. Kuznets did not assert that this period of increasing inequality, lasting some fifty to seventy years, must be repeated by the developing countries. But he pointed out that the underdeveloped countries might have a degree of inequality greater than the advanced countries and that many of them were much poorer than the advanced countries when they embarked on industrialization. So if the less developed countries experience the same growth in inequality during industrialisation, the hardships of the poor may likely to be much severe.

The above proposition is based on the logical hypothesis originally proposed by Kuznets (1955, 1963), that the secular behaviour of inequality follows an inverted 'U-shaped' pattern with inequality first increasing and then decreasing with development. Following Kuznets, the proposition that the distribution of income worsens with development, at least in the early stages, has received considerable attention.[5]

Kravis (1960) made an attempt to compare income inequality across nations and to explore the reasons why income inequality generally appeared greater in less developed countries than in developed ones; and confirmed Kuznets hypothesis of greater inequality in developing countries. Kravis computed four measures of inquality for pretax income among consumer units for ten developed and developing countries in the early 1950s; taking United States as the basis of comparison. He found that in three countries (Denmark, Netherlands and Israel) there was less inequality, in three other countries (Great Britain, Japan and Canada) there was about the same degree of inequality and in four countries (Italy, Puerto Rico. El Salvador and Sri Lanka) inequality was considerably greater. He concluded that the degree of equality tends to be positively correlated with the level of per capita income but that the correlation was not a simple one. The explanation of the greater inequality in developing countries was, therefore, to be sought in the greater dispersion in the upper part of the distribution scale.

Oshima (1962) joined the debate with a fourfold classification of the stages of development namely undeveloped, underdeveloped, semi-developed and fully developed and suggested that inequality was generally low at the underdeveloped stage and that the dispersion of incomes grows as countries, advance to the next stage. He further suggested that inequality increases during the semi-developed stage but inequality declines during the fourth stage. The main contribution of Oshima (1962) was that it laid the blame for income inequality on the shoulders of dualism. In his words, 'the major determinant of the dispersion of quintile shares between countries is the weight of farm or rural sector in the total economy' as well as the extent to which the agricultural and urban areas are economically integrated. Secondly, he found that within the rural and urban sectors the standard deviation of quintile shares was largely influenced by the dispersion of landholdings within the rural sector and the dispersion of capital per worker in the urban sector.

In an attempt to compare income distributions cross-nationally, Kuznets re-entered the discussion in 1963 by generating usable data on sixteen countries, nine of them developing. Classifying pre-tax family income in these countries by quintiles, observed that, (a) The share of the upper income groups was distinctly larger in the underdeveloped countries than in the developed countries. (b) The income share of the lowest quintiles is almost the same in developed and developing countries. From these two findings followed a third one, which indicated a greater concentration of income in the top group in the developing than in the developed countries and with the share of the lowest group being almost the same in both, the share of the middle group was lower in the developing than in the developed countries. Generally, in the developing countries income distribution was more equal below the level of the top 5 or 20 per cent of families.

A number of studies have compared income distribution in countries at different levels of economic development. Paukert (1973) examined data on income distribution at fifty to six countries and found a sharp increase in inequality (as revealed by Gini indices) and as one moved from the lowest per capita GDP countries upto those in the $300-$500 per capita range. (The $300-$500 range represents those countries with the most extreme inequality). As higher per capita income levels approached, inequality becomes progressively less. He pointed out that one should not generalize from the simple fact that the share of the poorest 20 per cent of families in countries below $500 per capita falls as income increases. Subsistence certainly sets a floor to family income; and in each of these countries, if the poorest 20 per cent are at subsistence level, their share of total income must fall as income increases.

It has also been observed that countries experiencing the most rapid rates of economic growth suffer from increasing inequality, Adelman and Morris (1973); Fishlow (1972); and Wells (1974) pointed out that increasing inequality accompanying rapid growth in Brazil in the late 60s and Arndt (1975) finds similar trends in Indonesia. Adelman and Morris (1973) examined data for forty-three developing countries, searching for relationship between patterns of income distribution and thirty-one indices of economic, political and social factors which could be expected to influence it. Their findings confirm the hypothesis that, at the lowest levels of development, growth tends to increase inequality. Broadly speaking in the poorest countries, growth works against the poorer segments of the population. The allocation of income to the poorest 60 per cent of the population is best 'explained' by the extent of socio-economic modernisation and the expansion of educational services, related variables found important by the World Bank.

Ahluwalia's study (1980), a summarized version of the recent work by the World Bank, provide some weak evidence that increasing inequality did not necessarily accompany economic growth. He compared the growth of income for the poorest 40 per cent income recipients with the GDP growth rate in 18 developing countries and found no clear pattern. In addition, cross-section regression analysis were run on data representing sixty-five countries where income recipients were divided into three groups—top 20 per cent, middle 40 per cent and lower 40 per cent and their respective income shares were used as dependent variables. They found that the growth rate of GDP was positively related to the share of the lower 40 per cent of income recipients which suggests that the dual objectives of growth and equity may not be in conflict. However, when regression was run again, separating countries by income level, it was found that the share of the poorest 40 per cent did decline with growth, up to the point where a per capita income level of about $400 was reached. After that, the share of this group increased concurrently the share of the top 20 per cent moved in an exactly opposite way, and that of the middle-income group remained unaffected. It is of interest that the World Bank study turned up two variables related to the quantity and quality of human resources as being most closely related to relative income shares. The level and availability of education was positively related to the income shares of the poorest 80 per cent. Oshima (2002) using the quintile deviation measure calculated the share of inequality attributable to each economic sector. He noted that changes in economic structure i.e. shift from a rural to an urban focus of economic activity as growth proceeds were more important than growth per se in explaining changing income distribution. His main conclusion was that undue policy emphasis on industrialisation could lead to unemployment, excessive urbanization, regional imbalance and widening inequality. Thus, he laid the blame for inequality squarely in the lap of dualistic development.

Deogaonkar (2004) Managing Director, Department of Neurosciences, Development Clinic Foundation USA has conducted a review on the effect of growing socio-economic inequality in Indian population and its effect on health care system. He observed that poverty is the result of socio-economic inequality in a society and is detrimental to the health of population. The indicators of health (Mortality, Morbidity and life expectancy) are all directly influenced by the standards of living of a given population. Hence, to him it is not the absolute deprivation of income that matters, but the relative distribution of income (Wilkinson, 1992). By considering on the aspects like unequal distribution of health care resources in India, geographical socio-economic and gender, effect on health indicators like IMR and MMR due to economic inequality etc., he found that since the emergence of free India in 1947, economic egalitarianism dominated the economic policies over time. Socialism and Government centered economic policies over time were favoured over the profit making private enterprises and capitalism. This basic inequality was magnified by the rapid but unequal economic growth that India has witnessed in the last two decades particularly during 1980s and 1990s. Amidst the rising standards of living, lie pockets of terrible poverty and deprivation. Hence, all these together have widened the gap between rich and poor.

Paraje (2005) has narrated a brief review on the concept of income non-response and inequality measurement. In countries where the proportion of income non-response is high, inequality, poverty or other measures constructed using income may give a distorted picture if non-response is not levelled appropriately. He found that the question of non-response to income data could be of paramount importance particularly in some Latin American countries where world's highest inequality exists. In countries like Argentina, Chile, Colombia, Costa Rica, Ecuador and Venezuela, income non-response rates are above 5 per cent and, in some cases, it is also higher than 10 per cent. In countries like Honduras and Panama, income non-response rates are relatively low in general, but are high (more than 10%) for particular labour categories such as self-employed and firm owners. He then quoted some comprehensive works on household surveys, such as Deaton (1997), who paid little attention to issues related to the effect that quality of the data has no economic inferences in general and inequality inferences in particular, Gottschalk and Smeeding (2000) in a work recognized that different pattern of income non-response (depending on the relationship between the probability of non-response and actual income level) may affect inequality measures differently and acknowledge the difficulties of knowing the exact pattern in each case etc., to show that these correction measures pay less attention.

Mac Arthur (2000) opines that the degree of income inequality in society may be related to the health status of a population. Greater income inequality has been linked to lower life expectancy in cross-national comparisons (Wilkinson, 1996); higher mortality rates, (Kalpan, et al., 1996 and Kennedy, et al., 1996) and worse self-rated health (Kennedy, et al., 1998) at the U.S. state level; higher mortality at the U.S. Metropolitan level (Lynch et al., 1998) as well as higher rates of obesity at the U.S. state level (Kahn et al., 1998). The mechanism linking income inequality to health still debated (Kawachi et al., 1999), but their association is found to be robust with respect to age, race, sex and adjustment for individual socio-economic characteristics [(Kennedy, et al., 1998 and Soobader and Lecfee, 1999)].

Grusky and Kanbur (2004) has done a comparative work on 'conceptual ferment in poverty and inequality measurement' by collecting the views (like Francasis Bourgugnon, Mortha Finemon, Douglas Massy, Mortha Nussbaum, Amartya Sen, and William Julius Wilson) on social and economic inequality. Using the views of above experts, the authors have developed a compressive series of last thirty years of research on various aspects of development economics. The series starts with the work 'on the measurement of inequality' (Atkinson, 1970), and end with (Atkinson et al., 2000) 'handbook of income distribution' which is a edited volume. These 30 years have been divided very roughly, into the first phase stretching from the 1970s to the mid-1980s and the second phase stretching from the mid-1980s to the end of last century. They named the first phase as the phase of conceptual ferment that is generally concentrates on answering four basic questions viz., (i) how should inequality and poverty be measured? (ii) should policy recommendations on issue of poverty reduction and equalisation rest on simple utilitarian premises? (iii) are households best treated as unitary entitles? and (iv) can the complicating effects of social interaction be readily be incorporated into analyses of poverty and inequality?.

### 2.3.1 *Evidence of Inequality in India*

Most of the early studies on income distribution in India based on income-tax data. But their reliability is vitiated by the narrow coverage of population and kind of income; also because of widespread tax evasion. These estimates are of limited value from the point of view of overall distribution. In spite of the absence of official figures on income distribution, several attempts have been made by institutions as well as researchers, to work out the patterns of distribution on a wider base with the increasing availability of data on consumer expenditure collected by the National Sample Survey. Some of these studies have confined only to consumer expenditure while others have tried to define distribution of personal incomes by incorporating simple hypothesis about saving behaviour.

Mahalanobis (1960, 1962) has been a pioneer in researches in the field of levels of living in India and had made significant contributions to methodology in course of his researches. He has developed the technique of the specific concentration curve. Another important innovation that goes in his credit is the method of fractile graphical analysis (FGA) which is specially useful for inter-temporal and inter-regional comparisons of data on levels of living.

Lydall (1960) estimated the distribution of income in India for the year 1955-56 by linking the income tax data with the consumer expenditure data of the National Sample Survey. He performed this exercise by assuming that the Pareto law of the distribution of income applies to India to the same extent as it does in most of the other countries. By comparing the pre- and post-tax fractile shares of income in India with U.K., he reached the conclusion that the final distribution of real income is more unequal in India.

Iyengar and Mukherjee (1961) made an attempt to study the distribution of household income for the year 1951-52, 1953-54 and 1956-57 using National Sample Survey and Reserve Bank of India data. Their estimates suggested that the top 10 per cent and the bottom 50 per cent of the population increased their share in the total income, implying thereby that the position of the middle-income group has worsened over the period.

The Reserve Bank of India study by Ojha and Bhatt (1963) is the first of its kind in building a meaningful pattern from unrelated data from different sources. It is based on integrating income tax data with the consumer expenditure data from NSS in their method of estimation. Analyzing the income structure in terms of three groups and comparing the pattern of income distribution in India with some of the developed as well as underdeveloped countries in terms of the concentration ratio, the study indicated that 'contrary to general impression, the degree of inequality in income distribution in India does not seem to be higher than in some of the advanced countries. This conclusion has been found to be at variance with the findings of the previous empirical studies and the limitations underlying the concept of income and the methodology employed in the study have been brought out.

The National Council of Applied Economic Research (1964) provided data on income distribution for both rural and urban areas. If these data were compared with the data for 1962, it would appear that the inequality in income in the rural areas had somewhat declined. In the urban areas, on the other hand, there seemed to be no definite indication of a change. The broad conclusion from this data set is that while there is a downward trend in inequality in rural sector, this is not true in the case of urban sector. But for the country as a whole the changes are so small that no definite conclusion can be drawn.

The National Council of Applied Economic Research (1967) conducted two comprehensive studies, one on the urban income and saving and the other on rural income and saving. The former was undertaken for the year 1960 and the latter for 1962. Subsequently the two studies were put together and the size distribution of income for the country as a whole was estimated. The results of the two indicated that among the rural household the top 10 per cent of the population had a share of 22 per cent of the total household income not very much different from the share of the bottom 50 per cent which had 22.7 per cent to its credit. To put it another way, the top 1 per cent of the rural households had a per capita income which was 12 time the per capita income of the poorest 5 per cent of the households. In the urban areas also the results showed almost the same picture. While the top 10 per cent of the urban households had a share of more than 40 per cent of the total household income, the share of the bottom 50 per cent was of the order of 17.5 per cent.

Swamy (1967) has examined the trend in the household consumer expenditure inequalities over the first decade of planning when there was price stability and the economy registered considerable growth. Adopting the various measures of inequality he concluded that the size distribution of income or consumer expenditure widened over fifties. He attributed 85 per cent of this increase in the size distribution of consumer expenditure to structural changes and the rest to inter-sectoral changes.

In an elaborate study focusing on the trends in income distribution (1953-54 to 1959-60) Ranadive (1968) drawn two broad conclusions (a) the income structure in India is comparable to that in other underdeveloped countries. The contention that Kuznets' hypothesis of greater income inequality in the underdeveloped countries than in the developed countries is seem to be not valid for India, (b) ten years of planning have not had any impact on the income structure in the direction of narrowing the disparity. It needs to be borne in mind that his estimates relate to the size distribution of money income and makes no allowance for the possibility of differential increases in the cost of living. Given the generally held belief that the impact of rising cost of living has been more severe on the low-income groups, he found that the richest 2 per cent have improved their relative position which would, therefore, merit further scrutiny.

In a cross section study focusing on inequalities in personal income distribution in India, Sarma (1970) found higher income disparities in the urban household sector than in the rural. He also looked into the income concentration among various socio-economic groups. Further, in an inter-country comparison of income distributions, he found the degree of concentration of income in India is higher than in the economically advanced countries, a finding in conformity with Kuznets' earlier results. Examining the changes in Income distribution among rural households in India during 1968-69 to 1970-71, Sarma found a decline in inequality over time.

Randive's (1971) estimates of consumer expenditure inequalities are spanning a period of fifteen years. Four of her measures indicate a decline in the expenditure inequality between 1953-54 and 1968-69. The fall in the share of the bottom decile suggests an increase inequality between all four groups above the poorest whose position worsened. The studies by Bardhan, Vaidhyanathan, Ojha and Bhatt also broadly indicate a decline in the expenditure inequality measured by Gini ratio.

In a study Ahmed and Bhattacharya (1974) estimated the personal income distribution in India for three different periods 1956-57, 1960-61 and 1963-64 by integrating the size distribution of consumer expenditure obtained from NSS with the size distribution of income before tax obtained from Income tax data on certain simplifying assumptions. They followed the technique developed by Lydall.

In an extensive study Radhakrishna and Sarma (1976) estimated the disparities in consumer expenditure over a long period for 17 years (1952-53 to 1968-69) adopting quintile shares and Gini concentration ratio for both rural and urban India separately. The inequality measures have been computed for total expenditure at current prices as well as at constant prices: Adjustments were also made for differential price impact across fractile classes. They concluded 'differential price effects have started operating against the bottom decile classes at a progressively higher pace down the rung ever since 1963-64'. As against these trend differentials, the average per capita expenditure of all classes at current prices has been increasing both for rural and urban India, the real per capita expenditure in urban areas has fallen and that in rural areas has increased marginally. Inequalities in the level of living considered in terms of current prices have narrowed down whereas those measured at constant prices (Base as 1952-53) taking into account price differentials have widened in the period beginning from 1963-64. With no appreciable improvement in real per capita expenditure on the one hand and widening disparities on the other, the level of living of the people in the bottom decile classes has fallen in absolute terms.

Nair (1983) termed the period from 1950-1967 as the period of 'increasing regional awareness'. Nair pointed that the rising inequality in agricultural NSDP was clearly brought out with decreased in NSDP from registered manufacturing. He found Punjab (including Haryana), Gujarat and West Bengal were among the top four states in terms of per capita NSDP in 1950-51, 1960-65 and 1971-76 while Bihar, Orissa and Uttar Pradesh were found to be with lower NSDP during the same period.

To make inequality comparisons one needs to make interpersonal comparisons. Welfare economics has been traditionally concerned to evaluate the goodness of any state of affairs solely in terms of the information provided by the ordinal, interpersonally noncomparable utilities which makes for a system of evaluation that would be subsumed under what Sen (1979) has called 'welfarism'. Welfarism, clearly speaking, is not a fertile ground for breeding inequality judgments. One way of relaxing the informal lightness of welfarism is to effect interpersonal comparisons of welfare without, however, moving away from 'ordinalism' through the device of what Arrow (1977) has called the 'extended sympathy'. This helps for making judgment of the form that 'it is no worse to be person 'j' in state 'x' than to be person 'k' in state 'y'. Basu (1995) put vital questions on the above issue by pointing out to the possibility that such judgment could be vitiated by certain problems of trivialness or ambiguity attending them using the 'intended sympathy' approach, Hammond (1976) has presented a social choice theoretic axiom of equity [a generalization of Sen's (1973) 'weak equity axioms'], which essentially demands that, given a pair of social states 'x' and 'y' and a pair of individuals 'j' and 'k', if 'k' is worse off than 'j' in both the states 'x' and 'y' with the rest of the society being indifferent as between 'x' and 'y', then society should defer to the relatively disadvantaged person 'k's performance between 'x' and 'y' in ranking the two alternatives (Subramanian, 1997).

Choudhury (1993) reported that for per capita consumption expenditure, the coefficient of variation first increased from 1967-68 to 1977-78 and then declined from 1977-78 to 1986-87, in both current prices and constant prices. Thus, between 1977-78 and 1985-86, while regional inequality in terms of NSDP worsened, the inequality lessened in terms of per capita consumption expenditure. Generally, regional inequality in consumption expenditure is found to be lower than in NSDP per capita.

Matlow (1995), analyzing the performance of 14 major Indian states during the period 1951-81, noted that Punjab (including Haryana), Maharashtra, Tamil Nadu and Karnataka emerged as the four fastest growing states in terms of aggregate output growth, whereas Uttar Pradesh, West Bengal, Madhya Pradesh and Orissa experienced the lowest rates of growth during the some period.

Panda (1996) conducted an econometric study on consumption pattern in Orissa based on 38th and 43rd rounds of NSS data. On the basis of 38th round of NSS data it is observed that the Engel ratio for all food items is the highest for ST with the lowest average per capita income compared to SC and general category of households. It is also found that the Engel ratio for SC is closer to ST which indicates a lower level of standard of living compared to general households.

Das and Barua (1996) noted that Punjab, Haryana, Gujarat, Maharashtra and West Bengal were among the major states with the highest per capita income in 1970. In 1980s, nearly the same configuration remained, but in 1990s, Tamil Nadu ranked higher than West Bengal in terms of its share of income relative to population. Bihar, Orissa, Madhya Pradesh and Uttar Pradesh remained at the bottom of the states in terms of income per years of 1970, 1980 and 1990. Thus, Das and Baura's study found worsening of regional inequality for the short post-reform period of 1990s.

The EPW Research Foundation (1997) besides bringing together a variety of data on national accounts in India has also published data on NSDP in current and constant prices for the various states for the period 1980-81 to 1995-96. The study pointed to differences in performances of different states that could be attributed to changes in relative prices as well as performance of different sectors.

A recent study of income convergence done by Rao, Kalirajan and Shond (1998) supported that the relative pattern of state level growth appears to suggest that the slower growing and low income states have continued to grow at slower rates in contrast to the states with higher income. Rao et al., however find lack of convergence in per capita NSDP for the period 1970-90.

Another study of Bhide, Kalirajan and Shond (1998) reported convergence in agricultural growth rates, which suggests reduction in the disparities of growth rate but not convergence of per capita NSDP from agriculture. In this sense, rising regional inequality in per capita agricultural NSDP is reflected in the findings of a number of studies.

The most influential support for Kuznets' hypothesis has come from the study of Ahluwalia (1974, 1976a, 1976b) and Ahluwalia et al. (1979). In two comparison prices, Anand and Kanbar (1993a and 1993b) have undertaken a detailed critical scrutiny of the Ahluwalia's findings. A quick summary of the Anand-Kanbur critique would boil down to the judgment that there is much that is wrong and little that is right with the Ahluwalia (1976b) exercise. First, a cross section study (such as the one Ahluwalia conducted) is not apposite to the purpose at hand. Second, the functional form of the relation between (in) equality and income, which Ahluwalia specifies, is in no way dictated by the 'mechanics' of the Kuznets process, which is claimed to have spawned the relationship being tested.

Secular trends in the behaviour of the Gini co-efficient of inequality in the distribution of consumption expenditure have been studied by Ahluwalia (1978), Dutta (1980) and Sundaram (1987). Vaidyanathan (1974) takes note of the possibility that since consumers in different size classes typically consume different commodity bundles, they would be confronted with differential rates of inflation; both methodologically and substantively his efforts at reckoning inequality after deflating nominal expenditure levels with fractile specific price indices is an important contribution Suryanarana (1991) alerts the user of NSS data to the possibility that a combination of secular inflation and the relatively infrequent NSS reclassification of the expenditure size-classes in nominal terms could by understanding the convexity of the Lorenz Curve make for a built-in-bias towards progressively understanding inequality over time.

### A Survey of Literature on Rural Poverty

Poverty is not a recent phenomenon in India as well as in the globe. Ample evidence of its abject incidence among the masses is found in the literary and descriptive accounts of the pre-colonial and colonial times. The debate on Indian poverty in the last century vividly brought out the socio-economic conditions of the time and mercenary impact of the British rule in deepening the poverty of the masses (Gadgil, 1945, 1965). After the advent of independence, sustained attempts have been made at planned development and the elimination of structural imbalances and constraints in improving the levels of living of the masses. With this evaluation of the impact of the policies of development have been undertaken from time to time (Sastry, 1980).

Pradhan (1979) in his study has given some reflections on poverty and prosperity before and after the British rule in India. To him, the old economic order with its primitive socio-political-economic conditions can be equated with under development. In the ancient period villages in India were merely huts with reed and straw. Rhys-Davids' description of Budhist India (6$^{th}$ century B.C) is an eloquent testimony to the country's economic condition where there was no roads, there was constant fear of thieves and decoits and the number of wealthy persons by the prevailing standard was very limited. During the Gupta period (B.C., 300-550 A.D.) which was considered to be the golden age in the history of India, roads were considered to be dangerous for Caravan trades. Failure of crops, droughts, inundations, famines and diseases caused the sufferings and sorrows of the people of ancient India. Similar references also exist in regard to general conditions of poverty during the medieval period. It is reported that during the Mughal rule the common people remained extremely vulnerable to natural calamities like floods and drought and in such calamities certainty of starvation was there for them'. The common men were miserably poor and poorer. The poverty of the people was 'so great and miserable that it could be depicted as the home of stack want and the dwelling place of bitter woe'.

Researchers like Moreland (1973), Maddison (1970) and others examining the economic condition of the Mughal period gave emphasis to the general poverty of the masses. Discounting both the views Dutt concludes that prior to British rule, 'the balance of evidences and of popular tradition undoubtedly points to a wider area of well being'. Again the Indian economy and sociology all through the historical epochs was characterized by great inequality among classes of people and between rural and urban areas. The inequality in the villages was regulated by 'social sanctions', which in turn regulated the distribution of produce from land. The nobles were seen 'steeped in luxury' and the common men were miserably poor. The wealth and prosperity was, thus, found to be concentrated among a few classes and in urban areas (Pradhan, 1979).

Pradhan, Panda and Sarangi (2005) reviewed that the British Intervention in India mauled and truncketed the Indian economy beyond measures. The 'spread effects' of the British rule were swamped and dominated by its 'backwash effects'. Hence, Marx summed up the destructive part of the British Raj as a 'heap of ruins'. Hence, it is this destruction which gave turn and twist to the already existing poverty in the country and added new dimensions to it.

In July 1870 Dadabhai Naoroji presented a paper, 'The wants and means of India', before the East India Association in London in which he gave 40 shillings (Rs. 20) per capita as high estimate of the gross production of India'. Subsequently in 1876, he had presented a paper titled 'poverty of India' before the Bombay bench of the East India Association in which he worked out, with the help of available official and other data on production and prices, the value of production per head separately for the Central Provinces (43s 5d); Punjab (49s 5d); N.W. Provinces (35s 5d); Bengal (37s 5d); Madras (35s 5d); Bombay (79s 5d) and an average of 40s or Rs. 20 for the whole of India. For estimating the quality and value of agricultural production, he took the figures of the price yield per acre and area under cultivation of the principal crop or crops of each province and arrived at an average value of income per acre, which he thereupon applied to the total area under cultivation in that province. To this he added 'the annual value of manufacturing industry, net opium revenue, cost of production of salt, coals and mines, profits of foreign commerce' and £30,000,000 for contingencies.

More than half a century later, Rao (1938) in his easy on the national income of India, accepted Dadabhai's figure of the value of agricultural produce as an authentic estimate. By this time, the concept of national income and the methodology of estimating it had undergone considerable refinement. Even so, after making the necessary adjustments, Rao placed the per capita income in 1867-68 at Rs. 23 to Rs. 24 (Rs. 23.40), thus revising Dadabhai's estimate by just 15 per cent. Dadabhai estimates in his days had been criticized for omitting all references to the contribution of railways to national income, to profits of trade, to salaries and pensions to non-agricultural wages and all other sources from which a man who does not grow food himself may obtain the means of purchasing it.

Dutta (1950), with his practical experience of rural India, emphasized the inequality of the land tenure system (under British rule) accompanied by a heavy taxation of the impoverished agriculture resulting in the permanent poverty of the Indian people. Since independence, sustained attempts have been made at planned development and the elimination of structural imbalances and constraints in improving the levels of living of the masses. Also, evaluations of the impact of the policies of development have been undertaken from time to time.

Chatterjee et al. (1963), by using NSS 13$^{th}$ round consumption data for rural India, found about 53 per cent of the population to fall below the norm of 2,400 calories per capita per day. These scholars have taken into account the food items only, and by excluding the non-food expenditure they have underestimated the extent of rural poverty in India.

Mukherjee (1969) prepared a map of India delineating clusters of regions relatively homogeneous in respect of level of living and the incidence of poverty. He looked at the aerial distribution of poverty over 50 regions. Ranking persons by per capita expenditure, he formed a group comprising the poorest 10 per cent of India's rural population and then examined how many of these poor fell in different regions. Judging both the rural and urban segments of the states as a whole on the criteria of density of the poor, density of the rich and per capita expenditure, he found Orissa, Kerala, Bihar, Mysore and Andhra Pradesh among the poorer states in 1963-64.

Minhas (1970) on the basis of the figures recommended by the study group, i.e., Rs. 240 per annum for urban area, and for rural population, he takes a slightly lower figure of Rs. 200 per annum on the ground that the urban cost of living tends to be somewhat higher at 1960-61 prices. Using the latter figure he finds that between 1956-57 and 1967-68 the number of poor people in rural areas decreased from 173 million to 154 million. Expressed as a proportion of rural population, it decline from 52.4 to 37.1 per cent. When the higher level is taken, i.e. Rs. 240 per annum as the poverty line income, the number of poor decline from 215 million in 1956-57 to 210 million in 1967-68, while the proportion dropped from 65.0 per cent to 50.6 per cent (Table–2.1). Minhas concluded that the number of poor tends to rise in bad harvest years.

Ojha (1970) looks at both rural and urban poverty for 1960-61 and at rural poverty only for 1967-68. Adopting a calorie norm of 2,250 per capita per day for an average Indian, he assumed that 66 per cent of this must be obtained from food grains, cereals and pulses, in urban areas; 80 per cent was the corresponding figure for the rural sector. These percentages were worked out to 518 gm. and 432 gm. per person per day in rural and urban areas respectively. Ojha adopted these standards for studying the incidence of poverty and found that nearly 51.8 per cent of all persons in rural areas (184 million) and 7.6 per cent in urban area (6 million) fell below the poverty line. For the year 1967-68, he concluded that 70 per cent of the rural population were below the minimum level of food grains consumption. Ojha has excluded the expenditure on health, education and housing. Secondly, he adopted the same minimum nutritional requirements, i.e., 2,250 calories per person per day, both for the rural and urban population without taking into account the nature, type and intensity of work as well as the price differences between the urban and rural areas.

The findings of Bardhan (1970) are in direct contrast to those of Minhas while he used the same NSS data for the distribution of consumer expenditure. Bardhan uses a different minimum level of income of Rs. 15 per capita per month for rural area and Rs. 21 for urban areas at 1960-61 prices on the ground that rural prices are generally lower than urban prices. Bardhan estimated that 38 per cent (or about 135 million persons) in rural areas and 44 per cent (or 34 million people) in urban areas fall below poverty line. On the basis of the same minimum norms (both for the rural and urban areas) Bardhan suggested that in 1968-69 at 1960-61 price as many as 54 per cent of the rural population and 41 per cent of the urban population fall below the poverty line. Thus, Bardhan's time series profile of the rural and urban poor showed a sharp rise in the incidence of poverty over time. Bardhan used the official agricultural labour consumer price index for deflating the consumption of the rural poor and the official working class consumer price index for deflating that of the urban poor. The former is constructed on the basis of NSS rural retail prices and the weighing diagrams worked out by the second agricultural labour enquiry. In absolute terms, Bardhan found a 'staggering' rise in the number of rural poor from about 135 million to 230 million between 1960-61 and 1968-69.

**Table–2.1**

**Percentage and numbers of people below minimum levels of living in rural India**

| *Year* | *Below Rs. 240 per annum* | | *Below Rs. 200 per annum* | |
|---|---|---|---|---|
| | *Percentage* | *Millions* | *Percentage* | *Million* |
| 1956-57 | 65.0 | 215 | 52.4 | 173 |
| 1957-58 | 63.2 | 212 | 50.2 | 169 |
| 1960-61 | 59.4 | 211 | 46.0 | 164 |
| 1961-62 | 56.4 | 206 | 43.6 | 159 |
| 1963-64 | 57.8 | 221 | 44.2 | 169 |
| 1964-65 | 51.6 | 202 | 39.3 | 154 |
| 1967-68 | 50.6 | 210 | 37.1 | 154 |

**Source: Minhas, 1970.**

Rudra has seriously criticized Bardhan's procedure of calculating the low figure of Rs. 15 on the basis of the above-mentioned reasons, both from a conceptual and a methodological point of view. Dandekar and Rath (1971) are of the opinion that the NSS estimate of average per capita consumption in 1967-68 is an underestimate. They note that the NSS estimate of rural per capita consumption of Rs. 239.8 in 1967-68 at 1960-61 prices (using the national income deflator) is about 7 per cent 'below' the corresponding NSS estimate in 1960-61 and about 11 per cent 'below' the corresponding estimate for 1967-68 derived from official national level data. They assume a daily intake of 2,250 calories per adult male as the required minimum intake for subsistence. This is the figure estimated by Sukhatme (1965) for Indian conditions, and it is somewhat lower than the intake recommended by the Nutrition Advisory Committee of the Indian Council of Medical Research.

Dandaker and Rath (1971), after making a number of adjustments to the basic NSS data, estimated the level of poverty using a method similar to Ojha's with two differences. They used the NSS estimates of consumption of food grains (and substitute) without any correction. Secondly, they assumed a yield of 200 calories per capita per day from other items of food. They found that for rural areas in 1960-61, an annual per capita consumer expenditure of Rs. 170.8 was needed to ensure a diet equivalent at least to 2,250 calories per capita per day. For a number of reasons, the urban consumer would typically need to spend a higher amount to purchase the same amount of nutrition, i.e Rs. 271.7. Thus, according to Dandekar and Rath, the urban consumer would have needed to spend around 50 per cent more to attain the same level of nutrition, whereas the average urban income was only 37 per cent higher than their rural counterpart. It was accordingly estimated that in 1960-61 about 33.12 per cent of the rural population and 48.64 per cent of the urban population would have been living below the level of poverty.

Panikar (1972) has subjected the estimates of Dandekar and Rath for Kerala to careful scrutiny. He has worked out a series of models for deriving minimum cost diets, taking into account the local availability and use of food items of a diet which offers both 'reasonable' variety and palatability and its cost at 1970-71 prices. He concludes that in Kerala such diet would cost Rs. 28.30 per capita per month and the total per capita consumption expenditure corresponding to this diet would be Rs. 37.80. Panikar is largely concerned with the question of choice of a nutritional minimum or, more strictly, a low-cost diet for poor households. He does not say anything explicitly about numbers of the poor in Kerala, to which his study relates. He criticizes both the nutritional measures used by Dandekar and Rath, and by the Nutritional Advisory Committee. His basic conclusions are that by ignoring regional factors, they both reached wrong conclusions about the cost of a nutritionally adequate diet in Kerala. Dantwala (1972) pointed out that in 1961-62 prices this amount would be only about half, since the prices have nearly doubled during the decade. Thus, according to Panikar's estimates, the requisite calorie level in rural Kerala would be met when per capita consumption expenditure, at 1961-62 prices, reached Rs. 18.20 and not Rs. 34.40 as estimated by Dandekar and Rath.

Vyas (1972) found a decline in the incidence of rural poverty during the 1950s, and traced the combined impact of major institutional changes and considerable agricultural growth for such a decline of rural poverty during the period. The proportion of rural poor below the poverty line (Rs. 240 per capita per annum) decline from 45 per cent in 1954-55 to 38 per cent in 960-61. The period after 1960-61 witnessed neither agricultural growth nor institutional change, but an increase in poverty.

Vaidyanathan (1974) by using Rs. 21.44 as the average per capita consumption per month at 1960-61 prices found that about 15.65 per cent were living in poverty in the country. This would give a total number of about 56 million, which can be taken as some sort of numerical estimate (in millions) of poverty. His estimates are based wholly on NSS data showing a considerable rise during the sixties though the degree of inequality in distribution declined. For 1967-68 the price index (base: 1960-61) was found to be about 190 for the first five decile groups.

Bhatty (1974) adopted both 'Sen's poverty index' and the traditional 'head count ratio' in quantifying the incidence of poverty among the various rural occupational groups and found the incidence to be maximum among the agricultural labourers (89.56%) followed by non-agricultural workers (78.77%) and cultivators (70.28%). Bhatty's estimates of the proportion of the population below the poverty line are lower than those of Bardhan, Dandekar and Rath, Minhas and Ojha. For the lowest poverty level, i.e., Rs.180, his results correspond roughly to Vaidyanathan's. It reveals that, for all poverty levels above Rs. 480 per capita per annum, the incidence was found to be more severe among the agricultural labourers and the lowest among non-agricultural rural workers.

Rajaraman (1974) found deterioration in the absolute levels of living and rise in the incidence of poverty in Punjab over the decade of sixties, i.e., 1960-61 to 1970-71. She measured poverty by the percentage of population below the poverty line worked out specifically for the region using linear programming techniques. Taking a figure of Rs. 16.36 for 1960-61 and corresponding level of expenditure of Rs. 33.36 in 1970-71 as the poverty line and percentage of the population below the poverty line had increased from 18.4 to 23.3 per cent during the decade. The largest increase in poverty was among the agricultural labourers. In 1960-61 and 1970-71 agricultural labourers formed 17.5 and 23.2 per cent of all rural occupational groups.

Atkinson (1975) has pointed out that there is no single 'subsistence' level which can be used as a basis for the poverty line. Even in the case of food, it is difficult to determine requirements with any precision. There is no one level of food intake required for subsistence, but rather a broad range where physically efficiency declines with a falling intake of calories and proteins. Moreover, an individual's nutritional needs depend on the level of activity (for example the office worker requiring less than a farm worker). Thus, precisely where the line is drawn depends on the judgment of the investigator, and the idea of a purely physiological basis for the poverty criterion is lost. Secondly, in the case of non-food items there is an even greater degree of arbitrariness, because the minimum needs, norms and the other factors change from region to region due to the climatic and social factors.

Deepaklal (1976) found a decline in the incidence of poverty among rural labour households in the first five out of six states, i.e., Maharashtra, Orissa, Rajasthan, Punjab, Uttar Pradesh and Mysore, between 1956-57 and 1970-71. He adopted alternative estimates of the state level poverty lines of Dandekar, Rath and Bardhan, using the data of rural labour enquires of the NSS for

1956-57 and 1970-71. He noticed a significant negative correlation between the percentage change in the proportion of sample households below the poverty line and the percentage change in the average household income for the sample group as a whole; further, the former was also correlated (though at a fairly low level of significance) with the percentage change in the cereal output during this period.

In a study Ahluwalia (1978) examined the trends in the incidence of rural poverty over the period of fourteen years, spanning the period 1956-57 to 1973-74, for India as a whole as well as for the individual states. He adopted the per capita consumer expenditure of Rs. 15 per month at 1960-61 rural prices as the poverty line. He calculated the equivalent poverty lines for different years by using consumer price indices for agricultural labourers (as that of Bardhan's work). Ahluwalia estimated both Sen's poverty index (Ps) and the traditional 'head count ratio' (as that of Bhatty's work) in his analysis. Some of the estimates of poverty is derived in Table–2.2. In the Table–2.2, the time series showed fluctuations in the incidence of poverty in response to variations in real agricultural output per capita, though no significant time trend was discernible. He found a statistically significant inverse relationship between rural poverty and agricultural performance for India as a whole. This relationship was also observed in several states but there was also evidence of other factors at work, which tended to increase the incidence of poverty independently of variations in agricultural output per capita.

The National Institute of Nutrition (1980) recommended different minimum calorie requirements on the basis of the nature of work carried on by different groups, i.e. sedentary, moderate and heavy work. If Dandekar and Rath had adopted different minimum caloric requirements separately for the rural and urban population by taking into account the nature, type and intensity of work carried on in two sectors, (i.e., higher minimum calorie requirements for rural population as compared to the urban population) their results might have been more reliable. Again Dandekar and Rath's study is based on NSS data which are collected only once a year, and do not give the reliable round-the-year information about the consumption pattern of the rural poor.

## Table–2.2

### Estimate of poverty in India

| | *Definition of 1960-61=100 poverty (Rs. per annum)* | *Period* | *Percentage of rural population below poverty line* |
|---|---|---|---|
| Ahluwalia | 180 | 1956-57 | 53.5 |
| | | 1960-61 | 38.4 |
| | | 1965-66 | 54.7 |
| | | 1967-68 | 56.5 |
| | | 1970-71 | 47.5 |
| | | 1973-74 | 46.1 |
| Bardhan | 180 | 1960-61 | 38.0 |
| | | 1964-65 | 45.0 |
| | | 1967-68 | 53.0 |
| | | 1968-69 | 54.0 |
| Dandekar and Rath | 180 | 1961-62 | 40.0 |
| Minhas | 200 | 1960-61 | 46.0 |
| | | 1964-65 | 39.3 |
| | | 1967-68 | 37.1 |
| Ojha | 2,250 Calories/per person/day) | 1960-61 | 52.0 |
| | | 1967-68 | 70.0 |
| Ranadive | 240 | 1953-54 | 38.0 |
| | | 1956-57 | 39.0 |
| | | 1961-62 | 37.0 |
| Vaidyanathan | 240 | 1960-61 | 59.5 |
| | | 1964-65 | 60.4 Based on NSS data |
| | | 1967-68 | 67.8 |
| | | 1960-61 | 58.8 |
| | | 1964-65 | 56.9 Based on official series |
| | | 1967-68 | 57.8 |
| Vyas | 180 | 1954-55 | 65.6 |
| | | 1960-61 | 63.2 |
| | 240 | 1954-55 | 45.5 |
| | | 1960-61 | 38.5 |
| Bhatty (NCAER) | 300 (1968-9=100) | 1968-69 | 54.4 |
| | 360 (1968-9=100) | 1968-69 | 67.1 |

**Source: S.A.R.Sastry (1980).**

Sastry (1980) stated that national income includes both consumption and investment goods and there is no reason why consumption should be deflated by the national income deflator because it covers the prices of both agricultural and manufactured commodities. Over the last decade prices of agricultural commodities rose at a much sharper rate than those of finished manufacturing commodities. But since the weight of the manufactured consumables in the budget of the rural poor is likely to be much lower than the nation average (which includes the rich and the poor, the urban as well as the rural sector), the national income deflator is very much likely to have understated the rise in the prices paid by the rural poor. Even within the class of agricultural commodities particularly cereals, there is evidence that the average price paid by the poor rose at a faster rate than that of the average price paid by the rich (Mahalanobis Committee on the Levels of Living gives empirical evidence to this effect). Further, since the weight of services in the budget of the rural poor is likely to be low, the national income deflator, which includes the price of services (whose index has grown at a relatively small rate), is likely to understate the general price rise for the rural poor.

Desai (1980) stated that Dandekar and Rath have adopted a methodology which is open to criticism on many grounds. They are wrong in taking the average requirement as the minimum requirement. They are equally wrong in not taking into account the different requirements of different age groups, sex etc. and basing their calculations on an all India average of calories intake. They have not shown an awareness of what the averages reveal and how they conceal.

Balakrishna (1981) by using the data on net domestic product from agriculture for the period 1974-75 to 1977-78 concluded that during the four years ending in 1977-78 incidence of rural poverty was on the decrease, both in relative terms and absolute numbers. The Planning Commission's estimate of rural poverty for 1977-78 given in the draft plan (1978-83) as 47.85 per cent is higher by 4.35 per cent when compared with Balakrishna's estimate of 43.5 per cent. Balakrishna has used the data of net domestic product from agriculture (1960-61 prices) for 1974-75 and 1975-76 from the

Reserve Bank of India. Since the corresponding data were not available for 1976-77 and 1977-78, he used the data on net national product from agriculture (1970-71 prices). The regression relationship between the net domestic product from agriculture (1960-61 prices) and net national product from agriculture (1970-71 prices) has been worked out by using the data for the period (1975-76). The required net domestic product data for 1976-77 and 1977-78 were obtained from his regression equation. Balakrishna has used different data from different sources by using different base years. Hence, the validity of the percentage of rural poor calculated by him is doubtful.

In determining the extent of poverty on the nutritional scale, Iyengar and Gopalkrishna (1985) took a minimum requirement of 2400 K calories per consumption unit (not per capita) as recommended by the Nutrition Experts Groups (Gopalan et al., 1871) and reduced it by 100 calories, to compensate for any under-estimation. This 2300 calories cut off happens to coincide with the FAO recommendations (FAO, 1973) endorsed by Sukhatme (1977). Using the above norm, the authors estimated poverty line separately for rural and urban Karnataka at Rs. 52.72 and Rs. 65 respectively in 1973-74 at constant prices.

The Task Force on Minimum Needs and Effective Consumption Demand constituted by the Planning Commission (1979) defined the poverty line as per capita monthly expenditure of Rs. 49.09 in rural areas and Rs. 56.64 in urban areas at 1973-74 prices corresponding to the per capita daily calorie requirements of 2400 k. calorie in rural areas and 2100 k. calorie in urban areas. This calorie norm for the poverty line, which was used for sixth plan, has been used for the seventh plan. The poverty line defined in this way covers the expenditure on food and non-food items and ensures the adequacy of calorie consumption. The poverty line is updated using the implicit CSO private consumption deflator as proxy for price rise in the consumption basket of the persons near the poverty line. The updated poverty line for 1983-84 is Rs. 110.81 per capita per month in rural areas and Rs. 117.50 in urban areas. For the estimation of the percentage of poor, NSS distribution of private consumption per capita is adjusted to correspond to the National Accounts Statistics level of total private consumption in the absence of any other information to allocate the difference among different expenditure classes. These are based on the recommendations of the Advisory Group on Estimation of percentage of persons below the poverty line for the seventh plan.

The Expert Group (1993) of the Planning Commission has accepted the poverty line of Rs. 491 (rural) and Rs. 571 (urban) at 1973-74 prices anchored on the recommended per capita daily intake of 2400 calories and 2100 calories respectively with reference to the consumption pattern of 1973-74. The expert group suggested, construction of state specific poverty line using state specific consumer price indices. Government of India (2001) official estimates published by the planning commission suggests that India recorded one of the developing world's fastest reductions in poverty during the 1990s. As per the official estimates poverty falls from 36 per cent of the population in 1993-94 to nearly 26 per cent at the end of the decade 1999-2000).

Gangopadhyay and Dubey (1998) examined the appropriateness of official poverty lines, and on the basis of calculations carried out in 1998, questioned several assumptions used in calculating these lines [poverty calculations for India]. They found that poverty estimates were higher in 1993-94 than warranted due to inappropriately high official estimates of inflation.

Deaton (2003) as per the estimates published in 2001, showed a marked reduction in the fractions of people in poverty. Among rural households, the fraction estimated to be in poverty is 27.1 per cent in 1999-00 compared with 37.3 per cent in 1993-94, while among urban households, the fractions were 23.6 per cent in 1999-2000, compared with 32.4 per cent in 1993-94.

Bhalla (2003) questioned about the official growth, inequality and poverty figures for India during 1983 to 1999 based on the fixed official poverty line and NSS data. The Government of India's figure of poverty in India that has declined from 45 per cent in 1983 to 26 per cent level in 1999-2000, a decline of 19 percentage points is a matter of questioning whether this result is credible or not. He then asked a question on what happens to inequality?

Clarifying this, he said that NSS data for the two survey years indicates no increase in inequality. Indeed, the Gini declined over this time period, and the share in consumption of the poor increased. An estimate of the per capita consumption growth, therefore, can provide an upper-bound estimate of poverty in India in 1999-2000. This estimate is provided by growth in real wages of the poorest of the poor-unskilled workers in rural agriculture. And a very lower-bound conservative estimate of their growth (supplied by NSS data) suggests that poverty in India in 1999 was less than 12 per cent. This is in sharp contrast to official estimate of poverty of 26 per cent for the some years.

Deaton (2003) has studied the relationship between prices and poverty in India during 1987-2000 using the consumption data from the 43rd, 50th and 55th rounds of the N.S.S. and computed for both urban and rural sectors of India separately by taking a range of consumer prices indexes for 1999-2000 relative to 1993-94 and for 1993-94 relative to 1987-88. The main focus of the study is to explain the methodology underlying by using the new price indexes and to incorporate them into estimation of poverty line.

Dutt, Kozel and Ravallion (2003) have developed an econometric model of poverty incidence which is calibrated to 20 household surveys for India's 15 major states spanning from 1960 to 1994. They suggesting that the key determinants of the rate of poverty reduction at state level are agricultural yields, growth of non-farm sector (depending on states initial conditions) development spending and inflation. The model is used to predict the rates of poverty reduction over the period 1994-2000. The findings suggest that up to 1999-2000, the incidence of poverty has been falling in India. The overall rate of poverty reduction is 0.8 percentage points per year for the period since 1993-94. This ratio is a little more than half way between the rates of poverty reduction implied by the 7 day recall and 30 day recall period data from the 55th round NSS data. And it is about 43 per cent of the rate of poverty reduction implied by the latter source. The estimates suggests that for 1990s the rate of poverty reduction is found to be slightly lower than India experienced in the 1980s and lower than the expectation based on growth elasticities of poverty calibrated to the 'pre-reform' data.

Panda and Sarangi (2004) has estimated the incidence of tribal poverty among the tribals in Orissa. In this study two poverty lines such as the food poverty line and the income poverty line has been estimated using FGT methodology and four more poverty indicators along with HCR are estimated by using the NSS data of 55th round. The estimated HCR reflects that the incidence of poverty with reference to both the food and income poverty line is the highest for STs and the lowest for 'others' category. The study reveals that the poverty gap ratio, which measures the depth of poverty, is the highest for STs and lowest for 'others' with reference to the food poverty line and the pattern is found little different with respect to income poverty line. The squared gap ratio which reflects the severity of poverty is again found to be highest for STs followed by SCs in respect to both the poverty lines. The intensity of poverty is also highest for STs with reference to both the poverty lines followed by 'others' then by SCs. Sen's index is found to be highest for STs followed by SCs and then by 'others'.

Ghose (2004) observed that labour market in India depicts a peculiar situation. The poor and the unemployed, are two distinct groups. The poor are not unemployed and the unemployed are not poor. Employment in the labour market is supply driven. The supply of labour automatically creates its own demand and a labour accepts jobs at wages/income whatever they are provided. The poor cannot afford to remain unemployed. The corollaries of this situation are growing incidence of child labour (Basu et al. 2005), distressed outmigration (Sankaran, 1994; Radhakrishna, 2002; David and Gupta, et al. 2005), high female work participation rate (Sundaram and Tendulkar, 2004) depressed fertility (Anand, 1998) with high mortality, low skill level, illiteracy, more precisely the poor human resource base.

Pradhan, Panda and Sarangi (2005) have studied about dynamics of poverty and under-development in Orissa. They found that the poverty is rampart in the state. The incidence of poverty is very high in the southern part of Orissa, which is dominated by the tribal population. Though Orissa is self sufficient in food grain production, hunger and starvation death still prevails in Southern Orissa. Chronic poverty is found rampant among the tribal in southern, and northern regions of Orissa (as per NSS regions of Orissa).

## 2.2 Conclusion

The review of studies on consumption behaviour, estimation of poverty line and the magnitude and incidence of poverty reveals that a number of studies have been done in this area. But there is a gap in micro-level studies which links these two areas both at national and regional level. The coverage of studies using unit consumer scales in the estimation of poverty line is scanty. Particularly for Orissa, no such studies have been done so far using consumer unit scales for the estimation of poverty line and poverty indices in the state. Further, a few studies have been done so far using per capita income for estimating the poverty line for the state. The present study is an attempt to fulfill this gap by providing a wide ranging coverage of the estimation of poverty line using both per capita and per unit expenditure and to explore the variation in consumption pattern vis-a-vis the magnitude and incidence of poverty among the four different occupation households of the state.

Thus, this review of various studies on poverty in India has revealed that their major focus has been on the aspect of measurement. None of them, in fact, examined the conceptual issues underlying the definitions of poverty or explored into casual links in depth between the various factors underlying the phenomenon. Even in the aspect of measurement there are many issues to be resolved. Though the price dimension does not figure in cross-section studies, it possess serious problem in time-series explorations. The choice of a relevant price deflator is one of the thorny problems in these exercises when one works out estimates of poverty over time. As different socio-economic groups will in general be differently affected in real terms by the movement of prices, the quantification of poverty at an aggregate level ceases to be meaningful unless the focus is on clear-cut analytical socio-economic groups like the fractile classes and occupational groups. Perhaps the most satisfactory way of resolving this issue is to adopt fractile price indices for the respective categories.

To dwell for a while on the other issues raised above, in most of the measurement exercises, precision in quantification is confined mostly to the food component (based on per capita consumption expenditure and certain norms of nutritional level of diets) while no satisfactory method has yet been evolved in estimating the basic needs under non-food (e.g., health, education, clothing, housing, fuel and light, etc.) with precision. The current practice is to adopt the observed proportion of non-food expenditure for the non-food component of the poverty line. This implies circularity as what is observed is indicated as the defined need in arriving at the poverty line in measurement exercises.

Almost all the above-mentioned studies are based on NSS data which are collected once in a year which generally coincides with the agricultural year. Consumption pattern in rural areas is directly related to the cropping pattern of that region especially of the rural areas. Further, the same norms (in terms of Rs./calories per capita per day/month) have been adopted by each scholar for the country as a whole, ignoring the regional differences in the cropping pattern, climatic conditions, customs and traditions, eating habits, etc., some of them have used the same norm both for the rural and urban areas without taking into account the differences in the nature, type and intensity of activities carried on these two sectors.

## REFERENCES

1. Noteworthy Among Those Who Used the Linear form are Allen and Bowley (1935); Allen (1942); Stone (1954); Leser (1961) and Pollak (1971). Similarly, the Most Extensively used form is the Double-log or Constant Elasticity Engel Curve. Main Contenders of this Form are Tobin (1950); Stuvel and James (1960); Brown (1954, 1964); and Theil (1965). The Hyperbolic form Proposed by Praise and Houthakker (1955) Tried out by Several Researchers like Goreaux (1960); Leser (1963); Bowley (1982) and Panda (1996). Tornquist (1941) has Tried the General form of Hyperbolic Consumption Function, Separately for Necessary, Semi-luxury and Luxury Items. The Log-log-inverse (LLI) Function has Introduced by Goreaux (1964). Other Important Studies on Functional forms of Engel Curves Includes Aasness and Rodseth (1983); Witte and Cramer (1986); Keen (1986); Nicol (1993); Aasness, Biron and Skjerpen (1993) etc.

2. Mention may be made of Roy and Laha (1960), Roy and Dhar (1960), Sinha (1966), Gupta (1968), Singh (1968), Maitra (1969), Bhattacharya and Maitra (1969), Jain (1972), Jain and Tendulkar (1973) and Panda (1996).
3. Ganguly (1960), Singh (1968, 1969), Jain and Tendulkar (1973), Coondoo, Mukherjee and Rao (1974, 1979) and Coondoo (1975).
4. Systematic Research on the Distribution of Income by Size of Different Levels of Development was Undertaken Towards the Mid of 1940s Internationally. The Work of Kuznets (1963); Kravis (1962); Nicholson (1967); Soltow (1968); Stack (1972); Weisskoff (1970); and Fishlow (1972) Focuses on the Trends in Income Inequalities in a Number of Countries.
5. Kravis (1960); Oshima (1962); Adelman and Morreis (1973); Chenery and Syrquin (1975); Paukert (1973) and Cline (1975).

# 3

# HOUSEHOLD COMPOSITION AND MEASUREMENT OF UNIT CONSUMER SCALES

## 3.1 Introduction

Consumption pattern of a household, in general is affected by several economic and non-economic factors. Some of the important determinants/factors of the household consumption pattern are income, household size and composition, level of education, occupation, tastes and habits, psychological factors etc. All these variables are not quantifiable. Neither these variables are equally important nor is it possible to find out the individual effects of all these variables in a single model as they interact with each other. Because of this, researchers in the past have investigated the effects of one or two important variables depending on the purpose of their study.[1] Income has, generally, been singled out as the most important determinant of consumption pattern. But data on income are either highly unreliable or not available, total consumption expenditure is frequently used as a proxy variable for income.[2] Household composition, generally, defined as the age, sex and work activities of its members have been ignored in most of the studies because of the computational and analytical difficulties involved. Household composition influences not only the magnitude but also the structure of consumption expenditure of a household.

Since different types of household members have different needs and ability to consume, the actual decisions regarding expenditure by a household are considerably influenced by the composition of the household (in terms of age-sex, work activities etc.). Therefore, while analyzing the consumption pattern of a household, a simple and straight forward Engel curve analysis in per capita terms such as equation–3.1 may not be satisfactory and it is desirable to consider household composition as one of the determining factors in Engel curve analysis. The Engel curve in per capita terms is

$$\frac{Y_{ij}}{n_j} = f_i\left[\frac{X_j}{n_j}\right] \tag{3.1}$$

where $Y_{ij}$ is the expenditure on the 'i'th item by the 'j'$_{th}$ household, $X_j$ is the total consumption expenditure by the 'j'$_{th}$ household, $n_j$ is the number of person in the 'j'$_{th}$ household and ($f_i$) indicates the functional form of the relationship. $y_{ij}$ and $x_j$ are the per capita specific item and the total expenditure respectively.

There are two possible ways of considering the effect of household composition in Engel curve analysis: (i) Classify the households in different groups so that each group consists of households of identical composition. The Engel curve analysis is then applied to each group separately and the results are compared. (ii) Adjust for the differences in composition between households in the Engel function itself. This is usually done by assigning adult equivalent weight to each member of different age and sex are converted into equivalent adult units. Household composition, thus, quantified in terms of equivalent adult units is then treated as a variable in the same way as income and its influence as measured and/or eliminated using an appropriate technique. The first method is direct and relatively simple. But the efficiency of this method is constrained by the non-availability of adequate data. The second method though computationally difficult, is less data demanding. Its application is more suited to household survey data. We, therefore, follow the second method.

Broadly speaking, these scales are of two types: (i) normative scales and (ii) economic scales. Normative scales are constructed, generally, on the basis of calorie requirements of individuals. The scales are, thus, constructed reflected the relative calorie needs rather than relative costs involved. It is the fact that calorie requirement of infants and children are lower than that of adults, but the cost of providing calories to the former may be higher than to that of the later. This is because adult obtain a large proportion of calories from cheaper food items like cereals whereas children, generally, get calories from relatively costlier food items like milk, fruits etc. Thus, normative scales tend to underestimate cost of providing nutrition to children. On the other hand, the basis of constructing economic scales is the consumption expenditure rather nutritional needs. Hence, as compared to nutritional scales, economic scales are more appropriate and useful not only for demand analysis but also for adjusting the distribution of consumption expenditure for variation in household composition, determination of accurate level of poverty and inequality etc.

There are essentially two approaches for estimating these scales:

(i) *The discrete scale approach:* This approach assumes that the scales vary between broad age-sex groups but remain invariant within each group.

(ii) *The continuous scale approach:* This approach assumes that the scales very continuously with the age of the individuals.

The common approach in the construction of equivalent scales is to group household members into various age-sex categories so that the specific scales are stepwise discrete (Prais and Houthkker, 1955; Price, 1970). However, alternative adult equivalent scale designs suggested by Friedman (1952) and Blockland and Somermeyer (1970) in specifying the scales as continuous functions of age and sex of the household members (Blockland, 1976; Base and Salathe, 1978). This later approach overcomes the restrictiveness of the former approach. Changes in expenditure pattern are then explicit functions of the biological and psychological growth (life cycle specification—a continuous process) of individual household members. The above continuous equivalent scale specifications provide no explanation for the selection of the boundary values of the age classes and for the variation in consumption pattern at various stages of the lifecycle. Further, socio-demographic factors, which are generally the key determinants of household expenditure, are often excluded in equivalent scale models. To overcome these difficulties, Tedford, Capps and Havlicek (1986) developed an equivalent scale (called the TCH scale) where the concepts and components of lifecycle are based explicitly upon the research by Levinson et al., (1978) and upon the concepts from child and human development described by Duvall (1977) and by Vander Zaden (1978).

We follow the discrete scale approach in our analysis. The purpose of the present chapter is to estimate the 'specific' and 'income' unit consumer weights, which constitutes 'specific' and 'income' scales respectively using the first (discrete) approach. Several researchers[3] have proposed alternative methods of estimation of unit consumer scales but the systematic and well known among them is the method adopted by Prais and Houthakker for British workers. But this procedure of estimation is arbitrary with regard to the choice of the functional forms of Engel curves and also the choice of their parameters, thereby enhancing the bias. In addition to this, the Prais and Houthakker procedure cannot be applicable if, for any specific item, the Engel curve assumes a functional form with more than one explanatory variable. Therefore, an alternative iterative procedure proposed by Singh and Nagar (1973), which overcomes the above difficulties, is applied for the estimation of 'specific' and 'income' unit consumer scales in the study.

A number of approaches have been used to introduce household size and composition into the specification of Engel function (equation 3.1). In particular, economists have been concerned with the generation of adult equivalent scales to reflect consumption behavior and/or requirements of household members in different age-sex classification. Adult equivalent scales, alternative to per capita measures, provides information on the contribution of various household members to the consumption behavior of the household. The common practice is to assign the adult male a weight of one and to assign other household members fractional weights based on their relative consumption needs as compared to adult males. The weights can be based on physiological and nutritional requirements (Engel, 1957; Stone, 1953; Hymans and Shapiro, 1974) or on observed consumer behaviour (Sydenstricker and King, 1921; Wold and Jureen, 1953; Prais and Houthakkar, 1955; Forsyth, 1960; Barten, 1964; Price, 1970; Singh and Nagar, 1973). Finally, the Barten and Muellbauer scales are based on the basic consumption theory and useful in welfare analysis (Barten, 1966; Muellbauer, 1974, 1977; Bojer, 1977; Nelson, 1992). Prais-Houthakker, Blockland, Buse and Salathe scales are reduce form of parameters useful in forecasting the effect of changes in the household consumption on household expenditure, while the Barten and Muellbauer scales are structural parameters useful in the evaluation of cost of living due to changes in household composition. Household equivalent scales and aggregates of the adult equivalent scales are consequently weighted household size measures, with adjustments for difference in age-sex composition of the household.

Prais and Hauthakker (1955) recognized the need for introducing two types of unit consumer scales, viz. those for the expenditure on different items (specific scale) and that for the income/total expenditure of the household (income/overall scale). The specific scales measures the equivalence of different type of persons in respect of the consumption of different items of household budget, while the income scales are overall scale measures the proportion of the total household income/ expenditure assigned to any particular member of the household. Both the income and the specific scales may be called 'unit consumer scales'.

The revised formulation of equation equation-3.1 in per unit scales is,

$$\frac{Y_{ij}}{\sum_{r} w_{ir} n_{rj}} = f_i \left[ \frac{X_j}{\sum_{r} w_{0r} n_{rj}} \right] \tag{3.2}$$

where $w_{ir}$ is the value (or the weight) for the 'r'$_{th}$ (r = 1, 2,....., k) type of persons on the specific unit consumer scale for the 'i'$_{th}$

(i =1, 2,.......m) item, $w_{0r}$ is the value (or the weight for the 'r'$_{th}$ person on the income/overall unit consumer scale; and $n_{rj}$ is the number or 'r' type of persons in the 'j'$_{th}$ household (j = 1, 2,....N).

Obviously $n_j = \sum_r n_{rj}$ is the unweighted household size of the 'j'$_{th}$ household. Thus, $\sum w_{ir}n_{rj}$ and $\sum w_{0r}n_{rj}$ measures the household size in terms of number of unit consumers (or in terms of equivalent adults where the adult male is taken as numeraire) measured on the specific and overall scale, respectively. The weighted household size is denoted as $n^*_{ij} = \sum w_{ir}n_{rj}$, for the same household 'j'. So, in equation (**3.2**) the dependent variable is the per unit expenditure on the 'i'$_{th}$ item by the 'j'$_{th}$ household and the explanatory variable is the total per unit expenditure of the 'j'$_{th}$ household. In equation (**3.2**) the unknowns to be estimated are the ($w_{ir}$)s, ($w_{0r}$)s and the structural parameters of $f_i$. The Engel curve analysis can then be carried out in terms of per unit expenditure instead of per capita. Prais and Houthakker pointed out that for every 'r', the ($w_{0r}$)s related to corresponding ($w_{ir}$)s through the restriction,

$$w_{0r} = \sum_{i=1}^{m} \frac{Y_{ij}}{X_j} \cdot \frac{\sum w_{0r}n_{rj}}{\sum w_{ir}n_{rj}} . w_{ir} \qquad 3.3$$

which follows from the budget constraints $\sum Y_i = X$. This function derived in equation (3.3) constitutes the basis for many empirical studies on the effect of household consumption on household consumption pattern.[4]

The per unit figures may be used in several ways: (a) to determine the effects of different age-sex groups on the consumption pattern of the household which will enable us to make more efficient predictions of commodity-wise consumption pattern that are highly useful for policy purposes, (b) to facilitate investigations of the economics and dis-economics of scale operating on the consumption pattern of the household, (c) to help in investigating the distribution of various items among different consumer units and the welfare level of households more accurately which may, in turn, be used for matters of giving relief and subsidies in form of tax reduction, and (d) for international comparison of development between countries.

This chapter is organised into four sections. Section-3.1 is the introduction. Section-3.2 deals Methods of estimating unit consumer scales. In section-3.3, the empirical results of the estimates of 'specific' unit consumer weights for different food and non-food items of consumption and the estimates of income unit weights corresponding to five different age-sex classes are examined; and finally, the concluding comments of the study are represented in section-3.4.

## 3.2 Methods of Estimating Unit Consumer Scales

In the beginning, the effect of a single additional individual on the household consumption was used to investigate, by comparing group of households with identical composition except for the presence or absence of one member. This approach was soon abandoned in view of its inefficient results and various other difficulties (Kemsley, 1952). The limitations of this method are: (1) it is difficult to get sufficient number of households of the requisite type and (2) it is possible that consumption pattern of the households of this type may be different by several other factors such as income distribution, regional, climatic and social conditions etc. As a result, subsequent researchers in the field mainly considered child as a fraction of an adult. Although, this idea was originally propounded by Carrol and Bright (1875) and then by Engel (1857) but its scientific treatment was done by Sydenstricker and King (1921). Later Prais and Houthakker developed a more logical and scientific iterative procedure for estimating unit consumer scales which was further modified by Singh and Nagar (1973). In this chapter, we have used the Singh and Nagars' Iterative Method for estimating unit consumer scales, the brief description of which is given below.

### *3.2.1 Singh and Nagar's Iterative Method*

Singh (1968), Singh and Nagar (1973) adopted a modified version of Prais and Houthakker's iterative procedure to estimate both the specific and income scales independently of any such restrictions and assumptions as employed in the models of Forsyth (1960), Barten (1969) and Coondoo (1973, 1975). It is obvious that the same form of the Engel function (in per capita or per unit terms) may not describe the consumption pattern with respect to all the items of consumption. Prais and Houthakker choose to work with only the semi-log and the double-log in their study. However, Singh and Nagar's model need not be constrained by any particular form of the Engel function. Instead, they scan through eleven different functional forms[5] (viz. L, DL, SL, EX, LI, HYP, P, LP, LO, LLI and SLI) at each stage of the iterative procedure and select the best fit one which (i) provide initial and final critical levels of demand below and above which the consumer would not have any demand for the item in question however low or high his income may be, (ii) satisfy the Slutsky's conditions and (iii) explains the maximum variation in the dependent variable.[6] We have applied ordinary least squares method at each stage of the iterative procedure (for details refer Panda, 1996 and Sarangi, 2006).

In the present iterative procedure we estimate all the parameters from the sample data while Prais and Houthakker (1955) assigned arbitrary values in their method of estimation. Unlike Praise and Houthakker, we can use any functional form for the Engel curves. The estimates of ($w_{ir}$)s do not involve under or over-estimation because we are setting $w_{0r}$=1. Further, the proposed iterative procedure side-steps, the problem faced by Forsyth (1960). This has the advantage that at no stage does the number of parameters to be estimated exceeds the number of equations and also the mutual dependence of the ($w_{ir}$)s and ($w_{0r}$)s is preserved.

As it often happens in regression analysis, the investigator may come across estimates of parameters which are either too high or too low (values) or of wrong signs according to normal expectations. The procedure of estimating unit consumer scales outlined above is not free of this difficulty. The unexpected results obtained may arise for several reasons. For example, it may be that the basic specification of the model is wrong or that some of the assumptions underlying the theory of estimation have been violated. However, it may also be possible that not all the available information has been used. Many times are knows a priori, that particular coefficients in the given regression are positive or negative or they satisfy some linear constraints among them. This type of 'a priori' information may be derived from economic theory or may be used on empirical evidence available to the investigator. It is, therefore, desirable to incorporate all the available information in the estimation procedure to get sensible results. The estimates so obtained will be more efficient. Moreover, this technique helps in solving the problem of multi-co linearity in the regression, at least to some extent.

Considering the problem of determining unit consumer scales discussed above, it may be noted that negative values of ($w_{ir}$)s do arise and even though plausible explanations may be found for some of them, they may lead to inconsistencies in consumer demand relationship.[7] For example, it may so happen that $\hat{w}_{ir}$ associated with the r[th] age-sex groups may be high and negative such that $\sum_{r=1}^{k} w_{ir} n_{rj}$, the number of unit consumers in the j[th] (j = 1, 2, 3,...., N) household, itself may become negative. In such a situation, per unit expenditure on the i[th] item will be negative. This violates the basic assumption of non-negativity of expenditure underlying consumer demand theory. Therefore, it may be desirable to incorporate the following inequality constraints on ($w_{ir}$)s in the estimation procedure.

$0 \leq w_{ir} \leq 1$ for all *i* and r[(i = 1, 2, 3,...., m), (r = 1, 2, 3,..., k)] (3.4)

Further, since all the age-sex groups constituting the household size are responsible for total expenditure on a particular item, the individual effect of different age-sex group on the expenditure of a specific item added together to unity; i.e.,

$$\sum_{i=1}^{k} w_{ir} = 1, \text{ for all } (i = 1, 2, 3, \ldots k) \qquad (3.5)$$

## 3.3 The Empirical Results

In the present study, we have estimated the consumer unit scale for nine food item groups viz., cereals; pulses and its products; milk and its products; edible oil, meat, fish and egg; vegetables and fruits; sugar and gur; salt and spices and beverages and five non-food items viz., pan, tobacco, intoxicants; fuel and light; clothing; durables and miscellaneous non-food items using data of 600 rural households purposively selected from different NSS stratums of the state collected during its 55th round (1999-00).

Singh (1968) and Singh and Nagar (1973) in their study proposed four different age-sex groups. They combined boys between 14-19 years of age and girls between 4-14 years of age into one group assuming that the expenditure on a girl of 19 years is, normally, more than that on a boy of equal age. But, actually the consumption pattern of boys and girls of the above age categories is not the same. In Indian families, parents lay much emphasis on their sons and neglect their daughters. Sons are well fed, dressed and avail all educational facilities as compared to their daughter. Generally, expenditure on a boy for different items of consumption is supposed to be higher than a girl (for the above age-sex categories). Hence, in this present study, we have segregated boys between 13-18 years and girls between 13-18 years of age as two separate groups to test the hypothesis of sexual discrimination in the allocation of family budget. For the present analysis, we have classified the member of each household into six different categories of age and sex groups. These age sex groups are as follows:

(i) Group-1: Adult males above 19 years.

(ii) Group-2: Adult females above 19 years.

(iii) Group-3: Adolescent boys between 13-18 years.

(iv) Group-4: Adolescent girls between 13-18 years.

(v) Group-5: Boys and girls, between 5-12 years.

(vi) Group-6: Children between 0-4 years.

Apart from household size and age-sex composition of household, several socio-economic determinants and other non-economic determinants affect the consumption pattern of the household. We restrict our analysis to one important socio-economic determinant i.e. the occupation of the household. The effect of these determinants is of three types, viz., i) economic effects stems from the income differentials associated with different occupation. Thus, the co-efficient of total expenditure/income may serve as an index of this type of effects, ii) but the socio-cultural effects are long-term effects. It reflect the attitudes and motives acquired over and sustained for a long time. It is these deep seated habits, unique to each group which is reflected in the variation of consumer behaviour for different occupation groups, iii) household daily requirement of calories, the allowances recommended by Nutritional Experts Group. The Indian Council of Medical Research (ICMR, 1968) has classified human activities into three broad categories (a) heavy (b) moderate and (c) sedentary. Information on work activities of adults is not available. The NSS provides information only about household occupation. It would be reasonable to assume that the work activities of adult males in the family correspond to that household's occupation. Different occupation involves human labour in different degrees. Even within each occupation, different operations may involve human labour in different degree. Based on these considerations, the sample households are categorized into four groups. i) salary and regular wage earner households (type-A occupation) (ii) small business and traders households (type-B occupation) (iii) cultivator households (type-C occupation) and finally (iv) Agriculture and other labour households (type-D occupation). The salary and regular wage earner households (type-A) are involved in occupations with light physical labour. The business households (type-B) and the cultivator household (type-C) are involved in occupation with moderate physical labour and finally the agriculture labour and other labour households involve in occupations with heavy physical labour. So the calorie requirements of the household vary from one occupation group to another. The present sample of 600 households includes 160 households for each category of occupation type.

We have applied the Singh and Nagar's interactive procedure to estimate both the specific and income scales taking into account the six age-sex category of household composition separately for each occupation group relating to nine food items and five non-food item groups mentioned above. We have tried with five functional form of Engel functions viz., L, SL, EX, P, SLI and chosen the most suitable form of Engel function at each stage of iteration for adjusting the specific total item expenditures ($C_j'$) and total consumption expenditure to household composition. The iterative procedure was continued till the estimates of specific and income scales are stable i.e. the difference between corresponding specific and income scales in two successive iterations is negligible. The iterative procedure was found to converge faster in case of salary and regular wage earner households (type-A) and the convergence was slower in case of agriculture and other labour households (type-D). It was also observed that the linear, semi-logarithmic and parabolic are selected most frequently for different items of consumption for all the occupation groups. The semi-logarithmic form (SL) is found to be the most suitable form of Engel function for cereals, the linear form (L) is found to be the most suitable form for pulses and its products like edible oil; meat, fish and egg and miscellaneous non-food items. Finally, for vegetables and fruits; sugar and gur; salt and spices; beverages; pan, tobacco and intoxicants; fuel and light; clothing and durables, the parabolic form is found to be most plausible functional form in the initial and final stage of iteration.

The item-wise estimates of specific and income unit consumer scales are converted into adult equivalent scales for different categories of occupation groups and for all occupation are presented in Table–3.1 to 3.5. It is observed from Table-3.1 that the adult specific equivalent scales are the highest for adult males and the lowest for the children (0-4 years) for most of the items of consumption. For milk and milk products only the specific adult equivalent scale is the highest for the children (0-4 years). But the scales for cereals; salt and spices; fuel and light; clothing; durables are the highest for adult females. When we compare these scale between adolescent boys and adolescent girls, it is observed that the weights for adolescent boys are little higher than girls for all most all consumption items except cereals; vegetables and fuel and light.

It is noticed from Table–3.2 that the equivalence weights for adult males are also the highest for all most all items of consumption except cereals; milk and milk products; salt and spices; fuel and light; clothing and durable for the type–B occupation households. For pulses; edible oil; slat and spices; fuel and light and clothing; the equivalent scale are the highest for adult females. The adult equivalent scales for children (0-4 years) are the highest for milk and milk product and lowest for other items of consumption. When compared the adult equivalents scales between boys and girls (13-18 years) these scales are found to be higher for boys than girls. This clearly indicates the consumption pattern of (type-A) occupation and (type-B) occupation are almost similar.

Table–3.3 reveals that adult equivalent scales for adult males is the highest for most of the items of consumption except cereals; salt and spices; fuel and light; clothing and durables and the lowest for children for all these items except milk and milk products. The scales for cereals; salt and spices; fuel and light; clothing and durable is the highest for adult females. One interesting feature of the scales for clothing is that these scales are higher not only for adult females but also for boys and girls (13-18 years). For pan, tobacco and intoxicants these scales are negative for children and very low for boys and girls (5-12 years).

From Table–3.4, it is noticed that the adult equivalent scale for type–D occupation for adult males are again the highest for adults and except cereal; milk and milk product; salt and spice; fuel and light; clothing and durables. For cereals; salt and spice; fuel and light; clothing and durables, the scales are the highest for adult females and for milk and milk products, the scale is the highest for children. The scale of all items except milk and milk products are the lowest for children (0-11). From Table–3.5, it is observed that for all most all items except milk and milk products; sugar and gur; salt and spices; fuel and light and clothing, these scales are the highest for adult males but for milk and its products, these scales are the highest for children (0-4 years). The scales of miscellaneous items are negative for children. On the other hand, the income scales are the highest for adult male in all occupation groups except group B occupation. For households in group B occupation, this scale is the highest for adult females and for all households. The income equivalent scales are found to be more than 0.90 for all occupation group. But in the combined group this scale is less than 0.90 for a few items. When we observe the pattern of these scales, we find that the scales are descending from adult males followed by adult females than adolescent boys and girls and so on in all the occupation groups.

**Table–3.1**

**Itemwise estimates of specific and income adult equivalent unit consumer scales for type-A occupation**

| *Sl. No.* | *Consumption item* | *Specific Scales* | | | | | |
|---|---|---|---|---|---|---|---|
| | | $\hat{W}^*_{i1}$ | $\hat{W}^*_{i2}$ | $\hat{W}^*_{i3}$ | $\hat{W}^*_{i4}$ | $\hat{W}^*_{i5}$ | $\hat{W}^*_{i6}$ |
| 1. | Cereals | 1.000 | 1.0394 | 0.8179 | 0.8306 | 0.5588 | 0.2357 |
| 2. | Pulses | 1.000 | 0.7072 | 0.7599 | 0.5585 | 0.5531 | 0.3210 |
| 3. | Milk | 1.000 | 0.5526 | 0.7314 | 0.3637 | 0.7221 | 1.6140 |
| 4. | Edible oil | 1.000 | 0.8153 | 0.7650 | 0.5150 | 0.2345 | 0.2006 |
| 5. | Meat, Fish and Egg. | 1.000 | 0.8169 | 0.9678 | 0.6499 | 0.5945 | 0.3032 |
| 6. | Vegetables | 1.000 | 0.9597 | 0.8424 | 0.8410 | 0.4638 | 0.0820 |
| 7. | Sugar and Gur | 1.000 | 0.9018 | 0.9191 | 0.6961 | 0.4485 | 0.5879 |
| 8. | Salt and Spices | 1.000 | 1.0466 | 0.9033 | 0.6665 | 0.4337 | 0.1332 |
| 9. | Beverage | 1.000 | 0.7587 | 0.7897 | 0.4878 | 0.3039 | 0.3448 |
| 10. | Pan, tobacco and intoxicants | 1.000 | 0.4485 | 0.8423 | 0.3211 | 0.2196 | -0.2788 |
| 11. | Fuel and light | 1.000 | 1.0285 | 0.8775 | 0.9017 | 0.5803 | 0.2474 |
| 12. | Clothing | 1.000 | 1.2350 | 0.9237 | 1.0352 | 0.7187 | 0.6164 |
| 13. | Durables | 1.000 | 1.0410 | 0.9123 | 0.8093 | 0.4115 | 0.2364 |
| 14. | All miscellaneous non-food exp. | 1.000 | 0.9667 | 0.7051 | 0.5147 | 0.5038 | 0.2410 |
| | Income scale | 1.000 | 0.9142 | 0.7815 | 0.6871 | 0.5013 | 0.2789 |

### Table–3.2

**Itemwise estimates of specific and income adult equivalent unit consumer scales for type-B occupations**

| Sl. No. | Consumption item | Specific Scales | | | | | |
|---|---|---|---|---|---|---|---|
| | | $\hat{W}^*_{i1}$ | $\hat{W}^*_{i2}$ | $\hat{W}^*_{i3}$ | $\hat{W}^*_{i4}$ | $\hat{W}^*_{i5}$ | $\hat{W}^*_{i6}$ |
| 1. | Cereals | 1.0000 | 0.9670 | 0.8254 | 0.6621 | 0.6369 | 0.4334 |
| 2. | Pulses | 1.0000 | 1.0323 | 0.6744 | 0.6393 | 0.2235 | 0.1343 |
| 3. | Milk | 1.0000 | 0.4420 | 0.6643 | 0.7777 | 0.9756 | 2.2397 |
| 4. | Edible oil | 1.0000 | 1.0680 | 0.8985 | 0.6917 | 0.7128 | 0.5387 |
| 5. | Meat, Fish and Egg. | 1.0000 | 0.9276 | 0.8671 | 0.4598 | 0.4282 | 0.1708 |
| 6. | Vegetables | 1.0000 | 0.8079 | 0.6048 | 0.5477 | 0.5225 | 0.1688 |
| 7. | Sugar and Gur | 1.0000 | 0.8973 | 0.8020 | 0.6714 | 0.6505 | 0.4988 |
| 8. | Salt and Spices | 1.0000 | 0.9605 | 0.5886 | 0.6439 | 0.3477 | 0.2421 |
| 9. | Beverage | 1.0000 | 0.8614 | 0.6687 | 0.4563 | 0.4210 | 0.2237 |
| 10. | Pan, tobacco and intoxicants | 1.0000 | 0.6734 | 0.4867 | 0.3416 | 0.1918 | 0.1288 |
| 11. | Fuel and light | 1.0000 | 1.0355 | 0.8307 | 0.7941 | 0.7633 | 0.1198 |
| 12. | Clothing | 1.0000 | 1.0656 | 0.8482 | 0.9634 | 0.5098 | 0.2365 |
| 13. | Durables | 1.0000 | 0.8781 | 0.6355 | 0.7105 | 0.2982 | 0.2193 |
| 14. | All miscellaneous non-food exp. | 1.0000 | 0.9523 | 0.7348 | 0.5175 | 0.2290 | 0.2458 |
| | Income scale | 1.0000 | 1.1198 | 0.9062 | 0.7472 | 0.6143 | 0.3662 |

**Table-3.3**

**Itemwise estimates of specific and income adult equivalent unit consumer scales for type-C occupations**

| Sl. No. | Consumption item | *Specific Scales* | | | | | |
|---|---|---|---|---|---|---|---|
| | | $\hat{W}^*_{i1}$ | $\hat{W}^*_{i2}$ | $\hat{W}^*_{i3}$ | $\hat{W}^*_{i4}$ | $\hat{W}^*_{i5}$ | $\hat{W}^*_{i6}$ |
| 1. | Cereals | 1.0000 | 1.0387 | 0.9005 | 0.8160 | 0.5490 | 0.2315 |
| 2. | Pulses | 1.0000 | 0.7072 | 0.7599 | 0.5585 | 0.5531 | 0.3210 |
| 3. | Milk | 1.0000 | 0.5526 | 0.7319 | 0.3637 | 0.7221 | 1.6140 |
| 4. | Edible oil | 1.0000 | 0.8153 | 0.7650 | 0.5150 | 0.2345 | 0.2006 |
| 5. | Meat, Fish and Egg. | 1.0000 | 0.8169 | 0.9678 | 0.6499 | 0.5945 | 0.3032 |
| 6. | Vegetables | 1.0000 | 0.8281 | 0.7578 | 0.7726 | 0.4261 | 0.0753 |
| 7. | Sugar and Gur | 1.0000 | 0.9018 | 0.9191 | 0.6961 | 0.4485 | 0.5879 |
| 8. | Salt and Spices | 1.0000 | 1.0466 | 0.9033 | 0.6665 | 0.4337 | 0.1332 |
| 9. | Beverage | 1.0000 | 0.7587 | 0.7897 | 0.4878 | 0.3039 | 0.3448 |
| 10. | Pan, tobacco and intoxicants | 1.0000 | 0.7316 | 0.4896 | 0.1866 | 0.1276 | -0.1616 |
| 11. | Fuel and light | 1.0000 | 1.1291 | 0.9634 | 0.7964 | 0.6371 | 0.2716 |
| 12. | Clothing | 1.0000 | 1.3813 | 1.0923 | 1.1578 | 0.8038 | 0.6894 |
| 13. | Durables | 1.0000 | 1.0410 | 0.9123 | 0.8093 | 0.4115 | 0.2369 |
| 14. | All miscellaneous non-food exp. | 1.0000 | 0.9667 | 0.7051 | 0.5147 | 0.5038 | 0.2410 |
| | Income scale | 1.0000 | 0.9335 | 0.8106 | 0.6676 | 0.5013 | 0.2789 |

## Table–3.4

**Itemwise estimates of specific and income adult equivalent unit consumer scales for type-D occupations**

| Sl. No. | Consumption item | Specific Scales | | | | | |
|---|---|---|---|---|---|---|---|
| | | $\hat{W}^*_{i1}$ | $\hat{W}^*_{i2}$ | $\hat{W}^*_{i3}$ | $\hat{W}^*_{i4}$ | $\hat{W}^*_{i5}$ | $\hat{W}^*_{i6}$ |
| 1. | Cereals | 1.0000 | 1.0572 | 0.8268 | 0.8306 | 0.6479 | 0.2357 |
| 2. | Pulses | 1.0000 | 0.7072 | 0.7599 | 0.5585 | 0.5531 | 0.3210 |
| 3. | Milk | 1.0000 | 0.7872 | 0.9366 | 0.4653 | 0.9239 | 2.0653 |
| 4. | Edible oil | 1.0000 | 0.8153 | 0.7650 | 0.5150 | 0.2345 | 0.2006 |
| 5. | Meat, Fish and Egg. | 1.0000 | 0.7697 | 0.9678 | 0.6499 | 0.5945 | 0.3032 |
| 6. | Vegetables | 1.0000 | 0.8817 | 0.7578 | 0.7726 | 0.4261 | 0.0753 |
| 7. | Sugar and Gur | 1.0000 | 0.9018 | 0.9191 | 0.6961 | 0.4485 | 0.5879 |
| 8. | Salt and Spices | 1.0000 | 1.0466 | 0.9033 | 0.6665 | 0.4337 | 0.1332 |
| 9. | Beverage | 1.0000 | 0.7587 | 0.7897 | 0.4878 | 0.3039 | 0.3448 |
| 10. | Pan, tobacco and intoxicants | 1.0000 | 0.2306 | 0.5719 | 0.1651 | 0.1129 | 0.0735 |
| 11. | Fuel and light | 1.0000 | 1.0285 | 0.8775 | 0.9017 | 0.5803 | 0.2474 |
| 12. | Clothing | 1.0000 | 1.2350 | 0.9237 | 1.0352 | 0.7187 | 0.6164 |
| 13. | Durables | 1.0000 | 1.0410 | 0.9123 | 0.8093 | 0.4115 | 0.2369 |
| 14. | All miscellaneous non-food exp. | 1.0000 | 0.9667 | 0.7051 | 0.5147 | 0.5038 | 0.2410 |
| | Income scale | 1.0000 | 0.9173 | 0.7890 | 0.6871 | 0.5270 | 0.2891 |

**Table-3.5**

**Itemwise estimates of specific and income adult equivalent unit consumer scale for 'All Occupational Group'**

| Sl. No. | Consumption item | *Specific Scales* | | | | | |
|---|---|---|---|---|---|---|---|
| | | $\hat{W}^*_{i1}$ | $\hat{W}^*_{i2}$ | $\hat{W}^*_{i3}$ | $\hat{W}^*_{i4}$ | $\hat{W}^*_{i5}$ | $\hat{W}^*_{i6}$ |
| 1. | Cereals | 1.0000 | 0.7579 | 0.8638 | 0.9255 | 0.6485 | 0.5035 |
| 2. | Pulses | 1.0000 | 0.8947 | 0.8934 | 0.6537 | 0.8229 | 0.6092 |
| 3. | Milk | 1.0000 | 0.5356 | 0.4783 | 0.7059 | 1.6694 | 1.7778 |
| 4. | Edible oil | 1.0000 | 0.7086 | 0.8053 | 0.5001 | 0.7376 | 0.3293 |
| 5. | Meat, Fish and Egg. | 1.0000 | 0.8829 | 0.5825 | 0.1388 | 0.4095 | 0.0762 |
| 6. | Vegetables | 1.0000 | 0.8679 | 0.6059 | 0.8523 | 0.5723 | 0.4457 |
| 7. | Sugar and Gur | 1.0000 | 1.1719 | 0.8096 | 0.7083 | 0.7853 | 0.4643 |
| 8. | Salt and Spices | 1.0000 | 1.2818 | 0.5829 | 0.7130 | 0.6801 | 0.5343 |
| 9. | Beverage | 1.0000 | 0.5494 | 0.4949 | 0.4091 | 0.6619 | 0.2320 |
| 10. | Pan, tobacco and intoxicants | 1.0000 | 0.8739 | 0.7762 | 0.8501 | 0.8570 | -0.3355 |
| 11. | Fuel and light | 1.0000 | 1.4014 | 0.8719 | 0.8079 | 0.5640 | 0.5394 |
| 12. | Clothing | 1.0000 | 1.3257 | 1.3363 | 1.0608 | 0.6206 | 0.5165 |
| 13. | Durables | 1.0000 | 0.8718 | 1.6326 | 0.5160 | 0.2216 | 0.1967 |
| 14. | All miscellaneous non-food exp. | 1.0000 | 0.6279 | 0.7266 | 0.3204 | 0.4842 | -0.3834 |
| | Income scale | 1.0000 | 0.7528 | 0.7216 | 0.6479 | 0.5384 | 0.3202 |

## 3.4 Conclusion

For the above analysis of specific and income adult equivalent scales for fourteen broad consumption items estimated by Singh and Nagar's iterative procedure, we conclude the following separately for different occupation group of households:

The adult equivalent scales vary from one age-sex category to another and from one occupation group to another from one consumption item to another. The adult equivalent scales over different age-sex categories and also across the different occupation groups varies more remarkably in food items than non-food items.

One interesting feature of the income adult equivalent scales are that these scales are the highest for adult males followed by adult females then by adolescent boys, and girls (13-18 years) then by boys and girls (5-12 years) and finally by children. So these scales are arranged in a descending order from adult male to children except in occupation type-B where this scale is the highest for adult females.

The specific adult equivalent scale for pulses and its products; meat, fish and egg; vegetables and fruits; beverages; pan, tobacco and intoxicants and misc. non-food items are the highest for adult males (above 18 yrs.); for fuel and light and clothing are the highest for adult females (above 18 yrs.) and for milk and milk product is the highest for children (0-4 years); but for pan, tobacco and intoxicants, the scale is the lowest and even negative for children in each of the four occupation as well as for all households. The scales are generally, small for all most all items for the children. For the boys and girls (5-12 years), these scales are almost the 2$^{nd}$ lowest and adolescent boys and girls (13-18 years) are little less than adult males and females for most of the consumption items over different occupation groups.

When we compare the scales both specific and income between adult male and adult females and also between adolescent boys and adolescent girls, it is observed that the scales are higher for adult males and for adolescent boys in the consumption of most of the food and non-food items across all the occupation groups. This is a clearly indication of discrimination of females irrespective of there age in household consumption across households of different occupation groups in the rural sector of the state.

## REFERENCES

1. For Instance Iyengar, Jain and Srinivasan (1968) and Gupta (1973) have Examined the Effects of Income and Household Size; Singh (1968) and Jain and Tendulkar (1972) and Sarangi (2006) of Occupational Factors; Prais and Houthakker (1955) and Singh and Nagar (1973), Panda (1996) and Sarangi (2006) of Household Composition; Michel (1972) of Education Level and Kotona (1951) of Psychological Factors.
2. Some Other Reasons for Preferring the Use of Current Consumption Expenditure to that of Current Income are Discussed in Deaton (1980), Srinivasan (1977).
3. Sydenstricker and King (1921); Woodsburry (1944); Nicholson (1949); Henderson (1949); Friedman (1952); Wold and Jureen (1953); Brown (1954); Prais and Houthakker (1955); Forsyth (1960); Roy and Dhar (1960); David (1962); Singh and Nagar (1969); Barten(1960); Juckson (1967); Price (1971); Moshane (1971); Coondoo (1973); Blokland (1976); Nicholson (1976); Kaptesn and Praag (1976); Kakwanic (1977a); Bojer (1977); Mcclements (1977); Muellbauer (1974, 1975, 1980); Buse and Salathe (1978); Pallak and Wales (1979); Blundell (1980); Brown and Johnson (1984); Paul (1985); Tedford, Caps and Flavlicek (1986); Roy (1986a); Jargenson and Slesnick (1987); Fither (1987); Deton, Javier and Thamas (1989); Burney and Khan (1992); Jain and Patel (1990); Schiepers (1997); Conniffe (1997); Nelson (1997); Sehiepers (1997); Conniffe (1997); Nelson (1997); Dickers, Fri and Pathardes(1993).
4. This Formulation Ignores the Possibility of Economics/Dis-economics of Scale in Household Consumption. However, the Equation (4.2) could be Further Revised to Include Possibilities of such Economies/ Diseconomies (Parais and Houthakker, 1955, Chapter-10).
5. Eleven Alternative Functional forms of the Engel Function, viz., L, DL, SL, EX, LI, HYP, P, LQ, LLT and SLI are Considered at each State of the Iteration of the above Procedure.
6. Singh and Nagar (1977) has Shown that Identification can not be Achieved if the item, for which the Scale is Known, has Zero Income Elasticity.
7. The estimators, $\tilde{W}_i$ take into account both the inequality and equality.

   Constraints has been proposed on N. C. Kakwani in his 'Problem of Estimation and Forecasting in Econometric Modes', unpublished Ph.D. Thesis, Delhi, 1967, pp. 50-53.

# 4

# INTER-OCCUPATIONAL VARIATIONS IN HOUSEHOLD CONSUMPTION

## 4.1 Introduction

It is generally believed that poverty is a direct reflection of low levels of per capita income rather than skewed income distribution. However, available empirical evidences contradict this widely held view point. It follows, therefore, that development strategies which succeed in raising the level of per capita income may not have any impact on absolute poverty if they are accompanied by deterioration in relative income shares. It has been observed that during the post-reform period (1993-94 to 1999-2000) in India, the real per capita income has increased at a rate of little over 4 per cent per annum, while the incidence of poverty has been falling by a little less than 1 percentage point. This implies that the disparities in the food expenditure of people in different expenditure classes have been declined. This proposition follows from the fact that people in the higher expenditure class spend proportionally less of their income on food compared to those in lower expenditure class, as their per capita income increases. Further, if the people in the higher expenditure class have a tendency to save more and spend lesser amount of increased income on non-food items, then disparities in per capita expenditure may even decline for non-food items is a sign of rising prosperity for people in the lower expenditure group too. This obviously will tend to reduce absolute poverty in a country.

Poverty reduction, therefore, is not merely a function of rising per capita income but the extent to which increased per capita income has benefited the different sections of society.

This analysis will obviously throw light on the behaviour of disparities in the food and non-food consumption expenditure along with the overall income distribution. If these disparities over time have displayed a tendency to decline significantly, then it depicts that the benefits of economic development have been distributed among different classes rather than confining to upper class only. This has facilitated in lowering the absolute poverty levels in the country. In this chapter, an attempt is made to examine the pattern of disparities in food, non-food and overall consumption expenditure, along with the behaviour of the household savings-income relations so that one could comprehend the direction of change in the relative poverty levels over a period of time. In addition, the inter-sectoral and inter-occupational variation in household consumption of different items, which have a significant bearing on the disparity in living standards, and the level of poverty is also examined in this chapter.

This chapter is divided into seven sections. The chapter begins with a brief introduction presented in section-4.1. Section-4.2 deals with various functional forms of Engel and the methodological issues involved in the Engel curve analysis along with the procedure of using the Dummy Variable Interaction Model (DVIM). Section-4.3 depicts the trend and interrelationship among consumption, inequality and poverty in India. Section-4.4 deals with the pattern and trend of consumption and poverty in Orissa. Section-4.5 reveals the empirical analysis of inter-sectoral variation in household consumption in the state. Section-4.6 depicts the empirical analysis of inter-occupational variation in household consumption. Finally, section-4.7 is the conclusion of this chapter.

## 4.2 Household Consumption and Engel Curve Analysis: Methodological Issues

Empirical investigation on consumer behaviour started with the customary procedure of determining the suitable functional form of Engel function, showing the relationship between total expenditure and particular item expenditure. The problem of finding the most appropriate form of Engel function has no clear-cut solution which appears to have found general acceptance. Generally, it is true to say that the specification of the form of relationship attracted less attention than that of the methods of estimating parameters for specified equations. To some extent, the answer depends on the degree of emphasis placed on the various properties one desires the function to possess.

The choice of functional form depends on three propositions (i) a close connection with direct or indirect utility function which may appear desirable (ii) the function should ideally be valid for all positive values of total outlay and the variation in Engel elasticities entailed by the formula associated with a functional form should be plausible and (iii) finally, the function should fulfil economic, statistical and econometric criteria. Estimation of parameters should be simple, convenient, allowing an assessment of reliability of goodness of fit and the error of specification should also be reasonable. Praise and Houthakker (1955), Roy and Dhar (1960), Liviatan (1961), Singh (1968), Maitra and Bhattacharya (1970), Coondoo (1975), Shah (1980), Bowley (1982), Rao, Singh and Patel (1982), Hampton (1985), Tansel (1986), Witte and Cramer (1986), Giles (1988), Nicol (1993), Panda (1996), Panigrahi (1998) and other researchers in the field of consumer behaviour have experimented with a number of Engel functions. Their studies indicate that (i) no unique Engel curve suffices for the complete range of consumer goods (ii) different mathematical forms give rise to widely differing elasticities. We thus, confine our attention to the problem of finding those Engel curves which give the most adequate fit for various food and non-food items.

### *4.2.1 Various forms of Engel Functions*

Instead of using per capita income, per capita total expenditure is used as a proxy variable, which is considered to be the most important factor affecting expenditure for most of the consumption items in Engel curve analysis.[1] For this reason our first concern is to choose an appropriate algebraic relationship between per capita item expenditure and per capita total expenditure with other variables constant. Eleven functional form of Engel curves are considered for our investigation. All the relationships are expressed in per capita terms in order to ignore the effect of household size which is another important variable effecting consumption pattern. The commonly used two parameter forms are Linear (L), Double-logarithmic (DL), Semi-logarithmic (SL) Exponential (EX), Log-inverse (LI), Hyperbolic (HYP).

*Linear (L) Engel Curve*: It is the simplest of all as regards to estimation and interpretation of its parameters. It satisfies the adding-up, homogeneity and symmetry condition. It also assumes constancy of marginal propensity to consume. The magnitude of Engel elasticity ($\eta$) varies directly with the per capita total expenditure (x) and inversely with the specific item expenditure (y). Besides, it implies that Engel elasticity tend to unity as income/total expenditure tends to infinity. So, this functional form is favoured by researchers for its general applicability and easier interpretion. This form is suitable, generally, for necessary items.

*Double-log (DL) Engel Curve*: It is most popular in two parameter forms. Here Engel elasticity ($\beta$) is constant at all levels of income/total expenditure. It also provides convex and concave curvature of the Engel curves to the income axis according to $\beta_i \lessgtr 1^2$ and straight line for $\beta_i = 1$. It also provides an automatic correction for heteroscedasticity of disturbances. This form is suitable especially for luxury items.

*Semi-logarithmic (SL) Engel curve*: For necessities, this form of Engrel curve is often proved to be satisfactory. It is the non-additive form of Engel curve which gives good approximation of double-log form in the neighbourhood of average income/total expenditure. It implies a decline in the Engel elasticity with rising income/total expenditure particularly for the items having under-elastic demand. The Engel elasticity ($\beta$/y) decreases continuously to zero as consumption expenditure increases.

*Log-inverse (LI) Engel Curve*: For necessity items approaching saturation, the Log-inverse Engel curve is found to be the suitable one where the elasticity ($\beta$/x) declines to zero with rising income/total expenditure. It has a sigmoid-shaped curve passing through the origin which implies that it does not provide any initial critical level of income below which the consumer does not have any demand for that item.

The *Exponential (EX) Engel Curve:* This form of Engel curves which provides elasticity increasing with income level and marginal propensity to consume. The elasticity is also increasing with the level of consumption of a particular item. Intutively, it will represent well for luxury item. It is used to explain the behaviour of household consumption in underdeveloped regions.

*Hyperbolic (HYP) Engel Curve:*[3] This functional form is suitable for necessities. The marginal propensity to consume is inversely related to income squared and Engel elasticity is a decreasing function of income within a specified range.There is an income level for which Engel elasticity is equal to unity, the curve to its left represents the region of luxury items and to its right upto a point a region for necessicity items and beyond that point a region of inferior items. It may be mentioned that among these six forms only hyperbolic (HYP) form possess both a threshold and a saturation level. The semi-logarithmic form and linear form possess threshold but no saturation level. In log-inverse form, Engel elasticity is inversely related to income and it possess the saturation level. But double-logarithmic form possess none of these.

The two-parameter forms, though useful for many individual items for explaining variations in expenditures, some times prove to be inadequate as judged by their goodness of fit. It is worthwhile to refer to the three-parameter forms. The commonly used three-parameter forms are parabolic (P), log-parabolic (LP), log-quadratic (LQ), log-log-inverse (LLI) and semilog inverse (SLI). The three-parameter Engel curves are more flexible then two-parameter forms.

These three-parameter Engel functions are used for the purpose of adjusting and accounting for the abrupt changes in the movement of Engel curves (unaccounted by the two-parameter forms) if the data on income/total expenditure involve a wide range. For example, the *Log-log-inverse (LLI)* Engel curve rises (a) sharply for the initial values of 'x' (b) moderately for some further ranges of 'x' and (c) then, after the saturation point, it declines for very high values of 'x'. Thus, the curve can be divided into three segment's— first representing for luxury items, second for necessary items and third one for inferior items. In this function,

Engel elasticity is income increasingly if $\gamma$ is less than zero and income decreasing if $\gamma$ is more than zero. This form is widely used by the researchers as it shows sensible variation in Engel elasticity along the curve and also ensures satisfactory fit for all types of items. The *Semi-log inverse (SLI)*, also implies diminishing Engel elasticity for an item with rising income (for normal signs of the parameters). This tendency appears to be more marked in this form *(SLI)* than that of *Log-log-inverse (LLI)*. The tendency of increasing elasticity with the increase in the income/total expenditure level would be more pronounced in case of *Log-parabolic (LP)* than the *Parabolic (P)* form of Engel functions (for normal signs of the parameters). But in case of *Log-quadratic (LQ)* function, Engel elasticity is proportional to the logarithmic of total expenditure and thus changes in it are expected to be slow.

### 4.2.2 *Economic and Statistical Criteria for the Choice of the Engel Curves*

For the choice of a suitable Engel function, it involves certain economic or theoretical criteria, statistical criteria and econometric criteria. Unfortunately, the theory consumer behaviour offers very little in the context of specification of Engel curves (Coondoo, 1975). In fact the only theoretical restriction on the form of Engel curves stem from the budget constraint. Usually, this restriction is labelled as the adding-up criterion which proves to be too stringent and limits the choice to a few functional forms that may not fit actual expenditure data very well. The other restrictions are concerned with the shape of the Engel curve. First, the saturation criterion stipulated that the level of predicted consumption should approach a satiety level as income/total expenditure increases indefinitely (at given prices). Actually, if the adding-up criterion and the saturation criterion applied to item expenditures which are mutually inconsistent since the former may be true only when the later does not hold for at least one item. The second criterion, more pertinent for luxury items, suggests that the Engel curve should possess a threshold level of income below which the consumption of that specific item would be zero. Thirdly, since the empirical evidence frequently indicates a negative correlation between total expenditure and the Engel elasticity, it is expected that the nature of many items of consumption changes from luxury to necessary and even finally to inferior as total expenditure level rises.

The other economic-theoretical criteria are: first, it is desirable that the parameters of the Engel curve should have simple economic interpretation. Secondly, the estimated elasticities should confirm to theoretically plausibility in terms of its magnitude and sign. Finally, this criterion also includes (a) availability of graphical test (b) easy handling of heteroscedastic disturbances (c) treatment of zero observations (d) preference of a two-parameter Engel function to a three-parameter one.[4]

The principal statistical criteria governing the choice of the functional form centre around such properties as (a) goodness of fit i.e. the capability of explaining observed variation in item expenditure, (b) tractability in the context of demand projections and other applications, (c) simplicity of estimation of parameters.

The most important statistical criteria is that of the goodness of fit. The goodness of fit can be judged from (a) the extent of variation of the dependent variable of the Engel curve explained by the regressor (or regressors) and (b) the degree of randomness of the residuals around the fitted regression. As regard to (a) the coefficient of determination ($R^2$) is used frequently for two-parameter forms and adjusted coefficient of determination ($\overline{R}^2$) is used for three and more parameter forms. Another measure of goodness of fit is the 'F' statistic. It provides joint significance of the parameters of the Engel functions as well as the significance of $R^2$ and $\overline{R}^2$. The $R^2$ and $\overline{R}^2$ are the suitable measure of goodness of fit for comparing competing functional forms. (b) For examining the extent of auto-correlation and specification error if any, the Durbin-Watson (DW) statistic, Run test and other non-parametric tests are used very often (Paris and Houthakker, 1955 and Gupta, 1973).[5] Finally, the criterion of simplicity of estimation ordinarily means that a least-squares regression technique should be applicable after appropriate transformation of variables.

### 4.2.3 *Method of Estimation*

The regression models are useful in assessing the effects of both quantitative and qualitative factors. Effects of qualitative factors can be tackled by using the Analysis of Variance (ANOVA) model and the effects of both quantitative and qualitative factors can be tackled either by using the Analysis of Covariance (ANCOVA) model or Dummy Variable Interaction Model (DVIM). The latter two models are of mixed character which includes both qualitative and quantitative factors. We have made extensive use of the Dummy Variable Interaction Model (DVIM) for studying the inter-sectoral and inter-occupational variations in consumption pattern of different food and non-food items of consumption.

### *4.2.3.1 Dummy Variable Interaction Model*

To investigate the differential effect of sectoral/regional/occupational factors on the expenditure pattern of an household, we consider the following dummy variable interaction model[6],

$$y_j^r = \alpha_1 + \sum_{i=2}^{p} \alpha_i D_{ij}^r + \beta_1 x_j^r + \sum_{i=2}^{p} \beta_i Z_{iJ}^r + \varepsilon_j^r \tag{4.1}$$

where $D_{iJ}^r = \begin{cases} 1 & \text{when } i = r \ (i, r = 1, 2, \ldots\ldots, p) \\ 0 & \text{otherwise} \end{cases}$

and $Z_{iJ}^r = D_{iJ}^r x_j^r$

Here $y_j^r$ and $x_j^r$ represent the average monthly specific item expenditure and total expenditure, respectively in per capita terms for the households in the $j_{th}$ ($j = 1, 2, \ldots, n_r$) per capita total expenditure class and belonging to the $r_{th}$ ($r = 1, 2, \ldots\ldots, p$) group; $(\alpha_i)$s and $(\beta_i)$s are the parameters of the model and $E_j^r$ are the random disturbance term which have the usual assumptions of a linear regression model.

### *4.2.4 The Model and the Estimating Procedure*

For the purpose of comparing the consumer behaviour in the rural and urban sector of Orissa, it imperative to use the same functional form of Engel curves for both the sectors. This is necessary because different functional forms have different assumptions and also yielding different elasticity. In view of this, we choose the Linear (L) Engel function for meat, fish and egg; pan, tobacco and intoxicants and all non-food items; the Double-log (DL) Engel function for cereal and its products, edible oil, vegetables, fuel and light and all food items and the Exponential (EX) Engel function for durable goods and finally, the Parabolic (P) form for pulse and its products, milk and its products and clothing as the best-fit functional form of Engel curves in the Dummy variable interaction model for investigating the inter-sectoral/inter-occupational variation of consumption pattern.

The best fit functional forms of Engel curves used in the Dummy variable interaction model are estimated by the method of weight least squares (WLS). Estimated percentage of number of persons in each expenditure group is used as weights (these are provided in the NSS reports). Expenditure elasticities for each consumption item are computed at the corresponding average per capita specific item of expenditure and average per capita total expenditure of the sectors/occupation. The published NSS grouped data on consumption expenditure collected during the 55$^{th}$ round (1999-00), the sixth quinquennial survey constitute the data base for the empirical analysis of the study.

## 4.3 Trend of Consumption, Poverty and Inequality in India

It is generally observed that a study of income distribution over time is marred by the lack of proper data but still one can manage to draw inferences about pattern of relative poverty on the basis of trend of the disparities in consumption expenditure and behaviour of household savings of different expenditure classes. In India, since 1972-73 NSSO has been regularly publishing quinquennial round reports on the level and pattern of consumption expenditure. Moreover, NSSO is also regularly publishing data on sources of household income in India corresponding to different quinquennial round on consumer expenditure. The two data sets together will facilitate to draw inferences about the behaviour of relative poverty or income disparities in India.

It is clearly evident from that the two estimates almost match each other so that the difference between them is of around 1 per cent or even less than that. Thus, our methodology gives the precise, consistent and realistic estimates of Gini Coefficient and area below Lorenz curve. In the absence of even distribution of persons among different expenditure groups, where trapezoidal rule cannot be applied, our methodology can be effectively used to determine area below Lorenz curve and, hence, Gini coefficient to determine disparities with regard to any variable like consumption expenditure, income, wealth etc. The trend in absolute rural poverty and the extent of disparities in the food, non-food and total consumption expenditure among different expenditure classes on the basis of our methodology are presented in Table–4.1.

**Table-4.1**

**Gini coefficient and the Lorenz curve for food, non-food and total consumption expenditure (1999-2000)**

*(in per cent)*

| *Measures of inequality* | *Trapezoidal Rule* | | | *Our Methodology* | | |
|---|---|---|---|---|---|---|
| | *Food Exp.* | *Non-Food Exp.* | *Total Food Exp.* | *Food Exp.* | *Non-Food Exp.* | *Total Consumer Exp.* |
| Area Under Lorenz (Rural) | 39.76 | 33.65 | 37.28 | 39.71 | 33.59 | 37.25 |
| Area Under Lorenz Curve (Urban) | 38.02 | 28.43 | 33.04 | 38.12 | 28.16 | 33.05 |
| Gini Coefficient (Rural) | 20.48 | 32.70 | 25.40 | 20.58 | 32.83 | 25.50 |
| Gini Coefficient (urban) | 23.97 | 43.14 | 33.93 | 23.76 | 43.69 | 33.91 |

**Source: Estimated on the basis of NSSO report on Level and Pattern of Consumer Expenditure, 6th Quinquennial Survey 1999-2000, Government of India.**

The data in Table-4.2 provide some interesting facts about rural India. The real per capita NDP during 1970s, increased at a rate of around 0.32 per cent per annum while the level rural poverty declined marginally from approximately 56 per cent to 53 per cent only (NAS estimates). During the same period, disparities in food, non-food and overall consumption expenditure increased significantly, especially the disparities in non-food expenditure. Obviously, the benefits of economic development has favoured the rural rich and the marginal decline in rural poverty, that has occurred, is owing to some possible drift of benefits of the increased per capita income to lower expenditure classes of society. Thus, on account of increased disparities in household consumption expenditure among different classes and that savings are largely concentrated with the people in higher expenditure class, therefore, during 1970s, income disparities too have aggravated. Thus, our analysis fully corroborates the first part of Kuznets hypothesis that initially economic development will aggravate the inequalities in income distribution. Moreover, it also highlights the fact that initial decline in absolute poverty will only be marginal, especially in developing countries and which will possibly occur on account of insignificant drift of benefits of economic development towards the lower expenditure classes. The case of rural India is a testimony to it. Thus, mere rise in overall per capita income is not sufficient to reduce poverty rather its distribution is more important for absolute poverty to decline.

**Table–4.2**

**Poverty ratios and Gini coefficient for food, non-food and total consumption expenditure in India (1972-73 to 1999-00)**

*(in percentage)*

| *Quinquennial Rounds* | *Absolute Poverty level* | | *Gini Coefficient* | | | *Gini Coefficient* | | |
|---|---|---|---|---|---|---|---|---|
| | | | *Rural* | | | *Urban* | | |
| | | | *Food Expend.* | *Non-food Exp.* | *Total Expend* | *Food Expend.* | *Non-food Exp.* | *Total Exp.* |
| 1st Round 1972-73 | 56.4 | 49.1 | 22.16 | 41.09 | 26.80 | 16.70 | 28.17 | 25.84 |
| 2nd Round 1977-78 | 53.1 | 45.2 | 25.86 | 51.29 | 31.32 | 20.55 | 40.05 | 31.86 |
| 3rd Round 1983 | 45.7 | 40.8 | 20.42 | 41.01 | 28.05 | 24.08 | 48.24 | 33.96 |
| 4th Round 1987-88 | 39.1 | 38.2 | 21.93 | 41.24 | 30.36 | 24.32 | 46.19 | 33.73 |
| 5th Round 1993-94 | 37.3 | 32.4 | 20.51 | 39.76 | 27.46 | 23.55 | 46.13 | 33.55 |
| 6th Round 1999-00 | 27.1 | 23.6 | 20.58 | 32.83 | 25.50 | 23.76 | 43.69 | 33.91 |

**Source:** **Estimated from the data of six quinquennial rounds, Report on Level and Pattern of Consumption Expenditure in India, NSSO, Dept. of Statistics, Government of India.**

The estimated growth rate of per capita rural NDP in real terms for the period 1980-81 to 1993-94 is approximately 3.0 per cent per annum. It is worth to mention that this is a fairly long period, which we have to consider for estimating the growth rate of rural per capita NDP, as the data for rural and urban NDP was not available for other intervening years. The significant improvement in the per capita NDP growth rate from 0.3 per cent per annum to around 3.0 per cent per annum as well as considerable decline in disparities regarding food, non-food and overall consumption expenditure of different classes in rural areas has facilitated to reduce absolute rural poverty significantly. The absolute poverty which was 53 per cent in 1977-78 has come down to 37 per cent in 1993-94. There has been a gradual decline in absolute poverty between 1997-78 to 1993-94 but the decline in the disparities in consumption expenditure on food items of different classes is not so, during the same period. In such a situation, one may argue as to how the redistribution of the basic wage good (i.e. food) has not converged gradually among different income classes. It has declined between 1977-78 and 1983, but thereafter, it has increased marginally. This is also contrary to Engel's law which suggests that with the rise in income, proportion of income spent on food declines i.e. richer community tends to spend lesser proportion of income on food than the poor community. Since this did not happen, one may wonder whether redistribution has really helped in curtailing the absolute rural poverty. It is also observed that in between 1983 to 1987-88, there has been a major shift in consumption of food basket especially for rural rich. The shift is from the traditional items of cereals to more nutritious food items, such as milk and its products, meat, fish and egg etc. This shift is clearly evident from Table-4.2, which shows that although the MPCE (monthly per capita expenditure) on cereals has declined by 6 percentage points, but overall food expenditure has declined only marginally between 38$^{th}$ (1983) and 43$^{rd}$ (1987-88) NSS rounds. Prior to this, such a significant shift was not visible. It is also noticed that though MPCE on cereals during the 27$^{th}$ (1972-73) and 32$^{nd}$ (1977-78) NSS rounds has declined by about 8 per cent, but it has simultaneously led to a decline in overall food expenditure by about similar percentage points. This depicts the absence of any compositional shift in the food expenditure of different classes, especially the rural rich during 1972-73 to 1977-78. However, such a change in food basket is clearly visible during 1983 to 1987-88. It is on account of this visible change in the food consumption basket which occurred during 1983 to 1987-88 that the distribution of increased per capita NDP even to the lowest classes is not at all evident in terms of decline in the disparities in consumption expenditure on food among different classes but its impact in curtailing absolute poverty from approximately 46 per cent to 39 per cent can be well explained in terms of the major shift occurring in the composition of food basket, especially for rural rich in India.

Our detail analysis on poverty for urban households in India will facilitate to throw light on Kuznets inverted-U hypothesis. Moreover, the analysis will also examine the behaviour of absolute poverty to changes in per capita income, and trace the pattern of change in disparities in consumption expenditure on food, non-food and total expenditure components along with the overall distribution of income.

It is noticed that during 1970s, the per capita NDP in urban areas has declined from Rs. 1294 to Rs. 1267. This is in contrast to what has been observed in the rural areas. One important reason for the decline in the urban areas is that the population growth rate was more than double that of rural areas. This is possibly large scale migration of workers to urban areas. Moreover, an overall price increase of around 10 per cent in urban areas is also responsible for depressing the real per capita NDP in urban areas.

Despite the decline in real per capita NDP during 1970s, absolute poverty in urban areas declined from 49 per cent to 45.2 per cent while disparities in food, non-food and total consumption expenditure increased during major part of 1970s. The only plausible explanation for this contrasting pattern at the macro-level is the significant increase in the price of cereals, food and non-food items. For instance price of cereals between 1972-73 to 1977-78 increased at a rate of 5.6 per cent per annum while the price of overall food items increased at around 8.4 per cent per annum which forced people in the lower expenditure class to consume cereals rather than other food item which are more nutritious and which are a part of the consumption basket of the rich people. This has caused disparities in the food expenditure to widen. Moreover, the disparities in the non-food consumption expenditure rose more sharply than food consumption expenditure which is mainly on account of the fact that the price on non-food items showed an increase at a rate of 10.8 per cent per annum between 1972-73 and 1977-78. It is owing to such a steep rise in the prices of non-food items that the overall price index too displayed a rise at a rate of over 9 per cent per annum. This coupled with the fact that urban population increases at a rate of 3.75 per cent per annum caused the real per capita NDP to decline. However, since the price of basic wage goods like rice, wheat, etc. increased much slowly, therefore, consumption expenditure on cereals is not much affected as the consumption expenditure on other food and non-food items. Considering the fact that absolute poverty is mainly a function of the consumption expenditure on cereals in particular and all food items in general, its decline is not unusual despite the fall in real per capita NDP in urban areas during 1972-73 to 1977-78. Thus, the apparent contradiction between declining absolute poverty and real per capita NDP in urban areas is well explained by significant differential movements in the price indices of cereals, food and non-food items. This differential movement is also responsible for escalating disparities in food and non-food and overall consumption expenditure. Our analysis, thus, clearly revealed that mere low per capita income is not the cause of high absolute poverty rather it is influenced by other factors too. Moreover, rising disparities in consumption expenditure during the initial phase of economic development is at least an indicator of increasing income disparities or relative poverty too. Thus, the first part of Kuznets hypothesis is also corroborated by the available evidences from urban areas. This is in line with our findings for rural household sector of India.

The improvement in nominal per capita net domestic product is so much significant that despite the price of cereals, food and non-food items increased by over 12 per cent between 1977-78 to 1983, the per real per capita net domestic product increased on an average by about 3.28 per cent after 1981 and until 1993-94. The benefits of economic development during 1977-78 to 1983 is certainly experienced by all sections of the society, but is definitely biased towards urban rich. Our observations is based on the fact that though absolute poverty declined from 45.2 per cent to 40.8 per cent during 1977-78 to 1983 but the relative poverty has increased further as is evident from the residing disparities in the food, non-food and overall consumption expenditure.

Absolute poverty would have been declined still further and the disparities in consumption expenditure may not have increased, had the price of basic food items as well as of non-food items would have been of a tall order. Therefore, it is sufficient to suggest that mere increase in per capita NDP is not enough to make a substantial dent on the absolute poverty. Rather, redistribution of income and the extent to which price of basic food items increases during the process of economic development are reasonably important variables governing the level of poverty of a country. Furthermore, the disparities in all type of food, non-food and the overall consumption expenditure have increased during 1977-78 to 1983, therefore it is quite reasonable to infer that relative poverty during this phase in urban areas has increased i.e. the first part of Prof. Kuznets hypothesis, that rising disparities with increasing per capita incomes continue to hold good.

The shift in composition of food basket continued even thereafter, but the extent of change is not significant (Table-4.3). As a consequence, there is a marginal decline in the disparities of food consumption expenditure among different classes during the period 1987-88 to 1993-94.

Further, it is also evident from our analysis that in between 1977-78 to 1993-94, the disparity in the non-food consumption expenditure has declined from about 50 per cent to 40 per cent. The decline is fairly substantial but one should not interpret it as an indicator of declining income disparities too. There are three important reasons for it: (i) non-food expenditure in NSSO estimates represents a smaller fraction of total expenditure as compared to the food expenditure. Therefore, even smaller increases in non-food expenditure in money terms reflect large changes in percentage terms in it. On account of this, though the disparities in non-food expenditure has fallen from 51 to 40 per cent, yet the overall disparities in consumption expenditure has declined from just about 31 per cent to 27 per cent during 1977-78 to 1993-94; (ii) the household saving-income ratio has increased from 16.86 per cent to 23.08 per cent during 1977-78 to 1999-00.[7] This increase in household saving appears to be far more than the decline experienced in the disparities in consumption expenditure of different classes; and (iii) NSS estimates have been criticised for underestimation of consumption expenditure especially of the higher expenditure classes (Dandekar and Rath, 1971). Our analysis too has revealed it. This underestimation has been both for food and non-food item groups. The difference between in the NSS and NAS estimates is fairly low on food expenditure while it is relatively high on non-food expenditure especially the expenditure on miscellaneous items. What is indeed noteworthy is that the underestimation for non-food expenditure especially the expenditure on miscellaneous items has a tendency to increase.

**Table–4.3**

**Percentage distribution of monthly per capita expenditure (MPCE) on different food items over NSS rounds in rural India (1972-73 to 1999-00)**

| *Items* | *Average MPCE As Percentage of Total MPCE* | | | | | |
|---|---|---|---|---|---|---|
| | *27th* | *32nd* | *38th* | *43rd* | *50th* | *55th* |
| Cereals | 40.6 | 32.8 | 32.3 | 26.3 | 24.2 | 22.2 |
| Gram | 0.6 | 0.4 | 0.3 | 0.2 | 0.2 | 0.1 |
| Cereal Substitutes | 0.5 | 0.3 | 0.2 | 0.1 | 0.1 | 0.1 |
| Pulses and Products | 4.3 | 3.8 | 3.5 | 4.0 | 3.8 | 3.8 |
| Milk and Milk Products | 7.3 | 7.7 | 7.5 | 8.6 | 9.5 | 8.8 |
| Edible Oils | 3.5 | 3.6 | 4.0 | 5.0 | 4.4 | 3.7 |
| Mean, Fish and Egg | 2.5 | 2.7 | 3.0 | 3.3 | 3.3 | 3.3 |
| Vegetables | 3.6 | 3.8 | 4.7 | 5.2 | 6.0 | 6.2 |
| Fruits and Nuts | 1.1 | 1.1 | 1.4 | 1.6 | 1.7 | 1.7 |
| Sugar | 3.8 | 2.6 | 2.8 | 2.9 | 3.1 | 2.4 |
| Salt and Spices | 2.8 | 3.0 | 2.5 | 2.9 | 2.7 | 3.0 |
| Beverages | 2.4 | 2.5 | 3.3 | 3.9 | 4.2 | 4.2 |
| Food | 72.9 | 64.3 | 65.6 | 64.0 | 63.2 | 59.4 |

**Source: Level and Pattern of Consumer Expenditure, 6th Quinquennial Survey, 1999-2000, NSSO, Dept. of Statistics, Government of India, New Delhi.**

## 4.4 Pattern and Trend of Consumption and Poverty in Orissa

Orissa is a backward state characterized by persistent poverty, underemployment, low per capita income, inadequate development of socio-economic infrastructure, and recurrent natural calamities which have ravaged the state over the last four decade. The State Gross National Product at constant prices (1993-94) of Orissa increased from Rs. 8,536 crore in 1993-94 to Rs. 28, 685.68 crore in 2003-04 registering an annual growth rate of 4.46 per cent over the period which is much below the national growth rate. The state comprises of 36.08 million people accounts for 3.58 per cent of the population of the country. Nearly 87 per cent of its population live in rural areas and depend mostly on agriculture for their livelihood. Agriculture and its allied sector continued to be the main stay of the states economy with a contribution of about 25.97 per cent of the state domestic product during 2003-04 at 1993-94 prices. The decennial growth rate of population of the state during 1991-2001 was 16.25 per cent as against 20.06 per cent in the previous decade. The marginal decline in the growth rate of population in the state may be attributed to the rise in the literacy rate, effective dissemination of the massage about the benefits of small family. The density of population was 203 persons per square km in 1991 increased to 236 per square km in 2001. The urban population increased from 13.4 in 1991 per cent to 14.99 per cent in 2001. On the literacy front, the achievements have been remarkable. It has been noticed that the literacy rate increased from 49.09 per cent in 1991 to 63.1 per cent in 2001 as against the increase from 52.10 per cent to 64.8 per cent at the national level. The male and female literacy rate were 63.1 per cent and 34.7 per cent in 1991 have increased to 75.3 per cent and 50.5 per cent respectively in 2001. The percentage composition of households in ST, SC, OBC and others are 24, 22, 28 and 26 in rural Orissa as against 13, 17, 29 and 41 in urban Orissa respectively. It is observed that the distribution of social group was found to be homogenous in rural area, whereas it is heterogeneous in urban areas. Concentration of households belonging to other category is mostly found in urban Orissa.

Analysis of 55th round NSS consumption expenditure data reveals that the state of poverty in Orissa is worst. In comparison to the previous NSS round (50th round) in 1993-94, though there is marginal decline in the incidence of rural poverty from 49.8 to 47.8 per cent in Orissa, but the rate of escape from poverty in Bihar (where the incidence of poverty was highest in 1993-94) during the same period is from 57.9 per cent to 44.0 per cent which implies that the reduction of poverty in Bihar is much faster than Orissa. At all India level, during this period, there has been 10.3 per cent reduction in the incidence of poverty which is only 2 per cent in Orissa. In this background, the state of poverty in Orissa is very much discouraging. There is also a decline trend in the incidence of the poverty among all the social groups in both rural and urban areas of the state during the period 1983 to 1999-2000. At all India level, among the social groups, the reduction of poverty of SCs is marginally better by over 22 per cent than the other two social groups (ST and others) which is about 9 per cent. The decline in the incidence of poverty in Orissa is about 20 per cent for SCs, 14 per cent for STs and 23 per cent for other.

Table-4.4 shows per percentage distribution of households receiving income from different sources for a period of 365 days. It is observed that among the households engaged in cultivation in rural areas 58 per cent belongs to OBC and others category while the rest 42 per cent belongs to SC and ST category. This trend is also maintained in urban area i.e 69 per cent belonging to OBC and other social groups and 31 per cent from SC and ST groups. In rural Orissa, about 71 per cent households of SC and ST are receiving income from fishing and other agricultural activity, whereas in urban area only 16 per cent of households of ST and 45 per cent of SC households are getting their income from agriculture and other allied agricultural activities. This figure is 70 per cent in case of OBC and other groups.

## Table–4.4

**Percentage distribution of households reporting receipt of Income during a period of 365 days from different sources by Social Classes**

| *Sl. No.* | *Sources of Income* | *Rural* | | | | | *Urban* | | | | |
|---|---|---|---|---|---|---|---|---|---|---|---|
| | | *ST* | *SC* | *OBC* | *Others* | *All Classes* | *ST* | *SC* | *OBC* | *Others* | *All Classes* |
| 1. | Cultivation | 23.8 | 18.5 | 30.0 | 27.6 | 100 | 9.0 | 22.1 | 42.7 | 26.1 | 100 |
| 2. | Fishing & other | 41.0 | 30.2 | 18.3 | 10.5 | 100 | 7.3 | 22.6 | 39.6 | 30.6 | 100 |
| 3. | Agril. | 24.2 | 26.1 | 27.7 | 22.0 | 100 | 15.9 | 20.2 | 27.0 | 36.9 | 100 |
| 4. | Wage/Salary | 18.4 | 23.3 | 32.3 | 26.1 | 100 | 8.1 | 8.8 | 35.4 | 47.6 | 100 |
| 5. | Employment | 29.6 | 18.0 | 22.8 | 29.6 | 100 | 5.9 | 8.9 | 28.1 | 57.0 | 100 |
| 6. | Non-Agrl. | 39.2 | 16.4 | 15.3 | 29.1 | 100 | 3.3 | 5.3 | 28.2 | 63.2 | 100 |
| 7. | Enterprises | 10.9 | 20.0 | 30.8 | 38.2 | 100 | 3.0 | 14.6 | 15.7 | 66.7 | 100 |
| 8. | Pension | 33.6 | 11.6 | 15.0 | 39.8 | 100 | 1.1 | 11.3 | 25.4 | 62.1 | 100 |
| 9. | Rent | 28.1 | 21.9 | 23.5 | 26.5 | 100 | 15.5 | 28.8 | 23.9 | 31.7 | 100 |
| 10. | Remittance & Interest Divid. Etc. | 23.8 | 22.4 | 27.8 | 26.0 | 100 | 12.9 | 17.6 | 28.9 | 40.7 | 100 |

**Note:** **Computed from NSS data of 55th round, 1999-2000.**

In case of wage and salary, all the households are distributed equally between two broad social groups (of households) i.e. 50 per cent among OBC and others and 50 per cent among SC and ST households. In urban area it is 64 per cent and 36 per cent respectively. In case of non-agricultural enterprises, OBC and other groups dominated both in rural and urban areas. As regards to pension as source of income, nearly the same distribution of households is observed between two broad social groups—SC and ST group and OBC and other group in rural area, whereas in urban areas OBC and other group dominate the SC and ST group. When considered income from all sources, OBC and other social group constitute 54 per cent of the total household while SC and ST group constitute the rest 46 per cent in rural area. In urban area the percentage is 70 and 30 for these two broad groups respectively.

The percentage distribution of households and persons by social group into two broad MPCE class is presented in Table-4.5. It indicates that the percentage composition of households and persons in the lower MPCE classes is the highest for ST households than other categories of households i.e. 57 and 63 per cent in rural areas and 61 and 67 per cent in urban areas respectively. The percentage composition of households for SC, OBC and others categories are 43, 28 and 27 in rural areas and 54, 39 and 19 in urban areas in case of lower MPCE class. But the trend is reversed in both the sectors for higher MPCE class. This indicates that in both rural and urban households as well as among persons of different social group poverty is more rampant among ST households followed by SC then OBC and others households. Taking all social groups into account, it can be observed that on the whole 42 per cent of people in rural areas and 40 per cent in urban areas are below the poverty line taking MPCE as Rs. 325 as the cut off line for poverty.

**Table–4.5**

**Percentage Distribution of Households and Persons by Social Classes for broad MPCE Class**

| *Social Group* | *Rural* | | | | *Urban* | | | |
|---|---|---|---|---|---|---|---|---|
| | *MPCE up to Rs. 325* | | *MPCE Rs. 325 and more* | | *MPCE up to Rs. 325* | | *MPCE Rs. 325 and more* | |
| | *Household* | *Person* | *Household* | *Person* | *Household* | *Person* | *Household* | *Person* |
| ST | 56.8 | 62.9 | 43.2 | 37.1 | 60.5 | 67.0 | 39.5 | 33.0 |
| SC | 43.2 | 49.3 | 56.9 | 50.7 | 54.1 | 58.0 | 45.6 | 42.0 |
| OBC | 28.0 | 29.8 | 72.0 | 70.2 | 38.8 | 40.2 | 61.2 | 59.8 |
| Others | 26.9 | 30.4 | 73.1 | 69.6 | 18.7 | 23.7 | 81.3 | 76.3 |
| All | 38.0 | 41.5 | 62.0 | 58.5 | 36.0 | 40.0 | 64.0 | 60.0 |

**Source: Computed from NSS data of 55th round, 1999-2000.**

**Table–4.6**

**Percentage distribution of households and persons by calorie intake level**

| | | *Calorie intake level. Expressed as a percentage of a "norm" level of 2700 kcal per consumer unit per diem.* | | | | | | | | |
|---|---|---|---|---|---|---|---|---|---|---|
| | | *<70* | *70-80* | *80-90* | *90-100* | *100-110* | *110-120* | *120-150* | *>150* | *All* |
| 1 | 2 | 3 | 4 | 5 | 6 | 7 | 8 | 9 | 10 | 11 |
| Rural | Households | 13.2 | 12.6 | 15.8 | 14.4 | 10.8 | 9.7 | 14.3 | 9.2 | 100 |
| | Persons | 14.0 | 14.0 | 18.3 | 14.2 | 11.2 | 9.3 | 12.4 | 6.5 | 100 |
| Urban | Households | 10.4 | 11.2 | 15.5 | 18.3 | 15.7 | 10.3 | 13.1 | 5.5 | 100 |
| | Persons | 11.1 | 12.7 | 16.8 | 19.6 | 16.1 | 8.0 | 11.5 | 4.2 | 100 |

**Source: Computed from NSS data of 55th round, 1999-2000.**

The calorie intake levels per unit per day expressed as the percentage of the norm of 2700 kcal per consumer unit per day suggested by the nutritional experts are estimated. These estimates are further classified into eight percentage groups viz., 0-70, 70-80, 80-90, 90-100, 100-110, 110-120, 120-150, 150 and above. The group-wise percentage estimated are presented in Table-4.6. The figures in the table indicates that 42 per cent of rural households which accounted for 46 per cent of rural population had an intake of less than 90 per cent of the required level of 2700 kcal per consumer unit per day. The corresponding figures in urban areas indicate that about 37 per cent households which accounted for 41 per cent of urban population had an intake of less than 90 per cent of the required calorie norm. Thus, it can be said that more than 46 per cent in rural area and 41 per cent in urban area are living below poverty line in the state as per prescribed calorie intake norm. About 25 per cent of households and 25 per cent of the population had calorie intake level of '90-110' per cent of the required calorie norm (2700 kcal + 10 per cent fluctuation) in rural areas. But in urban areas, the corresponding percentages are 34 and 36 respectively.

To examine, the change of consumption pattern over time, the MPCE on food and non-food items separately for rural and urban areas of Orissa as well as at the all India level over different NSS rounds is presented in Table-4.7. The monthly per capita consumer expenditure in rural areas during 55$^{th}$ round of NSS was 373.27 as against the all India average of is 486.16. The MPCE (Monthly Per Capita Consumption Expenditure) in the rural Orissa under food items was higher being 64.12 per cent of the total expenditure as against 59.40 at the all India level. The expenditure under non-food items was 35.88 per cent of the total expenditure as against the all India average of 40.60 per cent. This indicates that the average living standard in rural Orissa as reflected by consumer expenditure is much below the living standard in rural India. In the Urban Orissa, the MPCE was 618.48 as against the all India average of Rs. 854.92. In urban area also, the percentage of expenditure under food items was 56.95 as compared to the corresponding all India figures of 48.66 per cent. The expenditure under non-food items to total expenditure in urban Orissa was 43.05 as against the all India level of 51.94 per cent. This shows that the living standard of the people in urban Orissa is also lagging behind the living standards in urban India. The percentage of expenditure under food and non-food items to total expenditure are 56.95 and 43.05 in urban Orissa against 64.12 and 35.88 in the rural areas of the state. This indicates the quality of life in urban areas is being better than that in rural areas. Although the expenditure on food items has always been higher than the expenditure on non-food items, the percentage expenditure on food items to total expenditure in Orissa has generally declined over the years. The expenditure on food items to total expenditure was around 75.1 per cent in the rural areas and 72 per cent in urban areas in 1972-73 (27$^{th}$ round of NSS) and these percentages have declined to around 64 per cent in the rural areas to 56 per cent in urban areas in the year 1999- 2000 (55$^{th}$ round of NSS). This is indicative of a gradual improvement in the living standards of the people in rural and urban Orissa.

## 4.5 Empirical Analysis of Inter-sectoral Variation in Household Consumption

In most of the cross-sectional studies based on NSS data, consumption pattern of rural and urban sector of the country have been separately examined. These studies revealed marked differences in the consumption habits in the two sectors of the country (Rudra and Roy, 1960; Sinha, 1966; Gupta 1968, 1970 and Mahajan 1970). In fact, several items appear to be luxuries in the rural sector happens to be the necessity items in the urban sector. For food grains, the Engel curves quickly reach a satiety level in the urban sector, while the curve for the rural sector shows very little of any such tendency. The factors responsible for such differences seem to be numerous. The principal ones being the difference in the standard of living between the two sectors, the difference in the relative prices and in the extent of monetisation prevailing in the two sectors, variation of the occupational pattern of the population and so on. Apart from the broad inter-sectoral differences in consumption pattern, considerable inter-regional differences in consumption pattern also exist within each sector. Natural resource endowments, physical and climatic conditions, economic factors such as opportunities for employment and income, demographic factors like the structure of the household and degree of urbanization, cultural factors and sociological factors vary wide across sectors also across regions and result in a considerable variation in the pattern and level of consumption.

Table–4.7

**Consumer expenditure of food and non-food items in rural and urban areas over different rounds of NSS for all Orissa and all India**

| Sl. No. | NSS Round and Period | All Orissa | | | | | | All India | | | | | | Per capita expenditure for Orissa as % of all India average | |
|---|---|---|---|---|---|---|---|---|---|---|---|---|---|---|---|
| | | Rural | | | Urban | | | Rural | | | Urban | | | | |
| | | Food | Non-Food | Total | Food | Non-Food | Total | Food | Non-Food | Total | Food | Non-Food | Total | Rural | Urban |
| 1 | 2 | 3 | 4 | 5 | 6 | 7 | 8 | 9 | 10 | 11 | 12 | 13 | 14 | 15 | 16 |
| 1. | 27[th] Round (1972-73) | 26.24 (75.06) | 8.72 (24.94) | 34.96 (100.0) | 44.77 (71.80) | 21.58 (34.61) | 62.35 (100.0) | 32.16 (72.81) | 12.01 (27.19) | 44.17 (100.0) | 40.84 (64.49) | 22.49 (35.51) | 63.33 (100.0) | 79.15 | 98.45 |
| 2. | 32[nd] Round (1977-78) | 37.47 (71.41) | 15.00 (28.59) | 52.47 (100.0) | 57.43 (66.02) | 29.56 (33.98) | 86.99 (100.0) | 44.33 (64.35) | 24.56 (35.65) | 68.89 (100.0) | 57.67 (59.98) | 38.48 (40.02) | 96.15 (100.0) | 76.16 | 90.47 |
| 3. | 38[th] Round (1986-87) | 72.72 (73.64) | 26.03 (26.36) | 98.75 (100.0) | 98.89 (65.31) | 52.51 (34.68) | 151.00 (100.0) | 73.73 (65.57) | 38.71 (34.43) | 112.44 (100.0) | 96.97 (59.12) | 67.06 (40.88) | 164.03 (100.0) | 87.82 | 92.31 |
| 4. | 42[nd] Round (1986-87) | 79.19 (69.35) | 35.00 (30.65) | 114.19 (100.0) | 135.52 (62.47) | 81.42 (37.53) | 216.94 (100.0) | 92.55 (65.67) | 48.38 (34.33) | 140.93 (100.0) | 128.97 (57.93) | 93.66 (42.07) | 222.63 (100.0) | 81.03 | 97.44 |
| 5. | 47[th] Round (1991-92) | 149.70 (69.82) | 64.72 (30.18) | 214.42 (100.0) | 204.57 (61.76) | 126.64 (38.24) | 331.21 (100.0) | 153.59 (63.08) | 89.91 (36.92) | 243.50 (100.0) | 207.77 (56.10) | 162.57 (43.90) | 370.34 (100.0) | 88.06 | 89.43 |

(Contd...)

*(Table 4.7 Contd…)*

| 1 | 2 | 3 | 4 | 5 | 6 | 7 | 8 | 9 | 10 | 11 | 12 | 13 | 14 | 15 | 16 |
|---|---|---|---|---|---|---|---|---|---|---|---|---|---|---|---|
| 6. | 51st Round (1994-95) | 164.51 (67.55) | 79.02 (32.45) | 243.53 (100.0) | 246.28 (56.04) | 193.21 (43.96) | 439.49 (100.0) | 188.89 (61.04) | 120.54 (38.96) | 309.43 (100.0) | 271.49 (53.44) | 236.58 (46.56) | 508.07 (100.0) | 78.70 | 86.50 |
| 7. | 52nd Round (1995-96) | 197.17 (63.90) | 111.38 (36.10) | 308.55 (100.0) | 283.81 (49.88) | 285.21 (50.12) | 569.02 (100.0) | 207.76 (60.34) | 136.53 (39.66) | 344.29 (100.0) | 299.98 (50.06) | 299.28 (49.94) | 599.26 (100.0) | 89.62 | 94.95 |
| 8. | 53rd Round (1997) | 192.62 (64.53) | 105.86 (35.47) | 298.48 (100.0) | 306.72 (54.55) | 255.57 (45.45) | 562.29 (100.0) | 231.99 (58.73) | 163.02 (41.27) | 395.01 (100.0) | 320.26 (49.62) | 325.19 (50.38) | 645.44 (100.0) | 75.56 | 87.11 |
| 9. | 54th Round (January-June 1998) | 194.80 (64.74) | 106.08 (35.26) | 300.88 (100.0) | 354.28 (55.23) | 287.21 (44.77) | 641.49 (100.0) | 232.40 (60.83) | 149.67 (39.17) | 382.07 (100.0) | 339.70 (49.64) | 344.57 (50.36) | 684.27 (100.0) | 78.75 | 93.75 |
| 10. | 55th Round (1999-2000) | 239.25 (64.12) | 133.92 (35.88) | 373.27 (100.0) | 352.23 (56.95) | 266.25 (43.05) | 618.48 (100.0) | 288.80 (59.40) | 197.36 (40.60) | 486.16 (100.0) | 410.84 (48.06) | 444.08 (51.94) | 854.92 (100.0) | 76.78 | 72.34 |

**Source:** **Economic Survey, 2004-05, Government of Orissa.**

### 4.5.1 *Analysis of Engel Curve for Inter-sectoral Variation*

Before applying the statistical and economic criteria to determine the suitability of a functional form of Engel curve, it is proposed to outline the main characteristics of rural-urban elasticities estimated for different Engel functions. Eleven functional forms of Engel curves are estimated by the method of weighted least squares. Out of the eleven forms estimated the results of only best-fit Engel curves are presented in Tables-4.8 and 4.9 for the rural and urban sector of the state respectively for each item of consumption. It is observed from the above tables that Engel elasticities widely vary from one functional form to another for each item. The elasticities obtained from the same functional form are also differing to a great extent between rural and urban sector. The rural elasticities, in general, are higher than the urban elasticities for most of the food items and the reverse is the case for most of the non-food items. Bearing this in mind about the behaviour of Engel elasticities, we now proceed to examine the suitability of different Engel functions on the basis of economic, statistical and econometric criteria for testing different hypotheses of inter-sectoral variation using the dummy variable interaction model.

We first exclude the Engel functions giving poor fits as indicated by the value of the determination ($R^2$) and adjusted coefficient of determination ($\overline{R}^2$). Then, we test the individual significance of the parameters β and γ using their 't' ratios and the joint significance of the parameters as well as the significance of $R^2$ and ($\overline{R}^2$) by 'F' values. These statistical criteria are applied to determine the most suitable functional form of Engel curves for all the items of consumption in both the rural and urban sectors of Orissa.

From a perusal of the values of the co-efficient of determination ($R^2$) of two parameter Engel functions and adjusted co-efficient of determination ($\overline{R}^2$) of the three parameter Engel function, 't' ratio and 'F' values of the co-efficient, it is observed that the functional forms such as SL, EX, LI, HYP and LP are found to be generally unsuitable for all most all the items of consumption. Only the exponential form (EX) is found to be the most suitable one for consumer durables in both the sectors of the state. All these five functional forms reflect very low values of $R^2$ and $\overline{R}^2$ with insignificant 't' ratio and 'F' values. The elasticity estimated from these five functional forms are also not plausible. These functional forms neither satisfy the statistical nor the economic criteria for the choice of a suitable functional form.

The results listed in Tables-4.8 and 4.9 indicate the general suitability of functions such as L, DL and P for all most all items. For cereals, edible oil, vegetables, all food items and fuel and light the double-log (DL) form is found to be the most suitable one with highly significant 't'ratio and F values and also high value of $R^2$ in both the sector of the state. The elasticity estimated from this functional form (DL) is also found to be plausible for these items. On the other hand, the linear (L) reflect low value of $R^2$ and the parabolic and other forms (Ex, LQ and LLI) reflect high value of $R^2$ for some items and low value $R^2$ for some other items. But the elasticities estimated for these items are not plausible in case of the linear and parabolic form.

The linear form (L) is found to be the most suitable one for meat, fish and egg; pan, tobacco and intoxicants and all non-food items with high value of $R^2$ and with highly significant 't' ratios and 'F' values. The parabolic form for these items also reflect high values of $\overline{R}^2$ with insignificant 't' values for the 'β' and 'γ' co-efficient and with slightly different value of elasticity compared to the linear form. For these items, the DL have low values of $R^2$ with insignificant 't' and 'F' values and highly unreliable estimates of Engel elasticities. The value of $R^2$ is also found to be high in case of other functional forms (LP, LQ, LLI) but the elasticities estimated from these forms are either high or negative, hence, not appropriate. On the other hand, the elasticity estimated from the linear form is found to be more plausible. So the linear form (L) is found to satisfy both the statistical and economic or a 'prior criteria' for these items in both the sectors of the states.

Finally, for the items like pulse and pulse products, milk and milk products and clothing, the estimated values of $R^2$ from L, DL, LP, LQ and LLI are although found to be high, the Engel elasticities are either negative or very low for the LLI and LQ and very high for LP. But the elasticities estimated from the parabolic form for these items are plausible and meaningful with high values of $\overline{R}^2$ and highly significant 't' ratio and F values. For durable items, the exponential (EX) is found to be the most suitable one with highly significant 't' ratio and F values. On the other hand, the functional forms like P, LP, LQ, L and LLI for this item (durables) either reflect low values of $R^2$ or low values of elasticities.

The above analysis indicates that the form of the Engel curve which may be suitable for the rural sector may not be suitable for the urban sector for some items of consumption. However, for the purpose of comparing consumers' behaviour for different items of consumption in rural and urban sector, it is imperative to use the same functional form for both the sector. This is because different functions make different assumptions, yielding different elasticities. For cereals, edible oil, vegetables, all food items and fuel and light the double-log form (DL); for meat, fish and egg; pan, tobacco intoxicants and all non-food items the linear form (L), for pulse and pulse products; milk and milk products and clothing the parabolic form (P) and finally for durables the exponential form appeared to be the most appropriate one.

### 4.5.2 *Characteristic and Magnitude of Inter-sectoral Variation*

The magnitude of average level of living of a region is measured in terms of per capita total expenditure. Table-4.10 represents the average per capita specific item expenditure to average total expenditure per capita (in proportional terms – it is the Engel ratio) and the Engel elasticities computed from the best fit Engel curves of different items of consumption for the rural and urban sector of Orissa. The per capita average total expenditure for the rural sector is Rs. 373.17 and for the urban sector is 618.48. The per capita average total expenditure in the urban sector is more than 1.7 times of the rural sector. This shows the disparity in the level of living of the people living in the rural and urban sector of the state.

**Table–4.8**

**Regression results of the most suitable functional form of Engel curve for various food and non-food groups for rural Orissa**

| | *Commodity/ Models* | $\alpha$ | $\beta$ | $t_\beta$ | $\gamma$ | $t_\gamma$ | $R^2/\bar{R}^2$ | $F$ | $\eta$ |
|---|---|---|---|---|---|---|---|---|---|
| Cereals | DL | -0.2272 | 0.9672 | 50.1381* | – | – | 0.9960 | 513.8321* | 0.7672 |
| Pulses and its Products | P | -1.5018 | 0.0426 | 5.4249* | -0.0021 | -4.3349* | 0.8923 | 46.5687* | 0.9642 |
| Milk & its Products | P | -23.3370 | 0.0255 | 1.6562 | 0.0003 | 4.3972* | 0.9211 | 65.1859* | 0.7590 |
| Edible Oil | DL | 2.2121 | 0.2695 | 6.1878* | – | – | 0.9929 | 38.2892* | 0.6695 |
| Meat, Fish & Egg | L | -26.0770 | 0.0600 | 7.8931* | – | – | 0.8617 | 62.3004* | 1.2471 |
| Vegetables | DL | -0.7368 | 0.9719 | 187.7184* | – | – | 0.9997 | 238.7911* | 0.8719 |
| All Food Items | DL | -0.7368 | 0.9719 | 187.7184* | – | – | 0.9997 | 238.7911* | 0.8719 |
| Pan, Tobac. & Intoxi. | L | 6.3670 | 0.0210 | 6.3266* | – | – | 0.8501 | 40.0254* | 0.8804 |
| Fuel & Light | L | 6.3670 | 0.0210 | 6.3266* | – | – | 0.8501 | 40.0254* | 0.8804 |
| Clothing | P | -9.7516 | 0.0803 | 12.2781* | -0.0002 | -3.6241* | 0.9676 | 165.1996* | 1.2366 |
| Durables | EX | 5.8982 | 0.0008 | 0.5911 | – | – | 0.0338 | 110.3494* | 1.2106 |
| All Non-Food | L | -340.5135 | 0.6711 | 8.6906* | – | – | 0.8802 | 74.6601* | 1.2652 |

**Source:** **Estimated from unit record data of 55th round (1999-2000).**

Table–4.9

**Regression results of the most suitable functional form of Engel curve for various food and non-food item groups for urban Orissa**

| | *Commodity/ Models* | $\alpha$ | $\beta$ | $t_\beta$ | $\gamma$ | $t_\gamma$ | $R^2/\overline{R}^2$ | $F$ | $\eta$ |
|---|---|---|---|---|---|---|---|---|---|
| Cereals | DL | -1.3313 | 0.8417 | 9.7810* | – | – | 0.9054 | 95.6689* | 0.6417 |
| Pulses and its Products | P | -1.5018 | 0.0426 | 5.4249* | -0.0001 | -0.3349 | 0.8923 | 46.5687* | 0.8750 |
| Milk & its Products | P | -65.3401 | 0.0830 | 7.0915* | -0.0002 | -0.1801 | 0.9523 | 110.9122* | 1.1354 |
| Edible Oil | DL | -0.2727 | 0.4718 | 8.1183* | – | – | 0.8683 | 65.9070* | 0.4718 |
| Meat, Fish & Egg | L | -47.2989 | 0.0707 | 6.8663* | – | – | 0.8250 | 47.1468* | 0.9286 |
| Vegetables | DL | -0.6797 | 0.6391 | 33.6027* | – | – | 0.9912 | 129.1437* | 0.6391 |
| All Food Items | DL | -0.6066 | 0.9486 | 43.3263* | – | – | 0.9947 | 877.1649* | 0.7486 |
| Pan, Tobac. & Intoxi. | L | 15.7138 | 0.0105 | 3.8752* | – | – | 0.6003 | 15.0169* | 0.9296 |
| Fuel & Light | DL | -0.3575 | 0.6364 | 20.1115* | – | – | 0.9759 | 404.4712* | 0.6364 |
| Clothing | P | -9.7952 | 0.0750 | 11.2830* | -0.0002 | -4.7324* | 0.9583 | 127.3490* | 1.3828 |
| Durables | EX | 5.1617 | 0.0010 | 3.2747* | – | – | 0.4714 | 10.7240* | 1.7445 |
| All Non-Food | L | -398.1143 | 0.6529 | 16.6803* | – | – | 0.9653 | 278.2312* | 1.8992 |

**Source: Estimated from unit record data of 55[th] round (1999-2000).**

It is noticed from the Table-4.10, that the Engel ratio of most of the food items such as cereals, vegetables and all food items is much higher in the rural sector as compared to the urban sector and the reverse is the case for pulse and its products; edible oil; milk and milk products and meat, fish and egg. But in case non-food items, the Engel ratio for clothing, fuel and light, durables and non-food items is higher in the urban sector as compared to the rural sector and reverse is the case for pan, tobacco and intoxicants.

The Engel elasticities for cereals; pulses and its products; edible oil; meat, fish and egg and all food items are higher in rural sector whereas these elasticities for milk and milk products, vegetables, pan, tobacco and intoxicants, fuel and light, clothing, durables and all non-food items are higher in the urban sector. The Engel elasticities are less than unity for cereals, pulses and its products, edible oil, vegetables, all food items, pan, tobacco and intoxicants fuel and light and greater than unity for clothing, durables and all non-food items. Indicating that all food items are necessary items and all non-food items are except pan, tobacco, intoxicants and fuel and light are luxury items. One peculiarity is that milk and milk product is a necessary item in the rural sector and it is a luxury item in the urban sector whereas meat, fish, egg is a luxury item in the rural sector and necessity item in the urban sector.

A perusal of the result of the Dummy variable interaction model presented in Table-4.11 for overall test of homogeneity ($F_1$) of the first hypothesis reveals significant inter-sectoral heterogeneity in the consumption pattern of all items except pan, tobacco and intoxicants. As the overall test indicates heterogeneity in the consumption pattern of all most all items, we now test the second hypothesis of slope homogeneity ($F_2$) which clearly indicates significant inter-sectoral heterogeneity in consumption of all items except cereals, edible oil and vegetables. Finally, the third hypothesis on intercept homogeneity ($F_3$) again reveals significant inter-sectoral heterogeneity in the consumption of all items except pulses and its products, meat, fish and egg and fuel and light.

The above analysis confirms the existence of significant inter-sectoral variation in the consumption pattern of milk and milk products; meat, fish and egg; all food items; clothing; durables; and all non-food items which is due to the variation in both the intercept and slope coefficient. This implies the variation in the consumption pattern of these items is due to the significant difference in the marginal propensity to consume and the mean level of total expenditure. The overall variation in the consumption pattern of pulse and its products, fuel and light is due to the variation in marginal propensity to consume between sectors. Finally, the overall variation in the consumption pattern of cereals, edible oil, vegetable is due to the variation in intercept coefficient which implies the variation in the consumption of these items is due to variation in their mean level of expenditure. But there is no such significance inter-sectoral variation in the consumption pattern of pan, tobacco and intoxicants.

## 4.6 Empirical Analysis of Occupational Variation in Household Consumption

Very little empirical study has been done in India to analyse the difference in the patterns of consumer expenditure among households belonging to different occupation group. Needless to say, the primary reason for this is the paucity of relevant expenditure data. The present study is based on the unit record data of 600 rural households spreading over different parts of rural Orissa. It is concerned primarily with the examination of the variations in expenditure pattern of rural households having different types of agricultural and other occupations. Rural households in Orissa are predominantly agricultural and are engaged in a variety of agricultural activities. It is, therefore, natural to expect considerable variation in the patterns of consumption among household having different types of activities.

## Table–4.10

**Sector-wise average specific item expenditure, percentage of average specific item expenditure and Engel elasticity for Orissa (1999-2000)**

| Sl. No. | Consumption Item | Rural | Rural | | | Urban | Urban | | |
|---|---|---|---|---|---|---|---|---|---|
| | | *Plausible Functional form* | *A.S.E.* | *Percentage* | $\eta$ | *Plausible Functional form* | *A.S.E* | *Percentage* | $\eta$ |
| 1. | Cereals | DL | 134.01 | 36.0104 | 0.7672 | DL | 140.39 | 22.6996 | 0.6417 |
| 2. | Pulses & its products | P | 10.54 | 2.8244 | 0.9642 | P | 19.51 | 3.1546 | 0.8750 |
| 3. | Milk & its products | P | 7.81 | 2.0929 | 0.7590 | P | 29.23 | 4.7262 | 1.1354 |
| 4. | Edible oil | DL | 10.83 | 2.9022 | 0.6695 | DL | 18.52 | 2.9945 | 0.4718 |
| 5. | Meat fish and egg | L | 13.57 | 3.6364 | 1.2471 | L | 28.73 | 4.6453 | 0.9286 |
| 6. | Vegetables | DL | 31.02 | 8.3126 | 0.5026 | DL | 46.80 | 7.5671 | 0.6391 |
| 7. | Other Food Items | DL | 31.10 | 8.3440 | 0.7604 | DL | 69.05 | 11.1646 | 0.8114 |
| 8. | All food items | DL | 239.25 | 64.1129 | 0.8719 | DL | 352.23 | 56.9518 | 0.7486 |
| 9. | Pan, tobacco and intoxicants | L | 9.98 | 2.6744 | 0.8804 | L | 12.07 | 1.9516 | 0.9296 |
| 10. | Fuel and light | DL | 29.88 | 8.0071 | 0.4836 | DL | 51.66 | 8.3529 | 0.6364 |
| 11. | Clothing | P | 24.48 | 4.6842 | 1.2366 | P | 38.36 | 6.2024 | 1.3828 |
| 12. | Durables | EX | 12.32 | 3.3041 | 1.2106 | EX | 15.38 | 5.4570 | 1.7445 |
| 13. | Other Non-food Items | L | 57.25 | 15.3430 | 1.4624 | L | 130.40 | 21.0843 | 1.6918 |
| 14. | All non-food items | L | 133.92 | 35.8871 | 1.2652 | L | 266.24 | 43.0482 | 1.8992 |
| 15. | Total Expenditure | | 373.17 | 100.00 | | | 618.48 | 100.00 | |

**A.S.E** → Average Specific Expenditure per capita.

% → Percentage of Specific Expenditure to average total expenditure per capita.

η → Engel Elasticity.

**Table–4.11**

**Item-wise inter-sectoral variations: Dummy Variable test for regression coefficients homogeneity.**

| *Sl. No.* | *Consumption Item* | *Plausible Functional Form* | $F_1$ | $F_2$ | $F_3$ |
|---|---|---|---|---|---|
| 1. | Cereals | DL | 8.3204* | 1.9436 | 14.7686* |
| 2. | Pulses & its products | P | 7.1467* | 5.6279** | 1.2136 |
| 3. | Milk & its products | P | 10.0188* | 3.9947** | 4.3646** |
| 4. | Edible oil | DL | 4.6546** | 0.6782 | 6.8272** |
| 5. | Meat fish and egg | L | 12.7975* | 6.4343** | 4.4536** |
| 6. | Vegetables | DL | 9.0593* | 1.3625 | 19.7867* |
| 7. | All food items | DL | 7.8436* | 4.6124** | 5.7273** |
| 8. | Pan, tobacco and intoxicants | L | 1.3624 | 0.2486 | 1.6083 |
| 9. | Fuel and light | DL | 7.4131* | 5.7624** | 6.8436** |
| 10. | Clothing | P | 12.5518* | 6.6346* | 12.1192* |
| 11. | Durables | EX | 22.5624* | 12.3642* | 8.1926* |
| 12. | All non-food items | L | 12.2423* | 8.4636* | 7.2316* |

**N.B.:** * : Significant at 1% level of significance.

**: Significant at 5% level of significance.

Jain and Tendulkar's study is elegant and satisfactory in many respects. They used all-India estimates of per capita item expenditure, cross-classified by levels of per capita monthly total consumer expenditure and occupation separately for rural and urban India, obtained from the 19th round NSS. Expenditure patterns for nine item/item groups were examined for each of five occupational categories, viz., (i) professionals, technical, administrative, executive, managerial and clerical and related workers, (ii) sales workers, (iii) farmers, fishermen, hunters, loggers and related workers, (iv) craftsmen, production process and related workers, and (v) miners, quarrymen, workers in transport and communication, services, sports and recreation workers and workers not classified elsewhere. For comparing expenditure patterns of different occupation groups in respect of specific items of expenditure, the authors insisted that in a sector the item-specific Engel curves must have the same form across occupation groups. They fitted six two-parameter forms of Engel curve, viz., linear, semi-log, double-log, log-inverse, hyperbola and exponential, for each item in each sector using all-occupation expenditure data and selected the best-fitting form as the one for which the weighted sum of squares of difference between observed and predicted item expenditures turned out to be minimum, the weights being the estimated population in individual per capita monthly total expenditure classes in the sector. In subsequent analysis, they applied the analysis of covariance tests of homogeneity to the occupation group-wise Engel curves for each item of expenditure in each sector. The results of these tests showed considerable inter-occupational difference in consumer expenditure patterns. Having established this, Jain and Tendulkar went further to identify what they called the 'dominant occupation' in the sense of having a consumption pattern, on the whole, different from the rest. This was done by performing occupation-pair-wise tests of homogeneity of Engel curves. Their results showed that the agricultural occupations and the professionals, technical related workers are the dominant groups in rural and urban India respectively. Other empirical studies on inter-occupational variation in consumption pattern in India include Ganguly (1960) and Singh (1968).

However, the NSS provides information about some broad categories of means of livelihood classes which depends on the household occupation. In case the members of a household have pursued more than one occupation, the broad categories (i.e. means of livelihood) have been determined on the basis of major source of income during the last 365 day. It would be reasonable to assume that the work activities of the adult males in the family correspond to that household in occupation. Different occupations involve different degrees of human labour. Even within an occupation, different operations may involve human labour in different degrees.

In this study, we have followed both Jain and Tendulkar's classification of occupation and National Classification of Occupation (NCO, 1986) with little modification. We have classified household occupation into four categories viz. (i) salaried and regular wage earner household (type-A occupation). (ii) small business and trader households (type-B) (iii) cultivator households (type-C) (iv) agriculture and other labour households (type-D) on the basis of means of livelihood of a household. The salary and wage Earner households (type-A occupation) include (a) professional, technical and related workers (b) administrative, executive and managerial workers and (c) clerical and related workers; The small business and trader households (type-B occupation) include shop-keepers traders and hawkers etc.; the cultivator households (type-C occupation) include cultivators owning land more than 2.5 hectares; and finally, agricultural and other labour households (type-D occupation) include small farmers owning land less than or equal to 2.5 hectares; fisherman, hunter, logger related workers; service workers, production and related workers; transport equipment operators; and all other workers. The modifications are made in occupation type-D by including small cultivators with fisherman, hunter, logger and related workers since all these activities involve strenuous work. We have compared the item-wise expenditure patterns across four occupational groups of rural households mentioned above for fourteen broad item groups of consumption.

### *4.6.1 Analysis of Occupation-wise Expenditure Patterns*

In this section we propose to present the results of comparison of occupation-wise Engel functions for different items [relating item specific per capita total expenditure (y) to (all-items) per capita total expenditure (x)]. Before proceeding to the detailed analysis, it would be worthwhile to discuss briefly the general characteristics of the occupational data.

Table-4.12 represents the occupation-wise and item-wise average specific item expenditure, Engel ratio and Engel elasticity for the 14 items separately for each of the four occupation groups for rural Orissa. It is seen that the average per capita monthly total consumer expenditure figures display a wide range of variation among occupation groups. It is highest for the type-A occupation households (Rs. 651.65), followed by type-B occupations (Rs. 500.64), type-C occupations (Rs. 412.59) and with type-D occupations (Rs. 370.87) in the bottom. It is clear, therefore, that in terms of average per capita consumer expenditure, type-A occupation households are much better-off as compared to the rest of the rural population. The type-D occupations (Rs. 370.87), on the other hand, are the worst sufferers. It is also seen that the Engel ratio for food is highest (69.51 per cent) for type-D occupation households and the lowest for type-A occupation households (50.03 per cent). This indicates that the standard of living of Type-A occupation households is better than other occupation households. But the households in Type-D occupation have a poor standard of living compared with the households of other occupation groups.

It is observed from Table-4.12 that the Engel ratio as well as Engel elasticities for cereals, vegetables, sugar and gur, salt and spices are the highest for Type-D occupation households and are the lowest for type-A occupation households. Further, these Engel ratios and elasticities of these items (cereals, vegetables, sugar and gur, salt and spices) are more for type-B and type-C occupation households as compared to type-A occupation households. Almost the reverse trend is observed for items like pulses and its products, milk and its products and meat, fish and egg and beverages. For these items (pulses and its products, milk and its products and meat, fish and egg), the Engel ratios and elasticities are higher for type-A occupation followed by type- B and type-C and except pan, tobacco and intoxicants and fuel and light these ratios and elasticities are high for type-D occupation and lowest for type-A occupation households. This clearly indicates the standard of living of type-A households are better as compared to all other occupation households and the standard of living of type-D occupation households is being the lowest. The standard of living of type-B and type-C occupation households is relatively much higher than Type-D occupation households and not higher than type-A occupation households.

One can analyse the level of poverty using Engel ratio and Engel elasticities. Generally, it is expected that the Engel ratio and the Engel elasticities for cereals, vegetables, sugar and gur, and salt and spices are high for poor households and low for the rich households. For all other food items, these ratios and elasticities are, generally, high for the rich and low for the poor. But for all non-food items except pan, tobacco, and intoxicants, these elasticities and the ratios are high for the rich and low for the poor households.

### 4.6.2 *Analysis of Engel Curve for Occupational Variation*

In the analysis of Engel curves we have considered six two-parameter forms of Engel curves, viz., linear (L), double-log (DL), semi-log (SL), exponential (EX) and log-inverse (LI) and the hyperbolic (HYP) and five three parameter Engel curves, viz., Parabolic (P), Log-parabolic(LP), log-log-inverse (LLI), Semi-log-inverse (SLI) and the Log-quadratic(LQ). All these forms have been fitted for each item and occupation group. In every case per capita item expenditure (y) or its logarithm has been regressed on per capita total consumer expenditure (x) and/or its transformations by the method of weighted least squares, the weights being the percentage of estimated population in different size classes of total consumer expenditure.

However, for the purpose of comparing consumer behaviour for different items of consumption for different categories of rural occupation households, it is imperative to use the same functional form for all occupations. This is because different functions make different assumptions, yielding different elasticities. For cereals, the Semi-log (SL); for pulses and its products; edible oil; and meat, fish and egg; and misc. non-food item, the Linear (L); and finally for milk and its products, vegetables and fruits, sugar and gur; salt and spices; beverages; fuel and light; pan, tobacco intoxicants; clothing and durables, the Parabolic (P) functional form appeared to be the most plausible functional form of Engel curves.

The $F_1$-statistic for the overall test on both slope and intercept homogeneity for occupational variation in the rural sector appear in column-4 of Table-4.13 confirms that the expenditure on all the items except sugar and gur; salt and spices; and pan, tobacco and intoxicants differs significantly over the occupations. The consumption of sugar and gur; salt and spices; and pan, tobacco and intoxicants reflect homogeneity across different occupation. As the overall test reveals homogeneity in expenditure on most of the food and non-food items, we test for slope homogeneity ($F_2$) for these items in the nest step. On review of Table-4.13 reveals that the slope homogeneity is observed for all items except meat, fish and egg across the occupations Finally, the $F_3$ statistics for intercept homogeneity reveals significant heterogeneity in consumption pattern of all items except beverage and fuel and light over the occupations.

The analysis of Table–4.13 reveals that in the rural sector the expenditure on all food and non-food items except meat, fish and egg; beverages and fuel and light has shown both slope and intercept homogeneity across different occupations. The overall occupational heterogeneity in the consumption pattern for cereals, beverages and fuel and light is due to variation in intercept but for meat, fish and egg, it is due to the variation in slope. For all other items, the overall occupational heterogeneity is due to the variation in both intercept and slope. It implies that the overall heterogeneity in the consumption pattern of all items except cereals, meat, fish and egg, beverages and fuel and light across different occupations is due to the variation in marginal propensity to consume and mean level of expenditure per capita. But the overall heterogeneity in the consumption pattern of meat, fish and egg over the occupations is due to variation in the marginal propensity to consume. Finally, the overall heterogeneity in the consumption of cereals, beverages and fuel and light over the occupations is due to the variation in the mean level of expenditure only.

Table–4.12

**Occupation wise & item wise average specific expenditure, percentage of average specific expenditure and Engel elasticities: Rural Orissa (1999-2000)**

| Consumption Item | Type-A Household | | | | Type-B Household | | | | Type-C Household | | | |
|---|---|---|---|---|---|---|---|---|---|---|---|---|
| | *Func. Form* | *A.S.E* | *%* | *h* | *Func. Form* | *A.S.E* | *%* | *h* | *Func. Form* | *A.S.E* | *%* | *h* |
| Cereals & its products | SL | 163.90 | 25.16 | 0.6398 | SL | 140.47 | 28.06 | 8.654 | SL | 148.45 | 35.98 | 0.668 |
| Pulses & its products | L | 32.63 | 5.01 | 0.6064 | L | 23.99 | 4.79 | 1.543 | L | 18.39 | 4.46 | 1.801 |
| Milk & its products | P | 33.20 | 5.09 | 1.393 | P | 16.76 | 3.35 | 1.950 | P | 9.51 | 2.31 | 1.353 |
| Edible Oil | L | 23.91 | 3.67 | 0.9984 | L | 18.48 | 3.69 | 0.871 | L | 15.28 | 3.70 | 1.724 |
| Meat, Fish & Egg | L | 26.46 | 4.06 | 0.9546 | L | 23.08 | 4.61 | 0.555 | L | 13.42 | 3.25 | 0.754 |
| Vegetables & fruits | P | 52.62 | 8.08 | 0.827 | P | 43.76 | 8.74 | 0.882 | P | 36.77 | 8.91 | 1.003 |
| Sugar & Gur | P | 11.43 | 1.75 | 0.841 | P | 9.11 | 1.82 | 1.764 | P | 8.004 | 1.94 | 0.971 |
| Salt and Spices | P | 18.66 | 2.86 | 0.966 | P | 13.59 | 2.72 | 0.449 | P | 11.79 | 2.86 | 0.783 |
| Beverages | P | 19.76 | 3.03 | 0.879 | P | 13.32 | 2.66 | -0.16 | P | 8.65 | 2.10 | 0.639 |
| Pan, Tobocco & Intoxicants | P | 12.06 | 1.85 | 1.374 | P | 7.69 | 1.54 | 0.576 | P | 7.93 | 1.92 | 0.285 |
| Fuel and Light | P | 53.68 | 8.24 | 0.788 | P | 42.51 | 8.49 | 0.617 | P | 36.64 | 8.88 | 0.646 |
| Clothing | P | 45.17 | 6.93 | 0.995 | P | 33.17 | 6.63 | 1.478 | P | 24.61 | 5.97 | 0.968 |
| Durables | P | 23.75 | 3.64 | 1.197 | P | 14.74 | 2.94 | 1.68 | P | 9.74 | 2.36 | 1.984 |
| Miscellaneous non food item | L | 134.42 | 20.63 | 1.373 | L | 99.97 | 19.96 | 1.281 | L | 63.41 | 15.36 | 1.747 |

*(Contd...)*

*(Table–4.12 Contd...)*

| *Consumption Item* | *Type-D Household* | | | | *All Household* | | | |
|---|---|---|---|---|---|---|---|---|
| | *Func. Form* | *A.S.E* | *%* | *h* | *Func. Form* | *A.S.E* | *%* | *h* |
| Cereals & its products | SL | 149.58 | 40.34 | 0.712 | SL | 145 | 33.43 | 0.579 |
| Pulses & its products | L | 14.36 | 3.87 | 0.866 | L | 19.03 | 4.39 | 1.61 |
| Milk & its products | P | 5.43 | 1.46 | 3.066 | P | 12.78 | 2.95 | 1.69 |
| Edible Oil | L | 12.36 | 3.33 | 0.645 | L | 15.57 | 3.59 | 1.233 |
| Meat, Fish & Egg | L | 10.54 | 2.84 | 0.565 | L | 15.20 | 3.5 | 1.316 |
| Vegetables & fruits | P | 34.3 | 9.25 | 1.215 | P | 38.63 | 8.91 | 1.035 |
| Sugar & Gur | P | 7.12 | 1.92 | 0.712 | P | 8.31 | 1.92 | 0.973 |
| Salt and Spices | P | 11.55 | 3.12 | 0.838 | P | 12.89 | 2.97 | 0.75 |
| Beverages | P | 6.92 | 1.87 | 1.173 | P | 10.24 | 2.36 | 0.791 |
| Pan, Tobocco & Intoxiconts | P | 7.38 | 1.99 | 1.068 | P | 8.52 | 1.96 | 1.99 |
| Fuel and Light | P | 34.47 | 9.29 | 0.668 | P | 38.64 | 8.91 | 0.784 |
| Clothing | P | 22.39 | 6.04 | 1.173 | P | 27.38 | 6.31 | 1.108 |
| Durables | P | 8.03 | 2.16 | 1.894 | P | 12.03 | 2.77 | 1.533 |
| Miscellaneous non-food item | L | 46.44 | 12.52 | 0.745 | L | 69.51 | 16.03 | 1.68 |

Table–4.13

**Item-wise inter-occupational variations: Dummy variable test for regression coefficients homogeneity (1999-2000)**

| *Sl. No.* | *Consumption items* | *Plausible Functional Form* | $F_1$ | $F_2$ | $F_3$ |
|---|---|---|---|---|---|
| 1. | Cereals | SL | 4.3868** | 1.2051 | 4.7051** |
| 2. | Pulses and its Products | L | 6.4770* | 6.9213* | 4.5259** |
| 3. | Milk and its Products | P | 4.6525** | 6.4314* | 4.4454** |
| 4. | Edible Oil | L | 4.5755** | 4.9352* | 5.7639* |
| 5. | Meat, Fish and Egg | L | 1.6180 | 4.1617** | 5.9337* |
| 6. | Vegetables and Fruits | P | 5.7396* | 4.3858** | 4.1371** |
| 7. | Sugar and gur | P | 1.2562 | 1.6782 | 2.0641 |
| 8. | Salt and spices | P | 1.3683 | 2.6582 | 1.3534 |
| 9. | Beverages | P | 4.5865* | 2.6892 | 5.3684** |
| 10. | Pan, Tobac. & Intoxi. | P | 1.5885 | 2.7048 | 1.4887 |
| 11. | Fuel & Light | P | 4.2278* | 2.6755 | 8.5865* |
| 12. | Clothing | P | 11.6266* | 16.2497* | 6.8022* |
| 13. | Durables | P | 4.9598* | 6.9415* | 6.0043* |
| 14. | Misc. Non-food items | L | 8.0137* | 11.1058* | 3.7940** |

## 4.7 Conclusion

The conclusions that emerge from the above exercise are as follows:

Before applying statistical criteria to determine the appropriateness of a functional form of the Engel curves, it is proposed to outline the main characteristics of sectoral elasticities computed from different functional forms for various food and non-food items. All the functional forms do not satisfy all the criteria postulated for the plausibility of Engel functions and very few of them meet Slutsky conditions. It would be, therefore, difficult to reject or accept any one of them on a priori basis. Thus, for this purpose, we use only those forms of Engel curves which are computationally convenient and also in line with the aim of two and three parameter functions in this study. For most of the items, the two-parameter functions are preferred to three-parameter ones except pulses and its products, milk and milk products and clothing.

In both the sectors, the two parameter Engel functions such as double log (DL) was found to be suitable for cereals, edible oil, vegetables, all food item and fuel and light; linear (L) form was found to be suitable for meat, fish and egg, pan, tobacco and intoxicants and all non-food items; the exponential form (EX) was found to be suitable for durable consumer goods. For the rest of food and non-food item the parabolic form (P) was found to be the most suitable one.

The elasticities estimated from various Engel functions for different items of consumption revealed that the magnitude of the elasticities for different items of consumption depends on the functional form chosen. Further the elasticities obtained from the same functional form are also different across the two sectors which is due to the difference in the consumption pattern caused by factors such as household income, household size and a host of sociological and psychological factors.

The Engel ratio for various food items except pulses and its products; milk and its' products; edible oil and meat, fish and egg are higher in rural areas as compared to urban areas of the state. On the other hand, the ratios for various non-food items except pan, tobacco and intoxicants are higher in urban areas as compared to rural areas. It is also observed that rural elasticities are greater than urban elasticities for various food items such as cereals; pulses and its products; edible oil and meat, fish and egg and all food items and the reverse is the case for milk and its products and vegetables. But the urban elasticities are higher than rural elasticities for various non-food items in the state.

The analysis of covariance based on cross-sectional data confirms the existence of significant inter-sectoral variation in the consumption pattern of various food and non-food items except pan, tobacco and intoxicants. The inter-sectoral variation in the consumption pattern of milk and its products, meat, fish and egg; all food items; fuel and light; clothing and all non-food items is due to the variation of marginal propensity consume and the mean level of expenditure. But the inter-sectoral variation in the consumption pattern of cereals, edible oil and vegetables is due to the significant difference in the mean level of expenditure and that of pulses and its products is due to the significant difference in marginal propensity consume.

The time-series analysis also confirms the inter-sectoral variation in the consumption pattern of all food and all non-food items in the state. In addition to this, it reflects the decline in the percentage of food expenditure and rise in the percentage of non-food expenditure over the period from 1972-73 to 1999-2000. This diversification of expenditure from food items to non-food items is a indicative of a gradual improvement in the living standards of the people of the state.

The occupational variation in the consumption pattern of rural households reveals that the expenditure on all food and non-food items except meat, fish and egg; beverages and fuel and light has shown both slope and intercept homogeneity across different occupations. The overall occupational heterogeneity in the consumption pattern for cereals, beverages and fuel and light is due to variation in intercept but for meat, fish is due to slope. It implies that the overall heterogeneity in the consumption pattern of all items except cereals, meat, fish and egg, beverages and fuel and light across different occupations is due to the variation in marginal propensity to consume and mean level of expenditure per capita. But the overall heterogeneity in the consumption pattern of meat, fish and egg over the occupations is due to variation in the marginal propensity to consume. Finally, the overall heterogeneity in the consumption of cereals, beverages and fuel and light over the occupations is due to the variation in the mean level of expenditure only.

## REFERENCES

1. The Term 'Engel Curve' is Generally Used to Express "The Relationship Between Expenditure or Consumption of An Item and Household Income".

   The Engel Law is Defined as "the Expenditure on Necessities (food etc.) Forms a Decreasing Function of Standard of Living, it Remains Constant on Clothing and Rent etc. and Expenditure on Luxuries form an Increasing Function of Income".

The Distinction Between Necessities and Luxuries are Highly Relative, the 'Engel Law May be Regarded as Providing Approximate Guidelines in the Theory of Consumer Behaviour. Since its Simplest form Involves Income/Total Consumer Expenditure as the Only Explanatory Variable, It May be Regarded as a Partial Relationship Subsuming the Effects of All Other Variables Under Error Term.

2. See Forsyth, F.G. (1960), pp. 372.
3. This Form of Engel Curve was Proposed by Prais and Houthakker. Latter it was Used by Bhattacharya (1963), Leser (1963) and Goreoux (1957).
4. For Details see Prais and Houthakker (1955).
5. See G.B. Gupta (1973).
6. See Suits (1957): *Journal of American Statistical Association*, Vol. 52, pp. 548-551: Johnston (1985), pp.225-233; Gujarati (1988), Chapter–14, pp. 450-451.
7. Refer National Statistics of India, 1950-51 to 2000-01, EPW research Foundation, Mumbai.

# 5

# MEASUREMENT OF INEQUALITY IN LIVING STANDARDS

## 5.1 Introduction

Development policies of the Government are increasingly judged not merely by their success in achieving a rapid expansion of aggregate real output but also in term of how the fruits of development are distributed between different classes and regions. So, a proper understanding of the nature and extent of inequalities, the manners in which it changes and the specific factors underlying these phenomena assume practical importance. In September 1994, the Program of Action at the Cairo International Conference on Population and Development asserted that despite decades of development efforts, both the gap between the rich and poor nations and inequality within the nations have widened. Widespread poverty remains the major challenge to development efforts. This view was echoed again and again at the United Nations World Summit for Social Development held in Copenhegon in March 1995. Elimination of widespread poverty and reducing the growing income inequality are at the core of all development problems and also the principal objective of development policy. There are two aspects to the measurement of income inequality across the world. The first is the inequality between the nations, which may be termed as 'international inequality'. The other one is the inequality between people across the world which also takes into account of the distribution of income within countries which may be termed as 'global inequality'.

The Norwegian Institute of International Affairs (2000) has conducted a study for measuring living standards using PPP (Purchasing Power Parity) estimates of 115 countries over the period 1965-1997 and observed that the gap between the richest and the poorest countries has increased but the overall Gini coefficient has decreased from 0.59 to 0.52. Milanovic (2002) has done a most comprehensive study using household survey of 91 countries covering 84 per cent of world's population and 93 per cent of world GDP. He derived the estimates of income distribution for 1988 and 1998 and found that global inequality was increasing and most of the increase in global inequality (88 per cent) was the result of the increase in between-countries inequality rather than within-countries inequality. The World Bank adopted three-fold classifications of countries such as 'low income', 'middle income' and 'high income' countries for measuring inequality. The World Bank Report (2002) reveals that low-income countries contain approximately 60 per per cent of the world's population and receive only 6 per cent of the world's income, the middle income countries contain 15 per cent of the world's population and receive 17 per cent of the world's income and the rich industrialised countries contain 25 per cent of the world's population yet receive 77 per cent of the world's income

In India, a considerable body of quantitative information on inequalities in the living standards has been accumulated over the years. The most important source is the National Sample Survey Organisation (NSSO) which provides data on per capita consumption and its distribution in urban and rural areas at the state and national level. The NCAER surveys of rural and urban savings conducted in the early 1960s provide estimates of income distribution at the national level. These surveys have been extensively utilised to assess the degree of income inequality and changes in inequalities over time. Mukherjee and Chatterjee (1967) using NSS earlier rounds data have observed the changes in the distribution of income and consumption over the period 1950-65. On the basis of the estimates of inequality in real consumption, they concluded that there was a higher level of disparity in the country during the second and third plan periods. Swamy (1967) using NSS data concluded that the inequality in consumption in the second plan was higher than the first plan. His estimates suggests that inequalities remain more or less stable in rural areas but increased in urban areas whereas the rural-urban disparities has been increased over this period. Regional variation in the degree of inequality have been examined by Mukherjee (1969) and a number of researchers.[2] These studies revealed that the degree of inequality is not uniform among the states. The Planning Commission's (1969) Report of the Committee on Distribution of Income and Level of Living is a remarkably detailed analysis of relative and absolute level of living of the poorer sections of the population with specific references to the quantity and quality of food consumption by them using certain early rounds of NSS data. Ahluwalia (1978), Dutta (1980), Sundaram (1987) and Srinivasan and Bardhan (1988) have examined the dynamic behaviour of the Gini coefficient of inequality in the distribution of consumption expenditure. The Gini coefficient of inequality in the distribution of consumption expenditure has been of the order 0.3 or more during the last four decades. It seems fair to suggest that there has been no dramatic secular decline of inequality in the distribution of consumption expenditure in the country. Datta Roy Choudhury (1993) indicated that the coefficient of variation of the per capita consumption expenditure first increases from 1967-68 to 1977-78 and then declined from 1977-78 to 1986-87 at both current and constant prices. During 1977-78 to 1986-87, regional inequality in term of NSDP worsens, but the inequality is lessened in terms of per capita consumption expenditure. Das and Barua (1996) reported a rising trend in regional inequality. Using Theil's entropy measure, inequality increased at a declining rate from 1970 to early 1980s and then rose at an increasing rate up to 1992. Bhide and Shand (2000) using Theil's Entropy measure and its sectoral decomposition observed downward phase of the inverted 'U' shape curve in the pattern of regional inequality over time following the economic reforms of the 1990s.

The intention of this chapter is to estimate different inequality measures for the analysis of disparities in the living standards of four occupational groups of households (classified on the basis of their means of livelihood) in the rural areas of Orissa, inter-state disparity in the living standards of the country and also to provide a brief international inequality scenario in the South-Asian countries.

This chapter is organised into **nine** sections. Section-5.1 is the introduction. Section-5.2 deals with the concept of inequality (relative poverty). Section-5.3 represents the axiomatic characteristics of a good inequality measure. Section-5.4 provides a vivid picture of income inequality in some developed and developing countries of the world. The inter-state inequality in living standards both in rural and urban areas explained using three inequality measures is presented in section-5.5. Section-5.6 deals with the measurement of inequality in the living standards using 55$^{th}$ round of NSS data. The choice of indices for measuring inequality is narrated in section-5.7. Section-5.8 deals with the empirical analysis of livings standards of four different types of occupations of rural households. Finally, section-5.9 is the conclusion of the chapter.

## 5.2 Concept of Inequality

Inequality signifies departure from the state of equality. The tools used for measuring the extent of such departure are known as measures of inequality. Measure of inequality is roughly be defined as a scalar representation of interpersonal income differences within a given population. Kuznets (1953) in his pioneering study stated that when we say income inequality, we mean simply differences in income, without regard to their desirability as a system of reward or undesirability as a scheme running counter to some ideal of equality of economic opportunity. Thus, measures of inequality are employed to study and compare the commonly recognised phenomenon of inequality in personal distribution of income or wealth which exists at different times and in different places. Poverty is a feeling of deprivation. Deprivation may be absolute or relative. Poverty, it may be argued, is necessarily relative because a person would be regarded as poor with reference to the society in which he lives (Meade, 1972). Sen (1976), Ahluwalia (1974, 1976) and Anand and Kanbur (1993) defined inequality as an unequal distribution of income, irrespective of the income level or the corresponding state of deprivation of the people at the bottom end of the income scale. According to United Nation Organisation (1975) relative poverty is the inequality in income distribution which changes with time, and is invariably different for each society. Varadarajan (1977) argued that relative poverty implies the extent of poverty in a society, which can be estimated in terms of the degree of general inequality. Jain (1981) defined a person is relatively poor who is above the poverty line with income above the absolute level, but below the income level required to meet the national average consumption expenditure. According to Altimir (1982) relative poverty is based on norms that attempt to take account of actual deprivation with respect to average level of needs of satisfaction in the society in question, which are, thus, taken as representative of the predominant lifestyle and at the same time attempt to reflect the average availability of resources in the society.

## 5.3 Postulates for the Selection of An Ideal Measure of Inequality

An ideal measure of inequality ought to satisfy a number of properties.

(a) *Mean or Scale independence:* The inequality Index remains invariant if everyone's income is changed by the same proportion (Sen, 1973 and Kolm, 1976). It should be homogeneous of degree zero in all incomes levels. It should be independent of the scale of measurement. This property is also called income homogeneity.

(b) *Population-size independence:* The inequality index remains invariant if the number of people at each income level is changed by the same proportion. The index depends only on the relative population frequencies at each income level. This property is also called population homogeneity.

(c) *Pigou-Dalton criterion:* A transfer of income from a richer to the poorer person that does not reverse their relative ranks reduces the value of the inequality index (Atkinson, 1970; Sen, 1973 and Kolm, 1976). There is, of course, a limiting condition of this criterion as pointed by Dalton, 'the transfer must not be so large as more than to reverse the relative position of the two income earners and it will provide maximum result when the transfer is equal to half of the difference of their incomes'. Degree of sensitivity to any transfer should also be reasonable.

(d) *Anonymity criterion:* This criterion is a symmetric inequality measure which implies that if any two individuals interchange their income positions, inequality index remains unchanged (May, 1952). Otherwise, the inequality index remains unaffected by any permutation of incomes.[3] This criterion ensures impartiality between individuals. The inequality depends on the frequency distribution of income and not on the order in which individuals are ranked within the distribution.

(e) *Translation criterion:* This condition corresponds to Dalton's principle of equal additions to income. Dalton (1920) and Cannon (1930), however, feel that equal additions to all income levels reduce income inequality, while equal subtractions increase it. But Kolm (1976) argued that equality measure should be invariant under equal absolute change in everyone's income.

(f) *Decomposability criterion:* The inequality measure should be decomposable so that inequality estimates of the sub-groups with minimum other information would help to estimate overall inequality (Theil, 1967 and Atkinson, 1970).

(g) *Normalisation criterion:* If the inequality index lies in the range of zero to one, the index is called as a normalized or standardized index (Champernowne, 1974). If we want to make the upper bound of equality measure independent of 'n', we can divide the measure by its maximum attainable value. But such normalization is obtained at the cost of the population-size criterion. It is satisfied if the inequality measure is zero only when every individual has equal income and it is unity when one individual is getting all the income. The merit of this criterion is to simplify the interpretation of inequality measures.

In addition, an inequality index should satisfy other properties such as (i) easy to calculate, (ii) have simple economic interpretation, (iii) depend on all income levels, and finally (iv) subject to statistical tests of significance like other statistical estimates.

## 5.4 International Inequality Scenario

Simon Kuznets initiated the discourse on the links between economic growth and income inequality in the mid-1950s, it had a multiplier effect on cross-country investigations on the determinants of income inequality. Results from a sample of recent studies are summarised in Table-5.1. Mostly the results are in line with a priori expectations, affirming, for instance, the positive impact of educational expansion and the negative impact of land concentration on income inequality. In one of the most comprehensive cross-country investigations, Li et al. (1998) start off with Gini coefficients for 112 developing and developed countries covering the period 1947-1994.

The final data on Gini ratios in Li et al. (1998) had for some of the Gini coefficient were for the distribution of expenditure and not income. The problem was to overcome by adjusting the expenditure Gini coefficient upwards by an average adjustment factor. Specifically, they adjusted for differences between income based and expenditure based coefficients by systematically increasing the latter by 6.6 per cent, this being the average difference between two components- income and expenditure (Li et al. 1998).[6] A consequence of this uniform adjustment is to believe that equal-expenditure Gini coefficient must mean equal income Gini coefficient with neither a theoretical nor intuitive basis.

For the first time, Gini ratios on the basis of per capita income for 49 countries are available in 1999 in the World Development Indicators Report (World Bank, 1999). Most of the Gini coefficients refer to a year from the late 1990s. Lowest Gini values of less than 0.3 are found in the regions of the former communist block and the welfare states of Western Europe. The same comment broadly holds good for Gini coefficient in the 0.3-0.4 range. Gini coefficients of a little over 0.4 are found for US and China. Latin America has always had very high Gini coefficient and the trend is continuing. Malaysia, the only East Asian economy in the data set, is in the high Gini category (Table-5.1). The pattern indicated by the groups of countries from the lowest Gini to the highest seems to affirm that the way to reduce the extent of income inequality is just to reduce it as a matter of policy via socialism or welfarism.

**Table–5.1**

**Gini ratios for per capita expenditure**

| *Countries* | *Year* | *Gini Coefficient* |
|---|---|---|
| Brazil | 1998 | 0.601 |
| Chile | 1998 | 0.571 |
| USA | 1998 | 0.401 |
| Bolivia | 1998 | 0.422 |
| United Kingdom | 1998 | 0.326 |
| Canada | 1998 | 0.315 |
| France | 1998 | 0.327 |
| Belgium | 1998 | 0.251 |
| German | 1998 | 0.281 |
| **East Asian Countries** | | |
| Hong Kong | 1998 | 0.451 |
| Korea | 1997 | 0.403 |
| Malaysia | 1998 | 0.484 |
| Taiwan | 1998 | 0.302 |
| Thailand | 1998 | 0.504 |
| China | 1998 | 0.415 |
| **South Asian Countries** | | |
| Bangladesh | 1992 | 0.28 |
| India | 1994 | 0.294 |
| Srilanka | 1990 | 0.301 |
| Pakistan | 1995 | 0.312 |
| Nepal | 1995-96 | 0.367 |

**Source: World Development Indicators, 1999.**

*East Asia*: A summary picture of the income Gini coefficient in East-Asian, South-East Asian and some other developed and developing countries of the world is provided in Table-5.1. These Gini coefficients have a serious limitation, since they are all based on income per household and not per capita household income. Notwithstanding the limitation for comparisons, it is possible to note that each economy has a 'normal' Gini ratio that characterised the income disparities typical to its economic and social structure and institutions, around which fluctuation take place over time (Rao, 2001).

One could discern three patterns of income inequality in East Asia. First, there is the Taiwan pattern that is due to the explicit pursuit of egalitarian policies, which included land reform and emphasis on the growth of small and medium enterprises to avoid the excessive growth of monopolies and conglomerates. Second, Korea falls into the middle pattern with a Gini of 0.4. The Koreans had their share of land reform but they relied on the so-called chaebols for their industrial development, deliberately fostering some degree of wealth concentration. Finally, there is the third pattern of the Gini of 0.45 to 0.5 in countries as diverse as Hong Kong and Malaysia and Thailand. These are the result of market forces coupled with minimal socialism/welfarism. It is to be noted that the Malaysian policy-makers had a focus on correcting racial income and wealth inequalities and not overall inequalities.

*South Asia:* Few countries in South Asia have data on income distribution. The consumption expenditure Gini coefficient in Table-5.1 does not provide an indication of high levels of inequality, but with poverty levels (that is, percentage of people in poverty) as high as 30 per cent or more in most of the countries. The low expenditure Gini coefficients are merely a reflection of shared poverty. It is to be noted that the expenditure Gini coefficient masks the considerable income inequality prevailing in these countries.

None of the South Asian countries have had the pervasive land reforms of the type implemented in China or Taiwan. In the South Asian economies in general and India in particular, there are a wide variety of subsidies on fertilizer, food, diesel oil, electricity, road and rail transport and education and health. In addition, trade unions are powerful in the organized sector. Despite subsidies and unionization, given the lack of targeting in case of the former and the limited coverage of the latter, their overall impact must be considered negligible and hence income inequality must be relatively high. Also, given the extent to which global forces are putting downward pressure on lower income groups and upward pressure at the top, it is unlikely that income inequality will decline significantly in the near future in the absence of rapid economic growth and institutional changes specifically aimed at lowering inequality.[7]

One important conclusion emerging from the above analysis is that it is public policy that matters: policy directly aimed at reducing inequality such as socialism or welfarism or a combination of the two. Market or state-mediated policies aimed at producing economic growth, including the promotion of education and economic freedom may not help to reduce income inequality.

Prospects are rather dim for reduced income/wealth inequalities because there is no convincing evidence that economic growth per se could lower income and wealth inequalities. Secondly, with acceptance and emulation of socialism and/or welfarism on the decline, institutions that work for the decline of inequalities such as land reform and fully Government funded public and social services get marginalised. Third, in the face of increasingly free global investment and trade flows, and the relatively negligible freedom for the flow of manpower, there is no prospect of the continuing partial globalisation to be a moderating force on inequalities. If anything, politicians and policy advisers could conveniently plead helplessness and point to the compulsions of globalisation. Finally, within Asia and probably elsewhere as well, a change that could eventually legitimize growing inequalities is the rapid growth of China coupled with growing income inequality, heralding perhaps a new brand of socialism.

## 5.5 Trends of Inequality at National and State Level

Poverty trends in India in the nineties have been a matter of intense controversy.[8] The debate has often generated more heat than light, and confusion still remains about the extent to which poverty has declined during the period. In the absence of conclusive evidence, widely divergent claims have flourished. Some have argued that the nineties have been a period of unprecedented improvement in living standards. Others have claimed that it has been a time of widespread impoverishment.[9] So far, the debate on poverty in the nineties has focused overwhelmingly on changes in the 'headcount ratio' – the proportion of the population below the poverty line. Accordingly, we begin with a reassessment of the evidence on headcount ratios, related poverty indices and inequality indices based on National Sample Survey (NSS) data. The broad picture emerging from these estimates is one of sustained poverty decline in most states (and also in India as a whole) during the nineties. It is important to note, however, that the increase in per capita expenditure associated with this decline in poverty is quite modest, e.g. 10 per cent or so between 1993-94 and 1999-2000 at the all-India level.

The evidence on inequality has focused mainly during the period between 1993-94 and 1999-2000. Based on further analysis of National Sample Survey data and related sources, Deaton and Dreze (2002) argued that there has been a marked increase in inequality in the nineties, in several forms. Firstly, there has been strong 'divergence' of per capita expenditure across states, with the already better off states (particularly in the southern and western regions) growing more rapidly than the poorer states. Secondly, rural-urban disparities of per capita expenditure have risen. Third, inequality has increased within urban areas in most of the states. The combined effects of these different forms of rising inequality are quite large. In the rural areas of some of the poorest states, there has been virtually no increase in per capita expenditure between 1993-94 and 1999-2000. Meanwhile, the urban population of most of the better-off states has enjoyed increases of per capita expenditure of 20 to 30 per cent, with even larger increases for high-income groups within these populations. Three aspects of rising economic inequality in the nineties have come up so far in most of the states. Firstly, there is strong evidence of divergence in per capita consumption across states. Secondly, the estimates of the growth rates of per capita expenditure between 1993-94 and 1999-2000 indicate a significant increase in rural-urban inequalities at the all-India level, and also in most individual states. Thirdly, the decomposition exercise of FGT poverty index has reflected the rising inequality within states, particularly in the urban sector, has moderated the effects of growth on poverty reduction.

Table-5.2 provides more systematic evidence on recent changes in consumption inequality within each sector of each state using two different measures of inequality. We show the logarithm of the difference of the arithmetic and geometric means (approximately the fraction by which the arithmetic mean exceeds the geometric mean), as well as the variance of the logarithm of per capita expenditure.

The direct use of the unit record data in the 55th Round, with no adjustment, shows a substantial reduction in inequality within the rural sectors of most states, with little or no increase in the urban sectors. With the correction, one can observe, within-state rural inequality has not fallen, and that there have been marked increases in within-state urban inequality. We suspect that the main reason why the unadjusted data are so misleading in this context is the change from 30 to 365 days in the reporting period for the low frequency items (durable goods, clothing and footwear, and institutional medical and educational expenditures). The longer reporting period actually reduces the mean expenditures on those items, but because a much larger fraction of people report something over the longer reporting period, the bottom tail of the consumption distribution is pulled up, and both inequality and poverty are reduced. Whether 365-days are a better or worse reporting period than 30-days could be argued either way, but the main point here is that the 55th (1999-00) and 50th (1993-94) rounds are not comparable, and that the former artificially shows too little inequality compared with the latter. Once the corrections are made in addition to increasing inequality between states, there has been a marked increase in consumption inequality with the urban sector of nearly all states (Banerjee and Piketty, 2001).

## Table–5.2

## Inequality measures

| | *Log (AM)-Log (GM)* | | | *Variance of Logs* | | |
|---|---|---|---|---|---|---|
| | *50th Round* | *55th Round* | *55th Round Adjusted* | *50th Round* | *55th Round* | *55th Round Adjusted* |
| 1 | 2 | 3 | 4 | 5 | 6 | 7 |
| Andhra Pradesh | 0.14 | 0.09 | 0.13 | 0.24 | 0.17 | 0.22 |
| Assam | 0.05 | 0.07 | 0.06 | 0.10 | 0.13 | 0.11 |
| Bihar | 0.08 | 0.07 | 0.08 | 0.16 | 0.13 | 0.16 |
| Gujarat | 0.10 | 0.09 | 0.11 | 0.17 | 0.18 | 0.18 |
| Haryana | 0.16 | 0.10 | 0.23 | 0.28 | 0.19 | 0.31 |
| Himachal Pradesh | 0.13 | 0.10 | 0.14 | 0.22 | 0.17 | 0.24 |
| Jammu and Kashmir | 0.10 | 0.06 | 0.07 | 0.16 | 0.12 | 0.14 |
| Karnataka | 0.12 | 0.10 | 0.12 | 0.21 | 0.18 | 0.22 |
| Kerala | 0.15 | 0.14 | 0.16 | 0.26 | 0.24 | 0.27 |
| Madhya Pradesh | 0.13 | 0.10 | 0.12 | 0.22 | 0.18 | 0.22 |
| Maharashtra | 0.16 | 0.11 | 0.16 | 0.27 | 0.20 | 0.28 |
| Orissa | 0.10 | 0.10 | 0.12 | 0.18 | 0.18 | 0.21 |
| Punjab | 0.13 | 0.10 | 0.14 | 0.22 | 0.19 | 0.24 |
| Rajasthan | 0.12 | 0.07 | 0.10 | 0.20 | 0.14 | 0.18 |
| Tamilnadu | 0.16 | 0.14 | 0.15 | 0.27 | 0.23 | 0.24 |
| Uttar Pradesh | 0.13 | 0.10 | 0.12 | 0.23 | 0.18 | 0.21 |
| West Bengal | 0.11 | 0.09 | 0.08 | 0.17 | 0.15 | 0.15 |
| All-India Rural | 0.14 | 0.11 | 0.14 | 0.23 | 0.21 | 0.24 |
| Andhra Pradesh | 0.17 | 0.16 | 0.17 | 0.30 | 0.29 | 0.33 |
| Assam | 0.13 | 0.16 | 0.14 | 0.25 | 0.30 | 0.27 |
| Bihar | 0.15 | 0.17 | 0.17 | 0.27 | 0.30 | 0.30 |
| Gujarat | 0.14 | 0.14 | 0.14 | 0.25 | 0.25 | 0.26 |
| Haryana | 0.13 | 0.14 | 0.15 | 0.24 | 0.27 | 0.28 |
| Himachal Pradesh | 0.38 | 0.16 | 0.42 | 0.37 | 0.29 | 0.40 |

*(Contd...)*

| 1 | 2 | 3 | 4 | 5 | 6 | 7 |
|---|---|---|---|---|---|---|
| Jammu and Kashmir | 0.13 | 0.09 | 0.12 | 0.24 | 0.16 | 0.21 |
| Karnataka | 0.16 | 0.18 | 0.17 | 0.31 | 0.32 | 0.34 |
| Kerala | 0.20 | 0.17 | 0.22 | 0.31 | 0.32 | 0.37 |
| Madhya Pradesh | 0.18 | 0.17 | 0.18 | 0.29 | 0.29 | 0.33 |
| Maharashtra | 0.21 | 0.21 | 0.21 | 0.40 | 0.36 | 0.40 |
| Orissa | 0.15 | 0.14 | 0.16 | 0.29 | 0.26 | 0.29 |
| Punjab | 0.13 | 0.14 | 0.14 | 0.23 | 0.25 | 0.25 |
| Rajasthan | 0.14 | 0.13 | 0.14 | 0.25 | 0.23 | 0.26 |
| Tamilnadu | 0.21 | 0.27 | 0.20 | 0.39 | 0.34 | 0.35 |
| Uttar Pradesh | 0.17 | 0.18 | 0.19 | 0.31 | 0.31 | 0.34 |
| West Bengal | 0.19 | 0.20 | 0.19 | 0.34 | 0.31 | 0.35 |
| Delhi | 0.29 | 0.21 | 0.30 | 0.43 | 0.39 | 0.46 |
| All-India Urban | 0.19 | 0.20 | 0.21 | 0.34 | 0.34 | 0.37 |
| All-India | 0.17 | 0.18 | 0.19 | 0.29 | 0.29 | 0.32 |

**Source: Deaton and Dreze, 2001.**

It is interesting to compare the growth rate of real wages for agricultural labourers with that of public sector salaries. The real agricultural wages have grown at 2.5 per cent or so in the nineties. Public sector salaries have also grown at almost 5 per cent per year during the same period.[10] Given that public sector employees tend to be much better off than agricultural labourers, this can be taken as an instance of rising economic disparities between different occupation groups. Since agricultural labourers and public sector employees typically reside in rural and urban areas, respectively, this finding may just be another side of the coin of rising rural-urban disparities. It also strengthens the evidence presented earlier on aspects of rising economic inequality in the nineties.

To sum up, except for the absence of clear evidence of rising intra-rural inequality within states, we find strong indications of a pervasive increase in economic inequality in the nineties. This is a new development in the Indian economy: until 1993-94, the all-India Gini coefficients of per capita consumer expenditure in rural and urban areas were fairly stable.[11] Further, it is worth noting that the rate of increase of economic inequality in the nineties is far from negligible. For instance, the compounding of inter-state 'divergence' and rising rural-urban disparities produces sharp contrasts in APC growth between the rural sector of the slow growing states and the urban sector of first growing states. This is further compounded by accentuation of intra-urban inequality which is itself quite substantial, bearing in mind that the change in measure relates a short period of six years.

**Table–5.3**

**Trends of inequality (Gini Coefficient) at national and state level**

| *States* | *Rural* | | | *Urban* | | |
|---|---|---|---|---|---|---|
| | *1983* | *1993-94* | *1999-00* | *1983* | *1993-94* | *1999-00* |
| Andhra Pradesh | 0.284 | 0.26 | 0.245 | 0.284 | 0.324 | 0.315 |
| Assam | 0.20 | 0.182 | 0.214 | 0.235 | 0.286 | 0.315 |
| Bihar | 0.257 | 0.236 | 0.225 | 0.283 | 0.324 | 0.341 |
| Gujarat | 0.25 | 0.226 | 0.226 | 0.255 | 0.281 | 0.281 |
| Haryana | 0.27 | 0.251 | 0.209 | 0.29 | 0.282 | 0.285 |
| Karnataka | 0.291 | 0.26 | 0.235 | 0.302 | 0.322 | 0.312 |
| Kerala | 0.288 | 0.239 | 0.213 | 0.301 | 0.305 | 0.314 |
| Madhya Pradesh | 0.291 | 0.271 | 0.259 | 0.274 | 0.313 | 0.315 |
| Maharashtra | 0.282 | 0.286 | 0.254 | 0.294 | 0.336 | 0.322 |
| Orissa | 0.272 | 0.258 | 0.280 | 0.278 | 0.315 | 0.313 |
| Punjab | 0.261 | 0.21 | 0.201 | 0.288 | 0.268 | 0.283 |
| Rajasthan | 0.343 | 0.236 | 0.203 | 0.282 | 0.296 | 0.277 |
| Tamilnadu | 0.331 | 0.273 | 0.256 | 0.301 | 0.321 | 0.313 |
| Uttar Pradesh | 0.282 | 0.271 | 0.241 | 0.292 | 0.329 | 0.339 |
| West Bengal | 0.294 | 0.23 | 0.226 | 0.29 | 0.326 | 0.314 |
| ALL India | 0.291 | 0.266 | 0.255 | 0.293 | 0.327 | 0.327 |

Table-5.3 provides systematic evidence on the recent changes in consumption inequality within each state with the use of Gini-Coefficient measure of inequality. It is evident from the table that during 1990s there is substantial reduction of rural poverty with a little increase in urban inequality. A perusal of the Gini coefficient figures for rural areas reveal that the inequality and the distribution of consumption expenditure was the highest in Orissa followed by M.P. It is even more than the all India figure in rural areas. For all most all the states, the inequality has declined except Orissa and Assam during the period 1983 to 1999-00. In the urban areas, the inequality figures show a rising trend. The inequality in the distribution of consumption rose in all most all states except Haryana and Punjab but it is marginally declined in urban Orissa during the above period.

The inequality figures in Table-5.3 conform that rural economy in most of the states are moving towards a homogeneous unit unlike the urban economy during the post-reform period, the urban attracts more private investment than the rural areas. That is why growth remains concentrated in urban areas of most of the states. Urban areas are viewed as the growth pole of the economy. But the fruits of growth reach a small section of population in the urban areas of most of the states.

## 5.6 Measurement of Inequality in Living Standards

In this Chapter, we shall examine the importance of household composition in the measurement of disparity in levels of living. Since consumption expenditure is taken as an index of economic well being, disparity in its distribution would represent disparity in the distribution of economic welfare. With this objective, consumption expenditure distributions based on family budget survey data have typically been defined over households and individuals. One such distribution is the distribution of households according to their total consumption expenditure (MPHCE). But it is generally agreed that two households incurring equal total consumption expenditure but differing in their family size are not equally well-off.[12] Hence, total consumption expenditure as a criterion for comparing the relative economic well-being of households differing in their family size is not satisfactory. Therefore, distribution of households according to their per capita consumption expenditure (MPCE) is generally used in preference to the distribution of households by their total consumption expenditure. And as, the data on individuals consumption expenditure are not available, the distribution of household consumption expenditure in per capita terms is often used for examining inequality in levels of economic well-being among individuals.[13]

However, per capita consumption expenditure is also not a very satisfactory index of economic well-being of household which depends not only on its total consumption expenditure and the number of its members but also on their age and sex structure. This is so because the consumption of household members varies with their age and sex characteristics. Hence the distribution of household consumption expenditure has to be adjusted for difference in relative needs between the households owing to the differences in their size and composition. This can be done with the help of income (or total consumption expenditure) equivalent adult scale. Income equivalent adult scale converts the household members differing in their age and sex into equivalent adults (for details see Chapter-III).

For the completeness of the analysis five different distributions of consumption expenditure[14] are examined. The five distributions of consumption expenditure are:

(i) The distribution of the households by per household consumption expenditure (MPHCE).

(ii) The distribution of households by per capita household consumption expenditure (MPCE).

(iii) The distribution of persons by per capita household consumption expenditure (MPCE).

(iv) The distribution of households by per unit (equivalent adult) household consumption expenditure (MPUE).

(v) The distribution of equivalent adults by per equivalent adult household consumption expenditure (MPUE).

All the five distributions will normally differ from each other except in a situation when household size and composition remain constant across the expenditure levels. Distribution-(i) through distribution-(iii) ignores household composition, whereas distribution-(iv) and distribution-(v) do not. We shall, therefore, rely upon distributions-iv and distributions-(v) for drawing conclusions about the degree of inequality in levels of living among households and individuals (equivalent adults) respectively. The relative performance of distributions-i and distributions-(ii) will be judged by comparing these two distributions with distribution-(iv) and that of distributions-iii by comparing with distribution-(v).

To be sure, both the distribution-(iv) and distributions-(v) are important in different contexts. The analysis of distribution-(iv) assumes important because household is the basic decision unit in our society because the redistributive policies of the Government are normally designed to deal with households. The merit of the distribution-(v) lies in the fact that it concerns the individuals, the ultimate units relevant for the measurement for economic welfare.[15]

## 5.7 Choice of Indices for Measuring Inequality

Among the more commonly used indices of inequality are: Gini coefficient, range, relative mean deviation, variance, coefficient of variation, log-variance, Theil's inequality index. All these indices, except the last one, are positive measure of inequality which makes no explicit use of the concept social welfare. The last one, namely, the Atkinson index, is a normative measure which is based on an explicit formulation of social welfare and the loss of welfare incurred from unequal distribution of an economic variable (say, income or consumption expenditure).[16]

It is, generally, agreed that a good index of inequality should satisfy at least the following two conditions.

(i) *Mean-Independence:* The value of the inequality index should remain unchanged if everyone's income increased (or decreased) by the same proportionate amount.

(ii) *Pigou-Dalton Condition* (or The Principle of Transfers): This requires that any transfer of income from a richer person to a poorer person (which, of course, does not reverse their positions) should be reflected into a reduction in the value of the inequality index.[17]

Not all the indices listed above satisfy both of these properties. Range, relative mean deviation, variance and log variance do not satisfy both the desirable properties and hence do not qualify as good measures of inequality. For analysing inequality, therefore, we select the other four indices, namely, the Gini-coefficient, the coefficient of variation, Theil's index and the Atkinson index, which satisfy both the desirable properties (the mean independence and the Pigou-Dalton condition) and hence qualify as good measures of inequality.

For comparing the relative inequality of different distributions, we shall first compare their Lorenz curves.[18] If the Lorenz curves for the two distributions do not interest, we can say that the distribution closer to the diagonal is unambiguously less unequal than the other, subject to the condition that we are ranking the distributions independent of their average level of income. And, in such cases, all the eight 'good indices' considered here will give the same ranking (viz., that given by the Lorenz curves). However, if the Lorenz curves of the two distributions intersect (at least once), the different inequality indices may rank them differently. Thus, the situations, where two Lorenz curves interact (also called the zones of ambiguity), will be analysed in terms of all the 'good inequality indices'.

## 5.8 Empirical Analysis

We have computed the mean, median and the lower and upper quintile shares in total expenditure and eight inequality indices viz., the Gini coefficient, Theil inequality index, (both entropy and second measure), the co-efficient of variation, the squared co-efficient of variation, log-variance, relative mean deviation, Kondor inequality index and the Atkinson's inequality index for all the five distributions separately for four occupation groups as well as for all occupation group using NSS data on consumption expenditure of 55[th] round, 1999-00. In this study, we have classified household occupation into four categories viz. (i) salaried and regular wage earner household (type-A occupation). (ii) small business and trader households (type-B) (iii) cultivator households (type-C) and (iv) agriculture and other labour households (type-D) on the basis of means of livelihood of a household. The classification of work activities of the households is based on the National Classification of Occupation (NCO) 1986 with little modification. The salary and wage earner households (type-A occupation) include (a) professional, technical and related workers (b) administrative, executive and managerial workers and (c) clerical and related workers; the small business and trader households (type-B occupation) include shopkeepers, traders and hawkers; the cultivator households (type-C occupation) include cultivators owning land more than 2.5 hectares; and finally, agricultural and other labour households (type-D occupation) include small farmers owning land less than or equal to 2.5 hectares; fisherman, hunter, logger related workers; service workers, production and related workers; transport equipment operators; and all other workers. The modifications are made in occupation type-D by including small cultivators with fisherman, hunter, logger and related workers since all these activities involve strenuous work. Atkinson's indices are computed for five different values of the inequality aversion parameter 'ε' (=0.5, 1.0, 1.5, 2.0 and 2.5) using household level per capita and per unit monthly expenditure data. Lorenz curves are drawn for each of the five distributions (in Chart-I, Chart- II, Chart-III and Chart-IV).

The descriptive statistics, the percentage distribution of income in different quintiles, the estimates of inequality measures (as mentioned above) are separately presented for each type of the expenditure distribution in Table-5.4 to 5.8 of the rural Orissa. For all the five distributions considered here for different occupations, we find medians of these distributions are much lower than respective means (Table-5.4 to 5.8). This implies that the consumption expenditure for each of the occupations of the rural households is positively skewed.

### 5.8.1 *The Distribution of the Household Consumption Expenditure (Distribution-i)*

The summary information and the inequality estimates presented in Table-5.4 reveals that the inequality in the distribution of households total consumption expenditure is the highest for type-A occupation households (Gini = 0.3862) and the second highest among the type-C occupation households (Figure-1 in

Chart-I). The Lorenz curve for type-B and type-C occupations almost coincide both on the lower and upper side of the distribution with slightly bulging out from the Lorenz curve of the type-B occupation households. Hence, there is no ambiguity in ranking the occupation distribution. The Gini coefficient is the lowest for type-D occupation households. All other measures of inequality provide the same ranking of the occupational distribution of the first category as mentioned earlier. The estimates of the measures like Theils measure (both entropy and second measure), squared coefficient of variation, relative mean deviation, Kondor inequality indices also provides higher values for type-A occupation households than type-C occupations which is then followed type-B and type-D occupation households. This is also evident from Lorenz curves in Chart-I. The estimate of Theils entropy and second measures are very close to each other. The relative mean deviation (RMD) and Kondor index provides the same value for all type of occupations. The Atkinson's inequality indices for different value of the inequality aversion parameter, provide the same ranking of inequality among the four occupation categories examined in the study.

### *5.8.2 The Distribution of Households by Per Capita Household Consumption Expenditure (Distribution-ii)*

As we move from distribution (i) to the present distribution (ii), the ranking of households changes in each occupation group. A quite large proportion of households are being reclassified from one decile to another. The proportion of households suffering from reclassification is roughly the same in the central and extreme deciles. The number households moving from decile 'i' by monthly household consumption expenditure (MPHCE) to decile 'j' by monthly per capita expenditure (MPCE) are less than those moving from 'j' by MPCE to 'i' by (MPHCE). That is because (MPHCE) and household size are positively correlated. This also explains why as compared to distribution (i), the present distribution shows less inequality in the most of the occupation groups and why at least shares of the lowest quintiles in the present distribution are higher than those in distribution-i in case of most of the occupation groups. Since the percentage of reclassification that occurs is not the same in all the occupations, the present distribution does not rank the relative inequality of rural occupation groups in the same order as distribution-i (Table-5.5).

For example, distribution-(i), shows highest inequality among occupation type-A and the second highest among occupation type-C; whereas according to the present distribution, occupation type-B reflect the second highest inequality instead of occupation type-C (Chart-I).

### 5.8.3 *The Distribution of Persons by Per Capita Household Consumption Expenditure (Distribution-iii)*

Generally distribution of per capita consumption expenditure among persons is relatively less unequal than among households in each of the rural occupations. The reason probably is that the household with higher per capita consumption expenditure tend to be smaller in household size in rural occupations. But this pattern is observed in rural Orissa. The inequality is same whether it is measured by households or by per persons. The Lorenz Cures in Chart-III (Figure 14 to 17) are closer to each other reflecting that household size has little effect in the inequality in the distribution of consumption expenditure among different occupation groups especially in occupation type-A and type-B. But in occupation type-C and type-D, the Lorenz curves are little away from each other indicating that household size have some effect in the inequality of distribution of consumption expenditure among the households of these two occupation groups (Table-5.6).

### 5.8.4 *Distribution of Adult Equivalent Units by Monthly Per Unit Consumption Expenditure (Distribution-iv)*

The distribution-iv provides a better picture of inequality in the level of economic well-being among households because it adjusts the households consumption expenditure for differences in age and sex structure of their members before they are ranked. According to this distribution, the lowest inequality (Gini = 0.1893) is observed among the type-D occupation households and the highest among the type-A occupation households (Gini 0.2969). The Lorenz curve for type-C and type-D occupation intersects to each other (see chart Fig.4). On the lower side, the Lorenz curve for type-C occupation households lies above the type-D occupation households and the converse holds on the upper side of the distribution. The Gini co-efficient, Theil Index (both the measures) and the Atkinson indices rank the distribution for type-A occupation as being more unequal than type-C and type-D occupations. The Theil index also ranks these two occupations in the same order. A comparison of distribution-(ii) with the present distribution brings out the following interesting points (Table-5.7).

(a) The ranking of household changes as we move from distribution-(ii) to distribution-(iv). But the total percentage of households reclassified from one decile to another in each occupation category is not the same. Most of the reclassifications are between adjacent deciles. A large proportion of households are reclassified in central deciles with a large majority of households in extreme deciles not changing their position. But since the percentage of reclassification and its pattern differ from one occupation to another occupation, distribution-(iv) does not rank our occupation groups in the same order as distribution-(ii). Unlike distribution-ii, distribution-(iv) shows highest inequality among households in type-A and the second highest in type-B occupation categories.

(b) Distribution-(ii) over states the degree of inequality in type-C and type-D occupation for most of the inequality measures. This needs to be explained. Since the needs of children are relatively less than adults in all occupations, per capita consumption expenditure figures tend to understate the relative economic status of households lying on the lower side of distribution-(ii). In the case for type-C and type-D occupations, the children requirements are relatively higher than the adults. Hence, per capita consumption expenditure figures tend to overstate the relative economic status of the households with higher children ratio lying on the lower side of distribution-(ii). This explains why distribution-ii understates the extent of inequality among type-C and type-D occupation households and overstates for type-A and type-B occupation households.

(c) In the case type-C occupation households, distribution-(i) overstates the degree of inequality on the lower side and understates it on the upper side. As we move from lower to higher deciles in distribution-(i), the children ratio first decreases and then tends to increase since children requirement are less than the adults, the per capita consumption expenditure figures tend to underestimates the relative economic status of the households on the extreme side of distribution-(ii). This explains why in this case distribution-ii overstates the degree of inequality on the lower side and understates it on the upper side.

### *5.8.5 Distribution of Adult Equivalent Units by Per Equivalent Adult Household Consumption Expenditure or Per Unit Consumption Expenditure (Distribution-v)*

As mentioned earlier, and comparing this distribution-(v) to distribution-(iii), the present distribution provides a better picture of inequality in levels of economic well-being among households differing in age and sex characteristics. According to this distribution the highest inequality is observed in type-A occupation households (Gini = 0.2791) and the second highest in type-B occupation households (Gini = 0.2731). The inequality is the lowest for type-C occupations households (Gini = 0.1838). The Lorenz curve for type-C and type-D occupation and type-A and type-B occupation are closer to each other (Chart-I, Figure-4). On the lower side, consumption is more equally distributed among type-C and type-D occupations whereas on the upper side it is mere equally distributed among type-A and type-B occupations (Table-5.8).

The conventional inequality indices namely, the Gini co-efficient, the co-efficient of variation, the Theil index and then Atkinson indices for all values of the inequality aversion parameter rank the distribution of type-A occupation higher than type-C occupations. The Lorenz curve for distribution-(iii) lies below the Lorenz curve for distribution-(v) in the case of all occupation households except type-A occupation whereas the position of the Lorenz curve are reversed (Chart-II). This implies that distribution-(iii) overstates the degree of inequality among households in all occupation groups except type-D occupation where the Lorenz curve is reversed. The reason is not difficult to be traced. The children ratio in the households on the lower side of distribution-iii is much higher than that of its upper side in all occupation groups. As noted earlier, the children requirement are less than adults in all occupations except occupation type-A. Hence, the per capita consumption expenditure figures tend to under state the relative economic status on the lower side of the distribution-iii. In the case of 'all occupations' except type-A occupation, the situation is reversed. This explains why distribution-ii is found to be over stating the degree of inequality among households in all the occupation groups except type-A occupation. Chart-IV shows that the per equivalent adult consumption expenditure in almost equally distributed among each of the rural occupation households except type-A occupation. The reason is that household with higher per unit consumption expenditure tends to be smaller in size in all the rural occupations except type-A occupation.

The intensification of regional disparities is only one aspect of a broader pattern of increasing economic inequality in the nineties. Two other aspects are rising rural-urban disparities in per capita expenditure, and rising inequality of per capita expenditure within urban areas in most of the states. Further, the real wages of agricultural labourers have increased more slowly than per capita GDP, and conversely with public sector employees, suggesting some intensification of economic inequality between occupation groups.

## 5.9 Conclusion

One important conclusion emerging from the international scenario is that public policy aimed for reducing inequality such as socialism or welfarism or combination of the two has significant influence in reducing income inequality. Market or state-mediated policies aimed at enhancing economic growth including promotion of the education, health and economic freedom may not help to reduce income inequality. There is no convening evidence that economic growth per se could lower income inequalities.

## Table–5.4

### Distribution of households by monthly per household consumption expenditure (MPHCE) in rural Orissa (1999-2000)

*(i) Distribution of Households by Monthly Per Household Consumption Expenditure (MPHCE)*

| *Sl. No.* | *Descriptive and Inequality Measures* | *Type A* | *Type B* | *Type C* | *Type D* | *All* |
|---|---|---|---|---|---|---|
| 1 | 2 | 3 | 4 | 5 | 6 | 7 |
| 1. | Mean Monthly Total Household Cons. Exp. (Rs.)(MTHCE) | 3270.16 | 3137.98 | 2484.29 | 1698.88 | 2299.06 |
| 2. | Median Monthly Total Household Cons. Exp. (Rs.) | 2512.94 | 2209.29 | 2004.04 | 1484.70 | 1812.63 |
| 3. | Geometric Mean of Monthly Total Household Cons. Exp. (Rs.) | 2546.21 | 2546.72 | 1999.51 | 1494.16 | 1854.32 |
| 4. | Mean Monthly Per Capita Household. Cons. Exp (MPCHCE) | 690.64 | 562.25 | 431.20 | 376.08 | 457.12 |
| 5. | Mean Monthly Per Unit Household Cons. Exp. (MPUHCE) | 798.62 | 641.50 | 501.73 | 436.63 | 528.99 |
| 6. | Mean Monthly Per Capita Expenditure (MPCCE) | 679.05 | 538.71 | 442.49 | 354.04 | 447.04 |
| 7. | Mean Monthly Per Unit (Equivalent Adult) Cons. Exp. (MPUCE) | 794.22 | 631.26 | 520.37 | 421.42 | 527.93 |
| 8. | Mean Household Size (MHS) | 4.82 | 5.83 | 5.61 | 4.80 | 5.14 |
| 9. | Mean Adj. HHS (MADJHHS) | 4.12 | 4.97 | 4.77 | 4.03 | 4.35 |
| 10. | % Share of Lowest Quintile | 6.44 | 7.31 | 7.34 | 8.47 | 7.39 |
| 11. | % Share of Lowest 40 % | 17.06 | 18.27 | 18.64 | 22.41 | 19.09 |

*(Contd...)*

*(Table 5.4 Contd…)*

| *1* | 2 | *3* | *4* | *5* | *6* | *7* |
|---|---|---|---|---|---|---|
| 12. | % Share of Highest Quintile | 46.91 | 42.95 | 43.19 | 38.43 | 42.87 |
| 13. | % Share of Highest 5% | 17.31 | 13.60 | 19.25 | 14.84 | 16.25 |
| 14. | Gini Coefficient | 0.3862 | 0.3526 | 0.3584 | 0.2766 | 0.3609 |
| 15. | Theil's Inequality Index (Entropy measure) | 0.2541 | 0.2043 | 0.2262 | 0.1297 | 0.2304 |
| 16. | Theil's Inequality Index (Second measure) | 0.2502 | 0.2088 | 0.2171 | 0.1284 | 0.2150 |
| 17. | Coefficient of Variation | 0.7840 | 0.6754 | 0.7791 | 0.5510 | 0.6131 |
| 18. | Squared Coefficient of Variation | 0.6147 | 0.4562 | 0.6070 | 0.3036 | 0.7820 |
| 19. | Log-variance | 0.4771 | 0.4124 | 0.4234 | 0.2562 | 0.3993 |
| 20. | Relative Mean Deviation | 0.3036 | 0.2774 | 0.2560 | 0.1955 | 0.2598 |
| 21. | Kondar Inequality Index | 0.3036 | 0.2774 | 0.2560 | 0.1955 | 0.2598 |
| 22. | Atkinson's Inequality Index | | | | | |
| | $\varepsilon = 0.5$ | 0.1194 | 0.0989 | 0.1045 | 0.0624 | 0.1055 |
| | $\varepsilon = 1.0$ | 0.2214 | 0.1884 | 0.1951 | 0.1205 | 0.1934 |
| | $\varepsilon = 1.5$ | 0.3057 | 0.2658 | 0.2763 | 0.1753 | 0.2678 |
| | $\varepsilon = 2.0$ | 0.3749 | 0.3306 | 0.3510 | 0.2271 | 0.3321 |
| | $\varepsilon = 2.5$ | 0.4324 | 0.3848 | 0.4210 | 0.2767 | 0.3894 |

## Table–5.5

**Distribution of households by monthly per capita consumption expenditure (MPCE) in rural Orissa (1999-2000)**

*(ii) Distribution of Households by Monthly Per Capita Consumption Expenditure (MPCE)*

| Sl. No. | Descriptive and Inequality Measures | Type A | Type B | Type C | Type D | All |
|---|---|---|---|---|---|---|
| 1 | 2 | 3 | 4 | 5 | 6 | 7 |
| 1. | Mean Monthly Total Household Cons. Exp. (Rs.)(MTHCE) | 3270.16 | 3137.98 | 2484.29 | 1698.88 | 2299.06 |
| 2. | Median Monthly Per Capita Household Cons. Exp. (Rs.) | 620.73 | 511.48 | 382.21 | 340.91 | 381.85 |
| 3. | Geometric Mean of Monthly Total Household Cons. Exp. (Rs.) | 596.67 | 484.48 | 397.81 | 352.50 | 407.13 |
| 4. | Mean Monthly Per Capita Household. Cons. Exp (MPCHCE) | 690.64 | 562.25 | 431.20 | 376.08 | 457.12 |
| 5. | Mean Monthly Per Unit Household Cons. Exp. (MPUHCE) | 798.62 | 641.50 | 501.73 | 436.63 | 528.99 |
| 6. | Mean Monthly Per Capita Expenditure (MPCCE) | 679.05 | 538.71 | 442.49 | 354.04 | 447.04 |
| 7. | Mean Monthly Per Unit (Equivalent Adult) Cons. Exp. (MPUCE) | 794.22 | 631.26 | 520.37 | 421.42 | 527.93 |
| 8. | Mean Household Size (MHS) | 4.82 | 5.83 | 5.61 | 4.80 | 5.14 |
| 9. | Mean Adj. HHS (MADJHHS) | 4.12 | 4.97 | 4.77 | 4.03 | 4.35 |
| 10 | % Share of Lowest Quintile | 8.67 | 8.80 | 11.25 | 11.60 | 10.08 |
| | % Share of Lowest 40% | 21.16 | 21.54 | 25.75 | 26.79 | 23.81 |
| | % Share of Highest Quintile | 38.78 | 38.55 | 33.96 | 33.51 | 36.22 |
| | % Share of Highest 5% | 11.67 | 15.70 | 12.71 | 11.76 | 12.96 |

(Contd...)

*(Table 5.5 Contd...)*

| 1 | 2 | 3 | 4 | 5 | 6 | 7 |
|---|---|---|---|---|---|---|
| | Gini Coefficient | 0.2969 | 0.2973 | 0.2268 | 0.2025 | 0.2693 |
| | Theil's Inequality Index (Entropy measure) | 0.1428 | 0.1576 | 0.0846 | 0.0673 | 0.1287 |
| | Theil's Inequality Index (Second measure) | 0.1462 | 0.1447 | 0.0806 | 0.0647 | 0.1158 |
| | Coefficient of Variation | 0.5588 | 0.6382 | 0.4383 | 0.3868 | 0.5738 |
| | Squared Coefficient of Variation | 0.3134 | 0.4073 | 0.1921 | 0.1496 | 0.3293 |
| | Log-variance | 0.2975 | 0.2661 | 0.1526 | 0.1242 | 0.2078 |
| | Relative Mean Deviation | 0.2162 | 0.2068 | 0.1631 | 0.1437 | 0.1944 |
| | Kondar Inequality Index | 0.2162 | 0.2068 | 0.1631 | 0.1437 | 0.1944 |
| | Atkinson's Inequality Index | | | | | |
| | ε = 0.5 | 0.0698 | 0.0727 | 0.0405 | 0.0325 | 0.0592 |
| | ε = 1.0 | 0.1361 | 0.1348 | 0.0774 | 0.0627 | 0.1094 |
| | ε = 1.5 | 0.1983 | 0.1884 | 0.1110 | 0.0908 | 0.1523 |
| | ε = 2.0 | 0.2569 | 0.2353 | 0.1414 | 0.1168 | 0.1895 |
| | ε = 2.5 | 0.3126 | 0.2768 | 0.1694 | 0.1416 | 0.2226 |

## Table–5.6

## Distribution of persons by monthly per household consumption expenditure (MPCE) in rural Orissa (1999-2000)

*(iii) Distribution of Persons by Monthly Per Household Consumption Expenditure (MPCE)*

| *Sl. No.* | *Descriptive and Inequality Measures* | *Type A* | *Type B* | *Type C* | *Type D* | *All* |
|---|---|---|---|---|---|---|
| 1 | 2 | 3 | 4 | 5 | 6 | 7 |
| 1. | Mean Monthly Total Household Cons. Exp. (Rs.)(MTHCE) | 3270.16 | 3137.98 | 2484.29 | 1698.88 | 2299.06 |
| 2. | Median Monthly Per Capita Household Cons. Exp. (Rs.) | 620.73 | 566.51 | 451.21 | 401.71 | 442.95 |
| 3. | Geometric Mean of Monthly Total Household Cons. Exp. (Rs.) | 596.67 | 562.42 | 462.14 | 412.07 | 474.52 |
| 4. | Mean Monthly Per Capita Household. Cons. Exp (MPCHCE) | 690.64 | 562.25 | 431.20 | 376.08 | 457.12 |
| 5. | Mean Monthly Per Unit Household Cons. Exp. (MPUHCE) | 798.62 | 641.50 | 501.73 | 436.63 | 528.99 |
| 6. | Mean Monthly Per Capita Expenditure (MPCCE) | 679.05 | 538.71 | 442.49 | 354.04 | 447.04 |
| 7. | Mean Monthly Per Unit (Equivalent Adult) Cons. Exp. (MPUCE) | 794.22 | 631.26 | 520.37 | 421.42 | 527.93 |
| 8. | Mean Household Size (MHS) | 4.82 | 5.83 | 5.61 | 4.80 | 5.14 |
| 9. | Mean Adj. HHS (MADJHHS) | 4.12 | 4.97 | 4.77 | 4.03 | 4.35 |
| 10. | % Share of Lowest Quintile | 8.67 | 8.80 | 11.25 | 11.60 | 10.08 |
| 11. | % Share of Lowest 40% | 21.16 | 21.54 | 25.75 | 26.79 | 23.81 |
| 12. | % Share of Highest Quintile | 38.78 | 38.55 | 33.96 | 33.51 | 36.22 |
| 13. | % Share of Highest 5% | 11.67 | 15.70 | 12.71 | 11.76 | 12.96 |

*(Contd...)*

*(Table 5.6 Contd…)*

| 1 | 2 | 3 | 4 | 5 | 6 | 7 |
|---|---|---|---|---|---|---|
| 14. | Gini Coefficient | 0.2954 | 0.2850 | 0.2275 | 0.1893 | 0.2609 |
| 15. | Theil's Inequality Index (Entropy measure) | 0.1428 | 0.1408 | 0.0852 | 0.0625 | 0.1205 |
| 16. | Theil's Inequality Index (Second measure) | 0.1462 | 0.1316 | 0.0821 | 0.0579 | 0.1087 |
| 17. | Coefficient of Variation | 0.5598 | 0.5895 | 0.4382 | 0.3834 | 0.5511 |
| 18. | Squared Coefficient of Variation | 0.3134 | 0.3475 | 0.1920 | 0.1470 | 0.3037 |
| 19. | Log-variance | 0.2975 | 0.2450 | 0.1577 | 0.1076 | 0.1954 |
| 20. | Relative Mean Deviation | 0.2162 | 0.2039 | 0.1657 | 0.1330 | 0.1885 |
| 21. | Kondar Inequality Index | 0.2162 | 0.2039 | 0.1657 | 0.1330 | 0.1885 |
| 22. | Atkinson's Inequality Index | | | | | |
| | $\varepsilon = 0.5$ | 0.0698 | 0.0658 | 0.0410 | 0.0296 | 0.0556 |
| | $\varepsilon = 1.0$ | 0.1361 | 0.1233 | 0.0788 | 0.0562 | 0.1030 |
| | $\varepsilon = 1.5$ | 0.1983 | 0.1736 | 0.1137 | 0.0805 | 0.1437 |
| | $\varepsilon = 2.0$ | 0.2569 | 0.2177 | 0.1458 | 0.1029 | 0.1792 |
| | $\varepsilon = 2.5$ | 0.3126 | 0.2569 | 0.1760 | 0.1242 | 0.2111 |

**Table–5.7**

**Distribution of households by monthly per capita unit consumption expenditure (MPUE) in rural Orissa (1999-2000)**

*(iv) Distribution of Households by Monthly Per Capita Unit Consumption Expenditure (MPUCE)*

| *Sl. No.* | *Descriptive and Inequality Measures* | *Type A* | *Type B* | *Type C* | *Type D* | *All* |
|---|---|---|---|---|---|---|
| 1 | 2 | 3 | 4 | 5 | 6 | 7 |
| 1. | Mean Monthly Total Household Cons. Exp. (Rs.)(MTHCE) | 3270.16 | 3137.98 | 2484.29 | 1698.88 | 2299.06 |
| 2. | Median Monthly Per Capita Household Cons. Exp. (Rs.) | 620.729 | 511.484 | 382.21 | 340.91 | 381.85 |
| 3. | Geometric Mean of Monthly Total Household Cons. Exp. (Rs.) | 685.46 | 561.76 | 479.18 | 399.05 | 398.98 |
| 4. | Mean Monthly Per Capita Household. Cons. Exp (MPCHCE) | 690.64 | 562.25 | 431.20 | 376.08 | 457.12 |
| 5. | Mean Monthly Per Unit Household Cons. Exp. (MPUHCE) | 798.62 | 641.50 | 501.73 | 436.63 | 528.99 |
| 6. | Mean Monthly Per Capita Expenditure (MPCCE) | 679.05 | 538.71 | 442.49 | 354.04 | 447.04 |
| 7. | Mean Monthly Per Unit (Equivalent Adult) Cons. Exp. (MPUCE) | 794.22 | 631.26 | 520.37 | 421.42 | 527.93 |
| 8. | Mean Household Size (MHS) | 4.82 | 5.83 | 5.61 | 4.80 | 5.14 |
| 9. | Mean Adj. HHS (MADJHHS) | 4.12 | 4.97 | 4.77 | 4.03 | 4.35 |
| 10. | % Share of Lowest Quintile | 8.74 | 9.37 | 11.13 | 12.30 | 10.48 |
| 11. | % Share of Lowest 40% | 22.01 | 21.97 | 25.55 | 27.69 | 24.31 |

*(Contd…)*

*(Table 5.7 Contd...)*

| 1 | 2 | 3 | 4 | 5 | 6 | 7 |
|---|---|---|---|---|---|---|
| 12. | % Share of Highest Quintile | 37.03 | 37.21 | 33.44 | 32.42 | 35.03 |
| 13. | % Share of Highest 5% | 11.99 | 14.80 | 12.46 | 11.55 | 12.72 |
| 14. | Gini Coefficient | 0.3091 | 0.3035 | 0.1900 | 0.2973 | 0.2911 |
| 15. | Theil's Inequality Index (Entropy measure) | 0.1456 | 0.1247 | 0.0826 | 0.0650 | 0.1242 |
| 16. | Theil's Inequality Index (Second measure) | 0.1527 | 0.1227 | 0.0785 | 0.0612 | 0.1137 |
| 17. | Coefficient of Variation | 0.5508 | 0.6382 | 0.4383 | 0.3868 | 0.5738 |
| 18. | Squared Coefficient of Variation | 0.3134 | 0.4073 | 0.1921 | 0.1496 | 0.3293 |
| 19. | Log-variance | 3.8977 | 4.2953 | 5.2240 | 4.6318 | 0.2069 |
| 20. | Relative Mean Deviation | 0.4380 | 0.4211 | 0.3669 | 0.2743 | 0.1954 |
| 21. | Kondar Inequality Index | 0.2920 | 0.2589 | 0.2385 | 0.2118 | 0.2633 |
| 22. | Atkinson's Inequality Index | | | | | |
| | $\varepsilon = 0.5$ | 0.0719 | 0.0594 | 0.0395 | 0.0311 | 0.0577 |
| | $\varepsilon = 1.0$ | 0.1416 | 0.1154 | 0.0755 | 0.0594 | 0.1075 |
| | $\varepsilon = 1.5$ | 0.2084 | 0.1668 | 0.1082 | 0.0854 | 0.1505 |
| | $\varepsilon = 2.0$ | 0.2718 | 0.2141 | 0.1377 | 0.1092 | 0.1878 |
| | $\varepsilon = 2.5$ | 0.3311 | 0.2570 | 0.1644 | 0.1312 | 0.2205 |

## Table–5.8

**Distribution of households by adult equivalence unit by monthly per unit consumption expenditure (MPUE) in rural Orissa (1999-2000)**

*(v) Distribution of Adult Equivalence Unit by Monthly Per Unit Consumption Expenditure (MPUCE)*

| *Sl. No.* | *Descriptive and Inequality Measures* | *Type A* | *Type B* | *Type C* | *Type D* | *All* |
|---|---|---|---|---|---|---|
| *1* | 2 | 3 | 4 | 5 | 6 | *7* |
| 1. | Mean Monthly Total Household Cons. Exp. (Rs.)(MTHCE) | 3270.16 | 3137.98 | 2484.29 | 1698.88 | 2299.06 |
| 2. | Median Monthly Per Capita Household Cons. Exp. (Rs.) | 648.99 | 566.507 | 451.213 | 401.712 | 442.949 |
| 3. | Geometric Mean of Monthly Total Household Cons. Exp. (Rs.) | 685.46 | 561.76 | 479.18 | 399.05 | 398.98 |
| 4. | Mean Monthly Per Capita Household. Cons. Exp (MPCHCE) | 690.64 | 562.25 | 431.20 | 376.08 | 457.12 |
| 5. | Mean Monthly Per Unit Household Cons. Exp. (MPUHCE) | 798.62 | 641.50 | 501.73 | 436.63 | 528.99 |
| 6. | Mean Monthly Per Capita Expenditure (MPCCE) | 679.05 | 538.71 | 442.49 | 354.04 | 447.04 |
| 7. | Mean Monthly Per Unit (Equivalent Adult) Cons. Exp. (MPUCE) | 794.22 | 631.26 | 520.37 | 421.42 | 527.93 |
| 8. | Mean Household Size (MHS) | 4.82 | 5.83 | 5.61 | 4.80 | 5.14 |
| 9. | Mean Adj. HHS (MADJHHS) | 4.12 | 4.97 | 4.77 | 4.03 | 4.35 |
| 10. | % Share of Lowest Quintile | 8.74 | 9.37 | 11.13 | 12.30 | 10.48 |
| 11. | % Share of Lowest 40 % | 22.01 | 21.97 | 25.55 | 27.69 | 24.31 |
| 12. | % Share of Highest Quintile | 37.03 | 37.21 | 33.44 | 32.42 | 35.03 |

*(Contd...)*

*(Table 5.8 Contd...)*

| 1 | 2 | 3 | 4 | 5 | 6 | 7 |
|---|---|---|---|---|---|---|
| 13. | % Share of Highest 5 % | 11.48 | 15.70 | 12.66 | 11.55 | 12.72 |
| 14. | Gini Coefficient | 0.2798 | 0.2731 | 0.1838 | 0.2506 | 0.2625 |
| 15. | Theil's Inequality Index (Entropy measure) | 0.1391 | 0.1176 | 0.0857 | 0.0597 | 0.1190 |
| 16. | Theil's Inequality Index (Second measure) | 0.1473 | 0.1166 | 0.0825 | 0.0546 | 0.1088 |
| 17. | Coefficient of Variation | 0.5830 | 0.5394 | 0.4352 | 0.3734 | 0.5511 |
| 18. | Squared Coefficient of Variation | 0.2841 | 0.3475 | 0.1920 | 0.1470 | 0.3037 |
| 19. | Log-variance | 0.3133 | 0.2304 | 0.1579 | 0.1003 | 0.1980 |
| 20. | Relative Mean Deviation | 0.2042 | 0.1937 | 0.1665 | 0.1283 | 0.1911 |
| 21. | Kondar Inequality Index | 0.2659 | 0.2619 | 0.2376 | 0.1958 | 0.2716 |
| 22. | Atkinson's Inequality Index | | | | | |
| | $\varepsilon = 0.5$ | 0.0690 | 0.0569 | 0.0412 | 0.0281 | 0.0553 |
| | $\varepsilon = 1.0$ | 0.1369 | 0.1101 | 0.0792 | 0.0531 | 0.1031 |
| | $\varepsilon = 1.5$ | 0.2042 | 0.1594 | 0.1139 | 0.0757 | 0.1445 |
| | $\varepsilon = 2.0$ | 0.2708 | 0.2045 | 0.1457 | 0.0964 | 0.1807 |
| | $\varepsilon = 2.5$ | 0.3355 | 0.2453 | 0.1747 | 0.1156 | 0.2126 |

In the South-Asian economies in general and India in particular, there are wide variety of subsidies right from education, health to rail and road transport. In addition, trade unions are powerful in the organized sector. Despite all this, the overall impact of these measures is found to be negligible and hence, income inequality is relatively high in those countries. Given the extent to which global forces are putting downward pressure on lower income groups and upward pressure at the top, it is unlikely that income inequality will decline significantly in the near future.

In the absence of clear evidence of rising intra-rural inequality within the states, we find strong indications of a pervasive increase in economic inequality in the nineties. There has been strong 'divergence' of per capita expenditure across states, with the better of states (particularly in the southern and western region) are growing more rapidly than the poorer states thereby widening the regional inequality. The rural-urban disparities of per capita expenditure, hence, also risen in most of the states. Inequality has increased within the urban areas of most of the states. The combined effects of these different forms of rising inequality are quite large. In the rural areas of some of the poorest states, there has been virtually no increase in per capita expenditure in the nineties. The compounding of the inter-state divergence and the rising rural-urban disparities produces sharp constructs in APC growth between the rural sector of the slow-growing states and the urban sector of first-growing states. This is further compounded of intra-urban inequality which is itself quite substantial especially during mid and late nineties.

The empirical findings on the ranking of households by per equivalent adult consumption expenditure (MPUE) differ significantly from the ranking by monthly per capita consumption expenditure (MPCE) in each occupation group. This implies that many households classified as poor according to the criterion of MPCE will not be so classified by the criterion of MPUE. Hence, the estimates of absolute poverty based on monthly per capita consumption expenditure distribution would be erroneous.

The distribution of per capita consumption expenditure over states the degree of inequality among individuals in all occupation categories except type-A occupation households. When households are taken as the relevant units, the distribution of per capita consumption expenditure is found to overstate the degree of inequality only in type-D occupation households. It, thus, follows that the distribution of household consumption expenditure, if not adjusted for household size and consumption effect, is likely to over/underestimate the extent of true in equalities among households. The bias could be on either side.

The contribution of occupational factor to per equivalent adult consumption expenditure inequality among adults is about 22 per cent in the rural sector. The distribution of household consumption expenditure which do not take into account for effects of household composition are likely to provide biased estimates of the contribution of occupational factors to overall inequality.

**LORENZ CURVE COMPARISON QF DIFFERENT OCCUPATIONS BASED ON DIFFERENT CONSUMPTION EXPENDITURE**

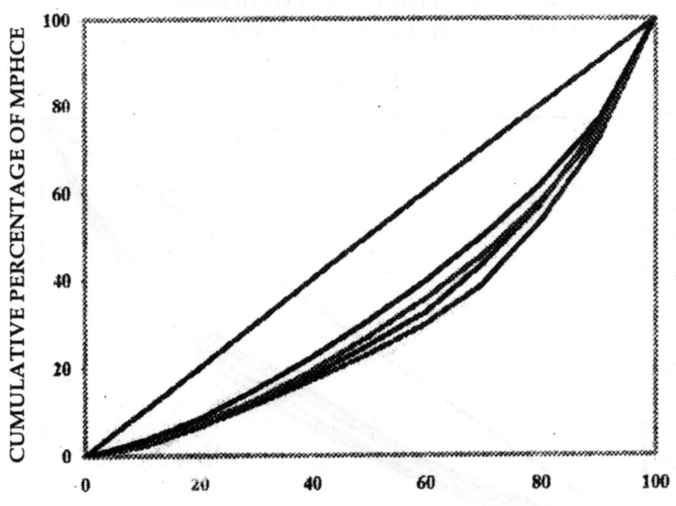


**DISTRIBUTION OF HOUSEHOLD BY MPHCE**

**CUMULATIVE PERCENTAGE OF HOUSEHOLDS**

**—E-LINE —TYPE-A —TYPE-B —TYPE-C —TYPE-D**

**FIG. 1**

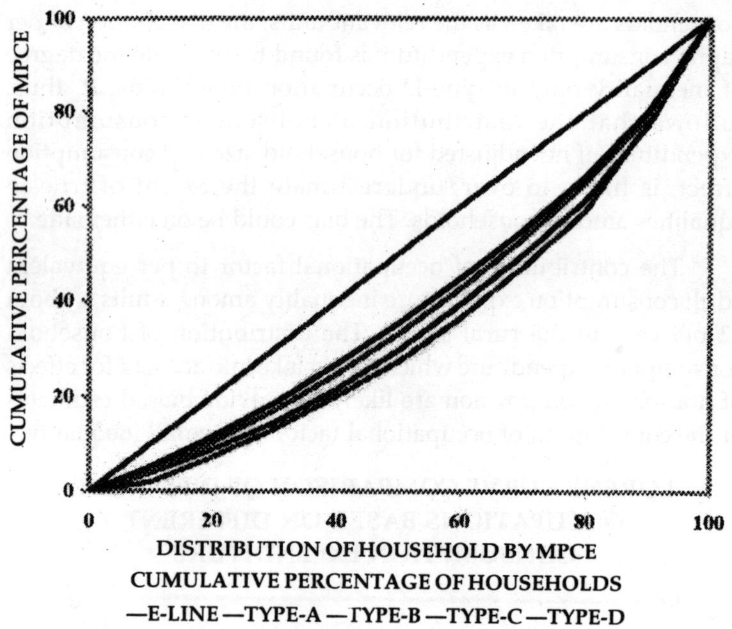
CUMULATIVE PERCENTAGE OF MPCE
100
80
60
40
20
0
0
20
40
60
80
100
DISTRIBUTION OF HOUSEHOLD BY MPCE
CUMULATIVE PERCENTAGE OF HOUSEHOLDS
—E-LINE —TYPE-A —TYPE-B —TYPE-C —TYPE-D

FIG. 2

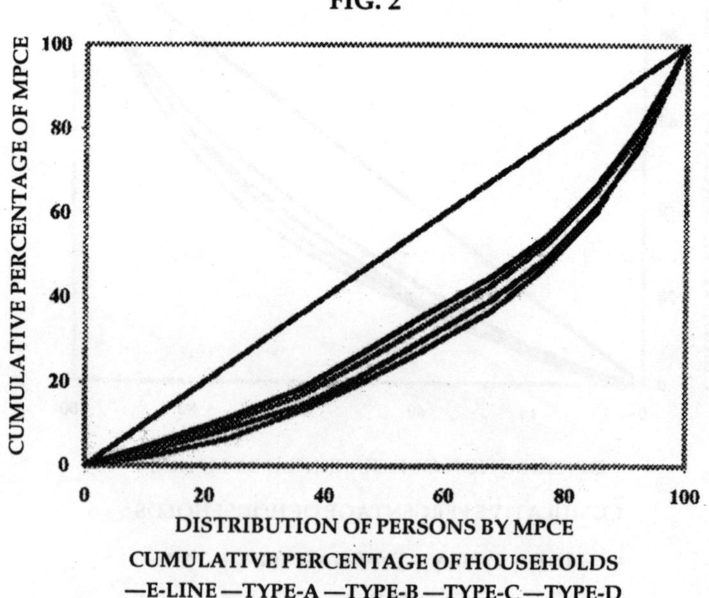
CUMULATIVE PERCENTAGE OF MPCE
100
80
60
40
20
0
0
20
40
60
80
100
DISTRIBUTION OF PERSONS BY MPCE
CUMULATIVE PERCENTAGE OF HOUSEHOLDS
—E-LINE —TYPE-A —TYPE-B —TYPE-C —TYPE-D

FIG. 3

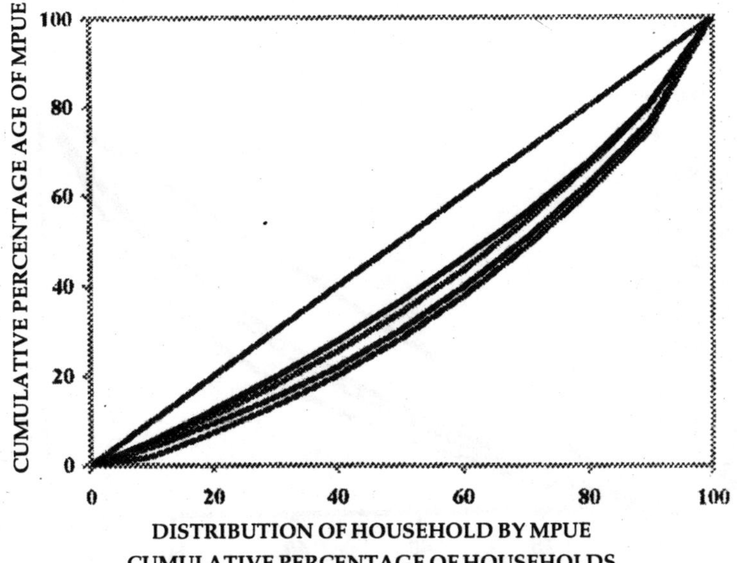
CUMULATIVE PERCENTAGE AGE OF MPUE
100
80
60
40
20
0
0
20
40
60
80
100
DISTRIBUTION OF HOUSEHOLD BY MPUE
CUMULATIVE PERCENTAGE OF HOUSEHOLDS
—E-LINE —TYPE-A —TYPE-B —TYPE-C —TYPE-D

FIG. 4

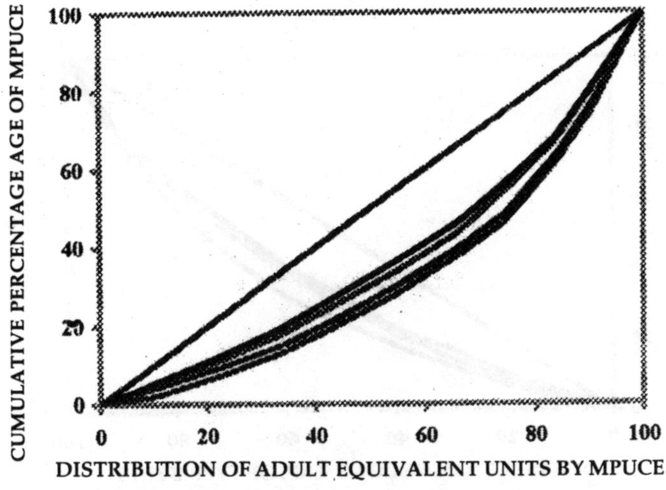
CUMULATIVE PERCENTAGE AGE OF MPUCE
100
80
60
40
20
0
0
20
40
60
80
100
DISTRIBUTION OF ADULT EQUIVALENT UNITS BY MPUCE
CUMULATIVE PERCENTAGE OF ADULT EQUIVALENT
—E-LINE —TYPE-A —TYPE-B —TYPE-C —TYPE-D

FIG. 5

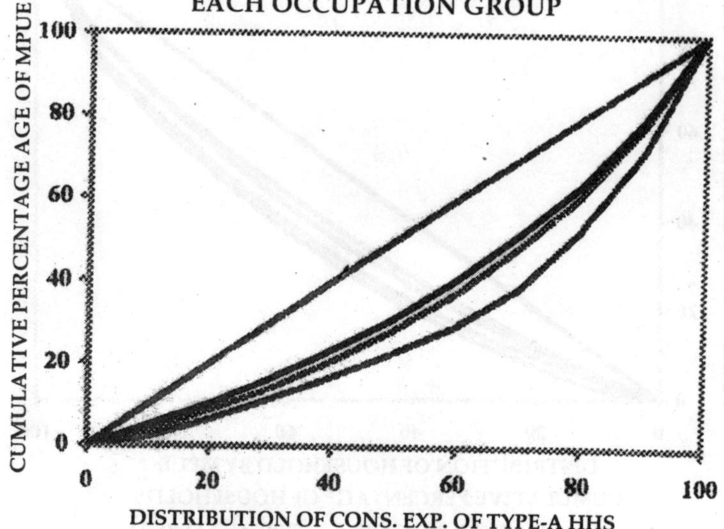
LORENZ CURVE COMPARISON OF DIFFERENT
CONSUMPTION EXPENDITURE DISTRIBUTIONS OF
EACH OCCUPATION GROUP
CUMULATIVE PERCENTAGE AGE OF MPUE
100
80
60
40
20
0
0
20
40
60
80
100
DISTRIBUTION OF CONS. EXP. OF TYPE-A HHS
CUMULATIVE PERCENTAGE OF HOUSEHOLDS
—E-LINE —MPHCE —MPCE —MPUCE

FIG. 6

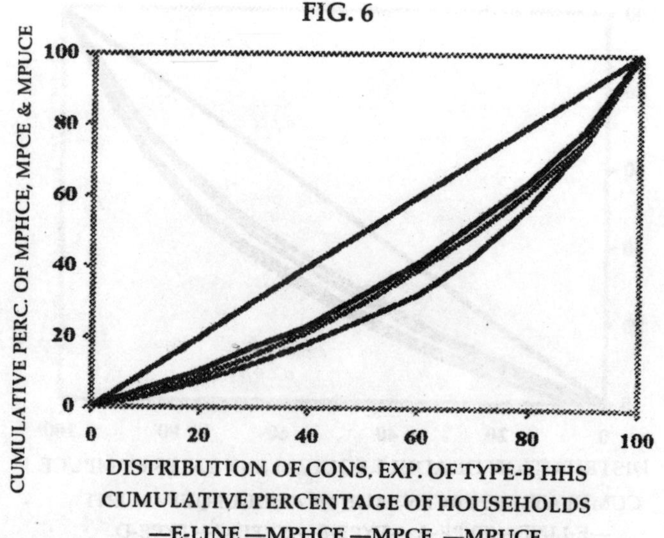
CUMULATIVE PERC. OF MPHCE, MPCE & MPUCE
100
80
60
40
20
0
0
20
40
60
80
100
DISTRIBUTION OF CONS. EXP. OF TYPE-B HHS
CUMULATIVE PERCENTAGE OF HOUSEHOLDS
—E-LINE —MPHCE —MPCE —MPUCE

FIG. 7

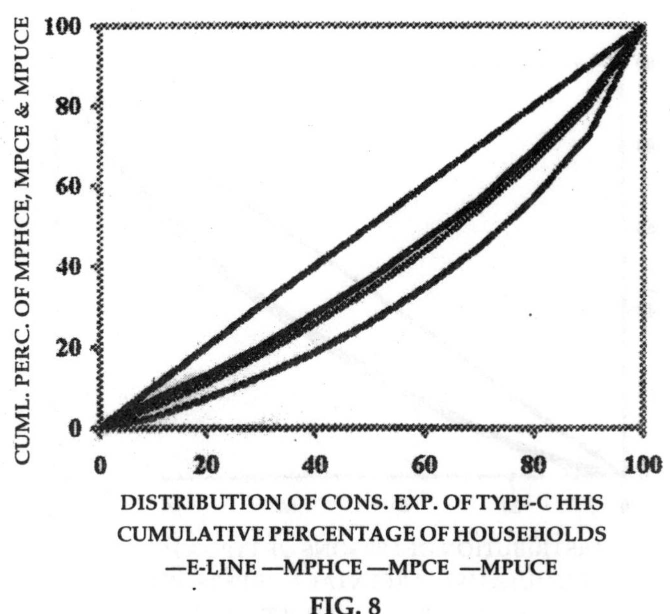


DISTRIBUTION OF CONS. EXP. OF TYPE-C HHS
CUMULATIVE PERCENTAGE OF HOUSEHOLDS
—E-LINE —MPHCE —MPCE —MPUCE

FIG. 8

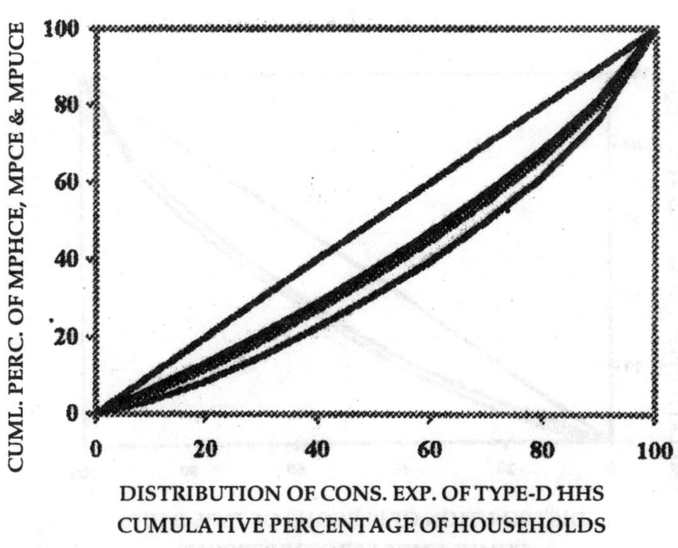


DISTRIBUTION OF CONS. EXP. OF TYPE-D HHS
CUMULATIVE PERCENTAGE OF HOUSEHOLDS
—E-LINE —MPHCE —MPCE —MPUCE

FIG. 9

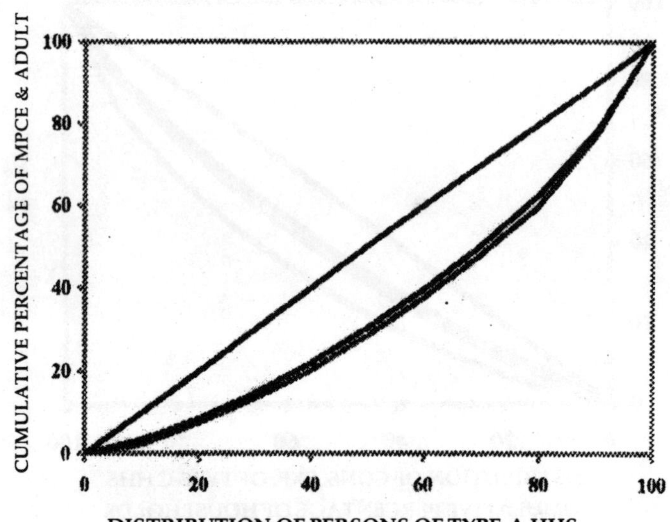


DISTRIBUTION OF PERSONS OF TYPE-A HHS
CUMULATIVE PERCENTAGE OF PERSONS
—E-LINE —MPCE —ADULT. EQUL

FIG. 10

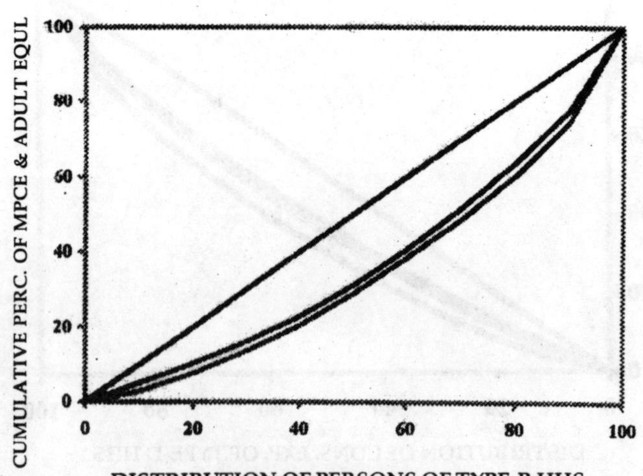


DISTRIBUTION OF PERSONS OF TYPE-B HHS
CUMULATIVE PERC. OF PERSONS
—E-LINE —MPCE —ADULT. EQUL

FIG. 11

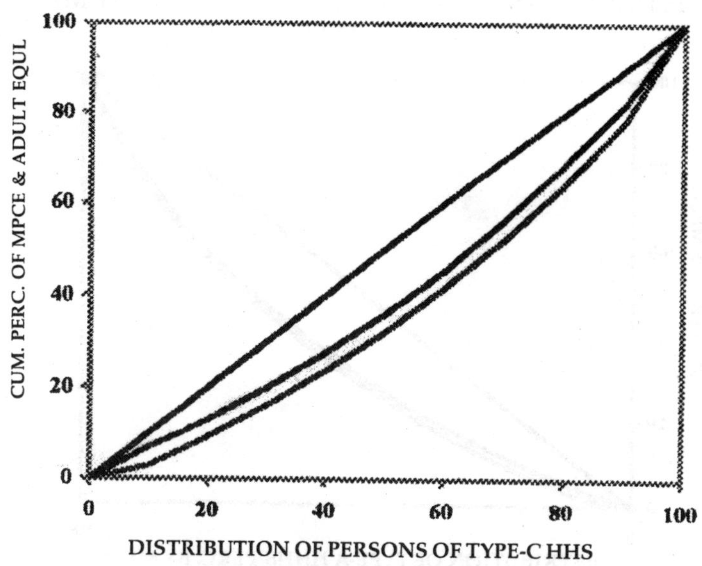


DISTRIBUTION OF PERSONS OF TYPE-C HHS
CUMULATIVE PERC. OF PERSONS
—E-LINE —MPCE —ADULT. EQUL

FIG. 12

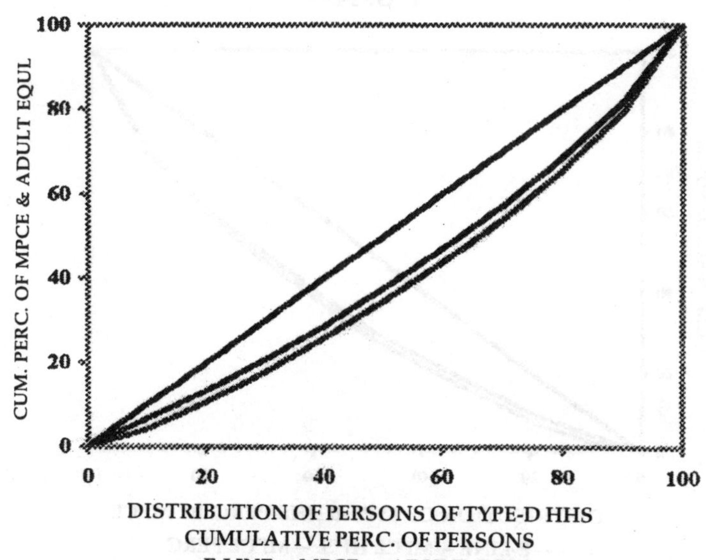


DISTRIBUTION OF PERSONS OF TYPE-D HHS
CUMULATIVE PERC. OF PERSONS
—E-LINE —MPCE —ADULT. EQUL

FIG. 13

## DISTRIBUTION OF HOUSEHOLDS/PERSONS BY MPCE (CHART-III, TYPE-ii & iii)

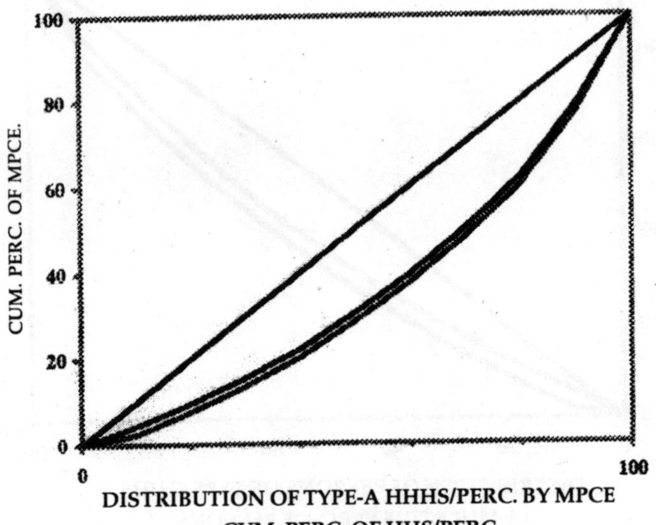


DISTRIBUTION OF TYPE-A HHHS/PERC. BY MPCE
CUM. PERC. OF HHS/PERC
—E-LINE —MPCE HHS —MPCE PERC.

FIG. 14

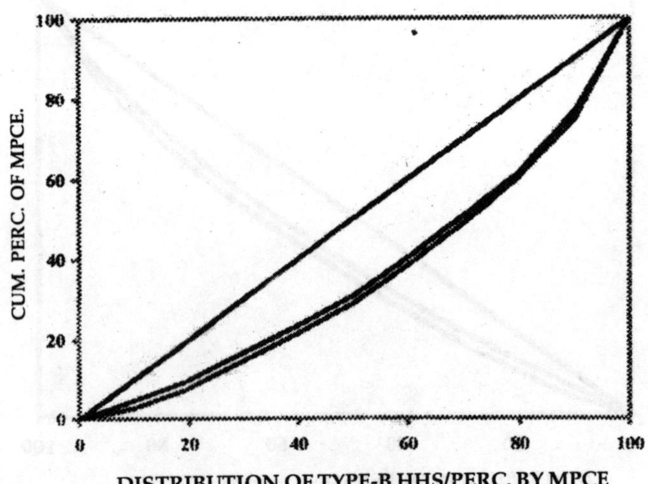


DISTRIBUTION OF TYPE-B HHS/PERC. BY MPCE
—E-LINE —MPCE HHS —MPCE PERC.

FIG. 15

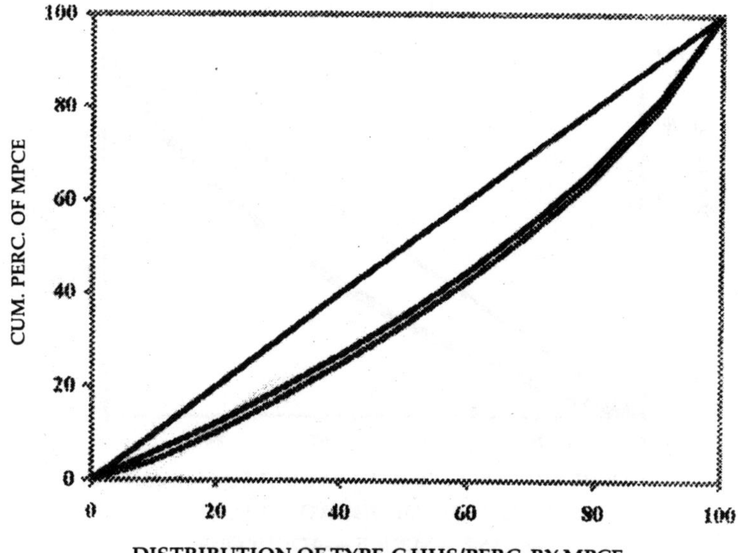


DISTRIBUTION OF TYPE-C HHS/PERC. BY MPCE
CUM. PERC. OF HHS/PERS.
—E-LINE —MPCE HHS —MPCE PERC.

**FIG. 16**

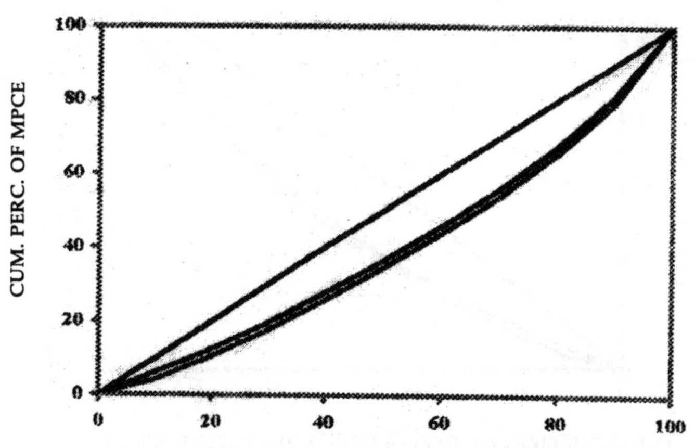


DISTRIBUTION OF TYPE-D HHS/PERC BY MPCE
CUM. PERC. OF HHS/PERC
—E-LINE —MPCE HHS —MPCE PERC

**FIG. 17**

## LORENZ CURVE COMPARISON OF DISTRIBUTIONS (CHART-IV, TYPE-iv & v)

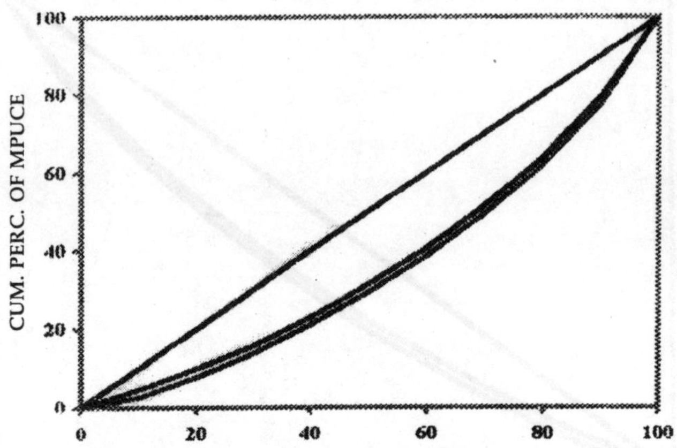


DISTRIBUTION OF TYPE-A HHS/ADULT EQUL. BY MPUCE
CUM. PERC. OF HHS/ADULT EQUL
—E-LINE —MPUCE —ADULT QUE.

FIG. 18

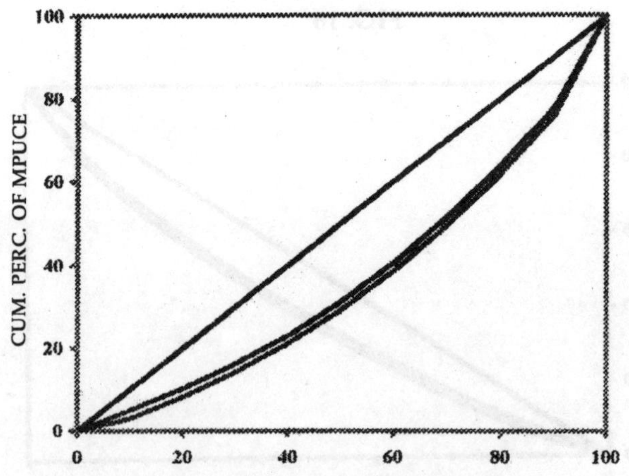


DISTRIBUTION OF TYPE-A HHS/ADULT EQUL. BY MPUCE
CUM. PERC. OF HHS/ADULT EQUL
—E-LINE —MPUCE —ADULT QUE.

FIG. 19

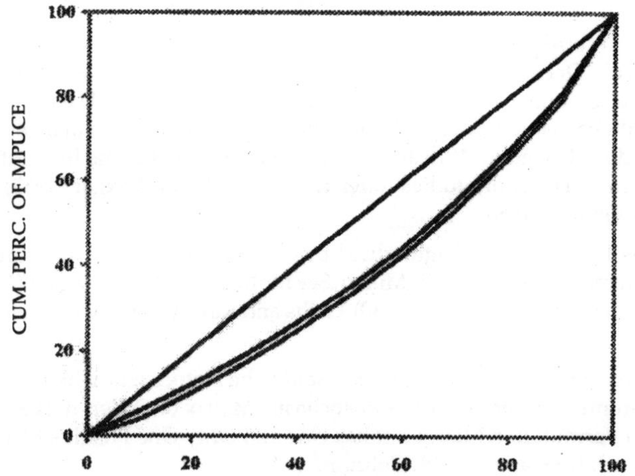


DISTRIBUTION OF TYPE-A HHS/ADULT EQUL. BY MPUCE
CUM. PERC. OF HHS/ADULT EQUL
—E-LINE —MPUCE —ADULT QUE.

FIG. 20

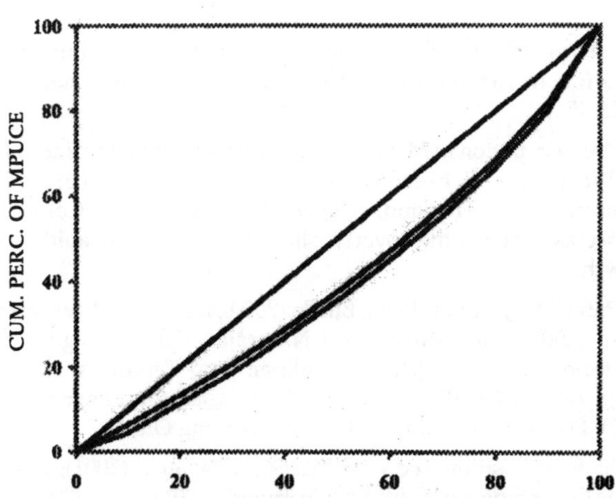


DISTRIBUTION OF TYPE-A HHS/ADULT EQUL. BY MPUCE
CUM. PERC. OF HHS/ADULT EQUL
—E-LINE —MPUCE —ADULT QUE.

FIG. 21

## REFERENCES

1. It is a World-wide Practice to Collect and Publish Data at the Household Level. Occasionally Attempts are being made to Explore the Demographic Factors while Analysing the Unit Record Data of NSSO (National Sample Survey Organisation) in Consumption and Inequality Studies (Coondoo, 1975 and Paul, 1988 &1989). For Some Illustrations of these Types of Studies Refer to Prais and Houthakker (1955) and Muellbauer (1980).
2. This Fact has been Highlighted by Various Researchers Working in Different Socio-economic Milieu. See for Instance Vaidyanathan (1974), Kuznets (1976), Krishnaji (1980), Gaiha and Kazmi (1981) and Sundaram (1990).
3. A Non-negative Square Matrix is said to be Bistochastic if all Row and Column Sums are Unity. A Bistochastic Matrix of Order 'n' is Said to be a Permutation Matrix if it has One and Only One Positive Element in Each Row and in Each Column.
4. A. Vaidyanathan (1974): 'Some Aspects of Inequalities in Living Standards in Rural India', in T.N. Srinivasan and P.K. Bardhan (eds.), Poverty and Income Distribution in India, Statistical Publishing Society, ISI, Calcutta.
5. See Ahmed, M. (1961); Ojha, P.D. and Bhatt, V.V. (1964); Iyengar, N.S. (1964); Mukherjee, M. and Chaterjee, G.S. (1967) and Mazumdar, Dutta (1969).
6. Li, Hongyi, et al. (1998): 'Explaining International and Inter-temporal Variation in Income Inequality', *The Economic Journal*, Vol. 108, pp. 26-45.
7. The Pre-occupation in Malaysia was with Correcting the Racial Income and Wealth Gap Between the Two Dominant (Malaya and Chinese) Communities. In Thailand, as in all Other Developing Countries, the Pre-occupation was the Poverty Alleviation Based on Rapid Economic Growth.
8. See Datt (1999), Gupta (1999); Bhalla (2000); Deaton and Tarozzi (2000); Dreze (2000); Lal, Mohan and Natarajan (2001); Nagaraj (2000); Ravallion (2000); Sen (2000); Sundaram and Tendulkar (2000, 2001, 2002); Vasaria (2000); Sundaram (2001); Chandrasekhar and Ghosh (2002); Datta and Ravallion (2002) and Among Others.
9. On the First Position, see Vhalla (2000); Bhagabati (2001); Das (2000). On the Other Side see Mehta (2001); Sainath (2001); Shiva (2001) Among Others.
10. Calculated from Government of India (2002). There have been Further Measure Increases in Public Sector Salaries After 1999-2000, with a Gradual Implementation of the Recommendations of the Fifth Pay Commission by Many State Governments.

11. See Draze and Sen (2002), Statistical Appendi, Table A.6, also Datt (1999).

12. The Terms 'Household' and 'Family' e Used Interchangeably Throughout the Analysis. We Also Used the Term 'Consumption Expenditure' to Refer to Total Consumption Expenditure for the Sake of Brevity.

13. See Dandekar and Rath (1971), Bardhan (1974), Vaidyanathan (1974). Rajaraman (1975), Ahluwalia (1976, 1978), Renuad (1976), Anand (1978). Meesook (1979) and Dutta and Meerman (1980).

14. The Definition of Different Types of Expenditures used in Five Expenditure Distributions of the Study are as Follows:

    (i) Mean Monthly per Household Total Consumption Expenditure (MHPCE): It is the Average of Monthly Total Household Expenditure.

    $$\text{Mean (MHPCE)} = \sum_{j=1}^{n} X_j / n$$

    (ii) Mean Per Capita Household Consumption Expenditure (MPHCE): It is the Average of Monthly Household Per Capita Expenditure of each Household.

    $$\text{Mean (MPHCE)} \ \frac{1}{n}\sum_{j=1}^{n}(X_j / n_j)$$

    (iii) Monthly Per Capita Expenditure (MPCE): It is the Monthly Total Consumption Expenditure of Each Household Divided by the Corresponding Household Size.

    $\text{MPCE} = (X_j/n_j)$

    (iv) Mean Per Unit (Adult Equivalent) Household Expenditure (MHPUE): It is the Average of Monthly Household Per Unit Expenditure of Each household.

    $$\text{MHPUE} = \frac{1}{n}\sum_{j=1}^{n}(X_j / n_j^*) \text{ where } n_j^* \text{ is the Adj. Household Size.}$$

(v) Monthly Per Capita Expenditure (MPUE): It is the Monthly Total Consumption Expenditure of Each Household Divided by the Corresponding Household Size.

$$\text{MPUE} = (X_j / n_j^*)$$

15. The Expenditure Approach has been Used More Extensively in Indian Studies on Poverty. See Ojha (1970); Minhas (1970, 1971); Bardhan (1970, 1971, 1973, 1974); Dandekar and Rath (1971); Panikkar (1972); Bhatty (1974); Rudra (1974); Raja Raman (1974, 1975); Rao (1977); Planning Commission, Government of India (1979); Paul (1984); Ahulwalia (1978, 1986); and Minhas, Jain, Kausal and Saluja (1987).

16. Notable Among the Attempts are those due to FAO (1946, 1950, 1952, 1957, 1959, 1961, 1962, 1963, 1973); FAO/WHO expert group (1965); Gopalan and Rao (1977); Indian Council of Medical Research (1968) and Patwardhan (1960).

17. Suppose θ is the Inequality Measure and if the Partial Derivative $\partial\theta/\partial z_j$ Exists for all 'j' then the Condition of Transfer may be written as:

$$D\theta = \frac{\partial\theta}{\partial z_i}(-dz_i) + \frac{\partial\theta}{\partial z_j}(dz_j) < 0 \text{ for all } z_i > z_j$$

That is

$$\frac{\partial\theta}{\partial z_i} > \frac{\partial\theta}{\partial z_j} \text{ for all } z_i > z_j$$

where $z_j$ is the Income of the jth (j=1, ..., n) Population Unit. For Details see Kondor (1975, pp. 313-315).

18. The Lorenz Curve Expresses the Relationship Between the Cumulative Proportion of Population Unit and Cumulative Proportion of Income.

# 6

# MEASUREMENT OF MAGNITUDE, INCIDENCE AND SEVERITY OF POVERTY

## 6.1 Introduction

The concern of this chapter is to provide a succinct, but self contained, discussion of a selection of measures of poverty that have been proposed in the literature. At the first blush the concept of poverty and the specification of the poverty line appear to be quite distinct. The analysis of inequality is concerned with the distribution of an economic cake among the members of a given population but the analysis of poverty is concerned with whether the resources of some members of the population fall below an acceptable minimum. A closer examination of these reveals a greater degree of overlap. The degree of overlap is most evident in the discussions of public policy in an 'unequal' economy; those at the bottom of the distribution are likely to be 'poor'. Thus, public policy directed at reducing inequality could also alleviate poverty in the limit providing an average income of the economy exceeding the poverty income. For alleviating poverty, the required feedback to the policy makers is the quantification or measurement of poverty. The quantification or measurement of poverty requires the solution of two distinct problems: (i) the problem of identification of the poor in the total population which involves the selection of an appropriate poverty line. A unit is identified to be poor if its income is below the poverty line; and (ii) the problem of aggregation which requires some method of combining the level of deprivation of different poor units into an overall indicator. There are various methods for combining the deprivation of the poor units into a single indicator.

Much of the theoretical debate on the measurement of poverty has been on the poverty measures rather than on the poverty line. While there has been considerable discussion on whether the poverty line should reflect 'absolute' or 'relative' view of poverty (see, for example, Sen, 1973), the literature is relatively thin on how to update the poverty line to account for inflation, changing consumption pattern and ensuring it's accuracy in terms of the original calorie based definition. The 'absolute' view of poverty indicates the poverty line as the expenditure required to purchase a 'subsistence' bundle of items by the individual. In the Indian context the 'subsistence' bundle was derived from the recommended minimum calorie or energy[1] requirement that was considered necessary for subsistence. However, with inflation and changing consumer preferences, the 'official poverty line' in India which was anchored on the minimum energy requirements three decades ago, has ceased to be an accurate, or even a reasonable indicator of the cost of acquiring the minimum energy requirement. In India, therefore, the debate on the 'relative' versus 'absolute' poverty line has given away to a debate on whether the poverty line should be money metric and expenditure based, as the 'official poverty line' is or whether it should be specified directly in term of minimum calorie requirement. This involves a significant methodological issue that is to be addressed in this chapter. This chapter also proposes alternative approaches to the construction of the poverty line and also provides a brief review of different poverty measures.

This chapter is structured into eight sections. Section-6.1 is the introduction. Section-6.2 deals with the concept of absolute poverty. Section-6.3 deals with the axiomatic requirements of a poverty index. Section-6.4 provides a picture of international poverty scenario, where as the inter-state poverty scenario is narrated in section-6.5. Section-6.6 deals with the estimation of poverty lines for different occupational households. The incidence, depth and severity of poverty is described in section-6.7.

Section-6.8 provides the empirical analysis of incidence, severity and depth of poverty using traditional, modern and the recent poverty measures. Section-6.9 is the conclusion of the study.

## 6.2 Concept of Absolute Poverty

People are poor in the absolute sense when their income is 'insufficient to obtain the minimum necessaries for maintenance of mere physical efficiency' (Rowntree, 1901).[2] If age, type of work, sex, climate, physique, dietary habits etc. are held constant then the same poverty standard would hold everywhere. This implies that income elasticity of the absolute poverty line is zero. Sen (1976) considers poverty as a matter of deprivation. Absolute deprivation relates to non-fulfilment of a basic sustenance of life. In case of absolute poverty a man's income fails to enable him to get the basic necessaries of life for physical existence. Atkinson (1989) defined absolute poverty as the inability to attain the minimum standard of living.

The concept of absolute poverty is, however, not as absolute and objective as it appears to be because the interpretation of the minimum necessities has been quite different across countries. For example, there have been attempts to draw absolute poverty lines for India (Planning Commission, 1981) and for the United States (Orshanky, 1965). But the same absolute poverty standard has not been adopted. It is because in a developing country like India, absolute poverty connotes a lack of subsistence level with reference to mere physical needs. On the other hand, in a developed country like the United States it connotes socially acceptable subsistence level. Absolute poverty norms, thus, seem to be related with average income introducing an element of relativity in the construction of the absolute poverty line which makes it quite difficult to draw a clear distinction between absolute and relative poverty notions. But in a strict sense, absolute poverty should be unrelated to the average income of the society and hence, this notion has to be linked to a mere subsistence level of living. This idea has prompted a number of authors (e.g. Rein, 1970) to designate absolute poverty as an objective notion. Thus, for studying the poverty situation in the low-income countries, it is necessary to draw an absolute poverty line. The poverty line in the absolute notion relates to a mere subsistence level of living as considered appropriate to the situation of the country concerned. Based on this concept, poverty is defined in terms of insufficiency of economic resources to meet the basic dietary needs namely food of an individual or a household.

The determination of basic dietary needs is a problem and is not free from ambiguities. First, we confronted with the problem of setting an appropriate 'basic needs' bundle of food, which is quantified in terms of energy. The second problem is to determine minimum dietary requirement for different socio-cultural groups. The list of food items varies from one society to another, or even in the same society, from one income group to another income group. The next problem is to estimate the minimum requirements of food intake to fulfil the required energy, protein and other micronutrients because such requirements may vary among individuals and over time for a given individual. In view of these problems, Rowntree (1901) considered a prison's diet as food bundle in his first study of poverty in York, which, however, appeared too stringent to him, and then he suggested a less stringent bundle of his own. Subsequently, different experts in this field have suggested several food bundles. Appropriate share of calorie that should come from cereal foods, non-cereal plant foods and animal foods is also not available in the literature. Even unanimous objective view of experts on a standard level of energy requirements is not available and it also varies with the variation of age, sex, region and activities (see e.g. Sukhatme, 1981). Therefore, one has to proceed by selecting a particular expert view. The selected view may be a planner's view or an individual researcher's view. In case of non-food needs, one has to face even greater difficulties (see for example Rowntree, 1941). In short, both number of needs and their quantities are matters of expert judgment.

## 6.3 Axiomatic Requirements of a Poverty Index

In the derivation of most poverty indices mentioned, an axiomatic framework is used to list the desirable properties of such an index or measure of poverty. Though, all researchers choose some of these properties as a matter, of course, other properties may be less easy to agree upon, as they reflect either value judgments or emphasis of the researcher on a certain aspect of poverty. This causes problems when a choice has to be made between two conflicting axiomatic requirements that are both believed to be desirable.

We will discuss the following axioms for the choice of a suitable poverty measure:

(i) *Monotonicity axiom:* A decrease in the income of a poor person should increase the poverty index, and vice versa.

(ii) *Transfer axiom:* A transfer from a poor person to a richer person should increase the poverty index, and vice versa.

(iii) *Proportion of Poor axiom:* An increase in the relative number of poor should increase the poverty index.

(iv) *Population symmetry axiom:* If two or more identical populations are pooled, the poverty index should not change.

(v) *Focus axiom:* The poverty index should be independent of the income levels of people above the poverty line.

(vi) *Transfer sensitivity axiom:* The increase of a poverty index as a result of a transfer of a fixed amount of money from a poor person to a richer person should be decreasing in the income of the donator, and vice versa.

(vii) *Decomposability axiom:* The poverty index should increase when poverty in a sub-group increases, other things being equal, and vice versa.

(viii) *Ranked relative deprivation axiom:* In addition, a stronger axiom, the ranked relative deprivation axiom which assumes that relative deprivation, depends on the rank order of welfare. The axiom is applied to poverty indices of a specific structure, i.e. weighted poverty gaps, where the weight of each person equals his rank order in the welfare distribution (Sen, 1976; Thon, 1979 and Takayama, 1979).

(ix) *Size-augmentation axiom:* If the given income vector is augmented by addition of an income less than z, then the poverty index should increase.

(x) *Normalisation axioms:* Often we want that the index should lie in the closed interval of 0, 1. For affecting it sometimes an interval axiom is stated, which is also referred to as sign and size axiom. Here we consider a class of axioms, some of which have been used in derivation of their respective indices by Sen, Kakwani and Takayama. The axioms used in derivation relate to some ideal situations. There exists possibility of five such situations.

($N_1$) when no body has income below z, then P = 0.

($N_2$) when everybody has zero income, then P =1.

($N_3$) when everybody has equal income but below z, then $P = I_P$.

($N_4$) when every poor has income equal to zero, then P = H.

($N_5$) when every body has equal income but below z, then $P = HI_P$.

We may note that the axioms ($N_1$) and ($N_2$) are often used as text axioms. But all of them may be used as derivation axioms. Takayama (1979) used $N_1$ and $N_4$ in his derivation as he employed two normalization parameters. Sen (1976, 1981) and Kakwani (1980) used only ($N_5$) in their derivations. According to Takayama (1979, pp. 757), $P_T = 1$ when any one unit monopolizes the whole income for considerably large 'n'. We can note the difference between Takayama's axioms and axioms ($N_2$). We may further note that these axioms may have to be modified if the derivation functions are not arithmetic ones.

## 6.4 Changing Scenario of International Incidence of Poverty

According to World Development Report (2000/2001) poverty implies lack of adequate food, shelter and other deprivations that keep them away from a decent standard of living which includes better housing, sanitation, access to safe drinking water and so on. It is a multidimensional concept. The main dimension are:

(i) lack of income and assets to attain basic necessities like food, shelter, clothing, and acceptable levels of health and education;

(ii) sense of voicelessness and powerlessness in the institutions of state and society;

(iii) vulnerability to adverse shocks, linked to an inability to cope with them.

Over the years a number of composite measures of poverty have been proposed. One such measure, the Physical Quality of Life Index (PQLI) has been superseded in recent years by the UNDP's Human Development Index (HDI)[3]; the latter being a composite of GDP per capita, life expectancy at birth and the level of education attainment. It is noteworthy that it is the UNDP, which has done the most to address poverty in all its dimensions. For example, as per an estimate made by UNDP, the cost of eradicating poverty across the world is relatively small compared to global income (not more than 0.3 per cent of world's GDP). Political commitment, not financial resources, is the real obstacle to poverty eradication. The United Nations Development Programme (UNDP) has also developed the Human Poverty Index (HPI)[4] which focuses on deprivation, especially, the deprivation in three basic needs of human life – longevity, knowledge and decent standard of living. The HPI is based on three main indices: the percentage of the population not expected to survive beyond the age of 40, the adult illiteracy rate, and a deprivation index based on an average of three variables (indicators)—the percentage of the population without access to safe drinking water, the percentage of population without access to health services, and the percentage of children under the age of 5 years who are underweight due to malnourishment. Though HDI is widely used, there are several criticisms labeled against it; such as variables included in the index, the arbitrary choice of weight in constructing the average, and the information list obtained combining three or four pieces of date into a single number. Thus, it is preferable to report a small range of social indicators rather than attempting to combine a group of indicators into an overall poverty index. Another way to separate the poor from the non-poor as proposed by the World Bank is to provide a minimum acceptable level of consumption. There are two ways of setting a consumption poverty line to measure poverty and make comparison across countries:

(i) the purchasing-power parity rate popularly known as the PPP method; and

(ii) the food energy method.

The World Bank estimated the PPP poverty lines at $1-a-day and $2-a- day. The food energy method of setting a consumption poverty line is one way of dealing with this problem by fixing a minimum internationally agreed calorie intake, and converting consumption bundles into calorie intakes using the nutritional values of food items in the bundle with non-food items having a zero values. The problem with this method is that consumers in different countries may choose different combination of food, which requires different income to meet nutritional requirements. Commodities, which are regarded as optional extras in some countries, may be necessities in others.

UNCTAD report (2002) 'On escaping the poverty trap' reviewed the nature of poverty in Less Developed Countries (LDCs) and defines 'poverty is a situation in which a major part of the population are at or below income level sufficient to meet their basic needs, and in which the available resources in the economy, even when equally distributed, are barely sufficient to cater to the basic needs of the population on a sustainable basis'. In general, poverty is defined as the inability to achieve minimally adequate levels of consumption. Incidence of poverty is calculated as a proportion of the total population living below the poverty line. Poverty gap index or depth of poverty is defined as the difference between poverty line and average level of consumption of those people living below the poverty line. International poverty is measured in term of $1-a- day and $2-a-day poverty lines. The $1-a-day norm (of international poverty line) is widely considered as extreme poverty and it is the focal concern of the International Development Goal of reducing poverty between 1990 and 2015 (UNCTAD, 2002).

### 6.4.1 *Magnitude and Incidence of Poverty Over Different Regions of the World*

Poverty amidst plenty is the world's greatest challenge of today. 'Widespread poverty remains the major problem to development effort' which has echoed again and again at the United Nations World Submit for Social Development in Copenhagen (March, 1995). The elimination of poverty is high and even growing income inequality is at the core of all development problems and the principal objective of development policy. Despite significant development effort over the past half century, extreme poverty remains widespread in the developing world. Of the world's 6 billion population, 2.8 billion (almost half) live in less than $2-a- day and 1.2 billion (about a fifth) live in less than $1-a- day. About 44 per cent of the world's poor are living in South Asia (WDR, 2001). It is much acute in less developed and developing countries than developed countries. These impoverished people often suffer from undernutrition and poor health, have little or no literacy, live in environmentally degraded areas, have little political voice, and attempt to earn a meagre living on small and marginal firms or in dilapidated urban slums. Therefore, the main problem for the researchers as well as the policy makers is an indepth analysis of the problems of poverty—its measurement, magnitude and incidence and the highly unequal distribution of income.

We now examine the incidence of poverty in less developed and developing countries of the globe. Developing countries have spread over different regions of the globe such as East Asia and Pacific; Europe and Central Asia; Latin America and the Caribbean; Middle East and North Africa; South Africa and Sub-Saharan Africa. In less developed and developing economies the incidence of poverty has varied over time and also across the regions. Estimates (Table-6.1) reveal that the share of the population in developing economies living on less than $1-a-day has declined from 28.3 per cent in 1987 to 24 per cent in 1998. There are large regional variations in the incidence of poverty. The incidence of poverty has declined in the regions in East Asia from 26.6 per cent to 15.3 per cent; in Middle East and North Africa from 2.4 per cent to 1.9 per cent; in South Asia from 44.9 per cent to 40 per cent; and marginally in Sub-Saharan Africa from 46.6 per cent to 46.3 per cent during the period 1987 to 1998. It is observed from Table-6.1 that though the poverty level has reduced in Latin America, South Asia and Sub-Saharan Africa, the number of people living on less than $1-a-day has increased in Latin America from 63.7 million to 78.2 million; in South Asia from 474.4 million to 522 million; and in Sub-Saharan Africa from 217.2 million to 290.9 million. In 1998, South Asia and Sub-Saharan Africa have accounted for around 70 per cent of the population living on less than $1-a-day. This is due to the geographical distribution of poverty. In East Asia the incidence of poverty in the 1990s has been influenced by the impact of the recent economic crisis. In most of the countries, poverty has risen as a result of the financial crisis of the late 1990s.

### 6.4.2 *Changing Scenario of Poverty in Less Developed and Developing Countries*

In less developed countries (LDCs), the average per capita private consumption per day during 1995-99 is $0.29 as per $1-a-day norm and $0.44 as per $2-a-day norm. The percentage of population living less than a dollar per day is 50 per cent and for $2-a-day is 81 per cent. Within LDCs, when we compare the African and Asian LDCs having higher incidence of 40 per cent and 46 per cent respectively, African LDCs are worst hit by poverty. The depth of poverty more or less is same for both the groups. However, the percentage of population below poverty line is very high in African LDCs. More than 65 per cent of population is living less than $1-a-day and almost 88 per cent of population is living on less than $2-a-day during 1995-99. As per $1-a-day norm, African LDCs has more number of people below poverty line than Asian LDCs. During 1965-69, about 56 per cent of population was living below poverty line. This percentage has increased to 62 per cent in 1985-89 and then to 65 per cent in 1995-99. Against this the Asian LDCs are able to reduce the percentage of population from 36 per cent during 1975-79 to 23 per cent during 1995-99. During this period (1965-99) number of people living below the $1-a-day norm has increased drastically for African LDCs. However, for the Asian LDCs number of people living less than $1-a-day had not increased much but in fact, it had declined from 46.5 million people in 1979 to 45 million people in 1999. The average consumption level of African LDCs has decreased indicating more depth in poverty gap. On the other hand, the average consumption level for Asian LDCs has increased showing a reduction in the depth of poverty. As per $2-a-day norm the incidence and depth of poverty is more for African LDCs, the incidence is about 82 per cent and unfortunately it is on the rise. In Asian LDCs, the incidence is about 79 per cent and it is showing a decline trend. The average consumption levels of those living below $2-a-day was falling for African LDCs which is less than $1 indicating more depth in poverty (gap). But Asian LDCs are relatively better than African LDCs. The average consumption level is more than $1 and it is on the rise (UNCTAD, 2002).

### *6.4.3 Poverty in Developing Countries*

The poverty situation in developing countries appeared to be slightly better than less developed countries (LDCs). The percentage of population living less than $1-a-day has drastically reduced from 44 per cent during 1965-69 to 7.5 per cent during 1995-99. The average consumption has increased from $0.86 during 1965-69 to $0.93 during 1995-99 indicating a reduction in the depth of poverty. As per $2-a-day norm, even though the populations living below the poverty line come down during the period 1965-99, the incidence is more. The average consumption level has also increased indicating a reduction in poverty gap (UNCTAD, 2002).

### *6.4.4 Poverty in South-Asian Counties*

South-Asia is one of the fastest growing regions. South Asia consists of India, Pakistan, Bangladesh, Bhutan, Nepal, Maldavis and Sri Lanka. This region has the average GDP growth of 5.2 per cent in 1998 and 5.4 per cent in 1999. As per $1-a-day norm, roughly 40 per cent of the poor in the world reside in this region. In South Asia poverty reduction has also varied in the 1990s. In Bangladesh poverty has decreased from 29.1 per cent in 1996 to 24.9 per cent in 1995-99 despite the worst flood situation. But Pakistan and Sri Lanka have made little or no progress in poverty reduction in the 1990s. In India, as per $1-a-day norm, percentage of population below poverty line has declined from 52.5 per cent in 1992 to 44.2 per cent in 1997. For Bangladesh and Nepal the incidence of poverty is low for $1-a-day norm and high as per $2-a-day norm (Table-6.2).

## Table–6.1

### Magnitude and incidence of poverty over different regions of the globe (PPP, 1985)

| *Region* | *People living on less than $1 a day (millions)* | | | | | *Percentage of population living on less than $1 a day* | | | | |
|---|---|---|---|---|---|---|---|---|---|---|
| | *1987* | *1990* | *1993* | *1996* | *1998* | *1987* | *1990* | *1993* | *1996* | *1998* |
| East Asia & Pacific | 417.5 | 452.4 | 413.9 | 265.1 | 278.3 | 26.6 | 27.6 | 25.2 | 14.9 | 15.3 |
| Europe and Central Asia | 1.1 | 7.1 | 18.9 | 23.8 | 24.0 | 0.2 | 1.6 | 4.0 | 5.1 | 5.1 |
| Latin America & the Caribb. | 63.7 | 73.8 | 70.8 | 76.0 | 78.2 | 15.3 | 16.8 | 15.3 | 15.6 | 15.6 |
| Middle East & North Africa | 9.3 | 5.7 | 5.0 | 5.0 | 5.5 | 4.3 | 2.4 | 1.9 | 1.8 | 1.9 |
| South Asia | 474.4 | 495.1 | 505.1 | 513.7 | 522.0 | 44.9 | 44.0 | 42.4 | 42.3 | 40.0 |
| Sub-Saharan Africa | 217.2 | 242.3 | 273.3 | 289.0 | 290.9 | 46.6 | 47.7 | 49.7 | 48.5 | 46.3 |
| All | 1183.2 | 1276.4 | 1304.3 | 1190.0 | 1198.9 | 28.3 | 29.0 | 28.1 | 24.5 | 24.0 |

**Source: World Bank Development Report, 2000/2001, pp. 23.**

## Table–6.2

### Poverty in some less developed and developing Asian countries (in percentage)

| *Country* | *Year* | *BPL - $ 1-a-day* | *PG - $ 1-a-day* | *BPL - $ 1-a-day* | *PG - $ 1-a-day* |
|---|---|---|---|---|---|
| Developing Asian Countries | | | | | |
| China | 1995 | 22.2 | 6.9 | 57.8 | 24.1 |
| | 1999 | 18.8 | 4.4 | 52.6 | 20.9 |
| Indonesia | 1995 | 11.8 | 1.8 | 58.7 | 19.3 |
| | 1996 | 7.7 | 0.9 | 50.4 | 15.3 |
| | 1999 | 12.9 | 1.9 | 65.5 | 21.5 |
| Philippines | 1991 | 28.6 | 7.7 | 64.5 | 28.2 |
| | 1994 | 26.9 | 7.1 | 62.8 | 27.0 |
| Thailand | 1992 | 1.8 | 0.7 | 23.5 | 5.4 |
| | 1998 | 1.7 | 0.5 | 28.2 | 7.1 |
| Turkey | 1994 | 2.4 | 0.5 | 18.0 | 5.0 |
| Developing South Asian Countries | | | | | |
| India | 1992 | 52.5 | 15.6 | 88.8 | 45.8 |
| | 1994 | 47.0 | 12.9 | 87.5 | 42.9 |
| | 1999 | 44.2 | 12.0 | 86.2 | 41.4 |
| Pakistan | 1991 | 11.6 | 2.6 | 57.0 | 18.6 |
| | 1996 | 31.0 | 6.2 | 84.7 | 35.0 |
| Sri Lanka | 1990 | 4.0 | 0.7 | 41.2 | 11.0 |
| | 1995 | 6.6 | 1.0 | 45.4 | 13.5 |
| Less Developed South Asian Countries | | | | | |
| Bangladesh | 1996 | 29.1 | 6.0 | 77.8 | 32.0 |
| | 1995-99 | 10.3 | 1.0 | 59.8 | 20.0 |
| Bhutan | 1995-99 | 24.9 | 5.0 | 77.0 | 30.0 |
| Myanmar | 1995-99 | 52.3 | 14.0 | 88.6 | 45.0 |
| Nepal | 1995 | 37.7 | 10.0 | 82.5 | 38.0 |
| | 1995-99 | 40.0 | 9.0 | 84.7 | 40.0 |

Table-6.2 presents data pertaining to incidence and depth of poverty in developing countries. A glance through the Table-6.2 reveals that as per $1-a-day norm the incidence of poverty is highest for India followed by Pakistan, Philippines and China. The incidence of poverty is more than 20 per cent for these countries. For other countries the incidence is around 10 per cent. The incidence is very high as per $ 2-a-day norm. The percentage varies between 18 per cent (Turkey) to 89 per cent (India). The depth of poverty is also relatively very high for $2-a-day norm than for $1-a-day norm.

## 6.5 Changing Scenario of Incidence, Depth and Severity of Poverty in India

The debate on poverty trend in Rural-India during nineties is inconclusive. There is a large variation in incidence of poverty among the states. Some states are extremely poor and their macro economic performance is not comparable with the relatively rich states. The inter-state disparity in rural per-capita consumption expenditure has widened during the post-reform period. Also there is difference in change in incidence of rural poverty among the states. The interdependence of state level per capita expenditure growth and poverty is not very clear. Growth is not evenly distributed within the states. Some states have experienced higher rural poverty than the others. The state level trend of rural urban disparity and rural-urban polarization is showing no relation with the trend of poverty. So the interdependence of rural poverty and rural development in the states of the country needs further examination.

Estimates of poverty in India are typically based on a normative minimum calorie intake method. More or less the calorie intake regarded as sufficient enough for a person to keep him alive (based on Sukhatme's estimates) is the calorie norms for determining the level poverty. Accordingly the Task Force constituted by the Planning Commission in 1979 fixed the calorie norms at 2400 calories per person per day for rural areas and 2100 calories per person per day for urban areas. This group accepted the calorie intake norms recommended by Nutritional Expert Group (1968) for fourteen age-sex categories. Based on these norms, poverty lines were estimated using the 28$^{th}$ round (1973-74) NSS consumption expenditure data for rural and urban areas. The estimates came out to be Rs. 49.09 monthly per capita consumption expenditure in rural areas and Rs. 56.64 in urban areas. Using the head count ratio as a measure of poverty, the incidence of poverty was estimated to be 56.4 per cent in rural areas and 49 per cent in urban areas. For subsequent rounds of NSS consumption expenditure data and the estimation of poverty line have essentially involves the updating of prices using state-wise price deflators for rural and urban population. Planning Commission's Expert Group (1993) under the chairmanship of Prof. Lakdawala, estimated that rural poverty declined from 56.4 per cent in 1973-74 to 39.1 per cent in 1987-88 and urban poverty ratio came down from 49.2 per cent in 1973-74 to 40.1 per cent in 1987-88. The overall poverty ratio, has therefore, declined from 54.9 per cent in 1973-74 to 39.3 per cent in 1987-88.

A major significant development for India's economic policy was Indira Gandhiji's extension of Nehruvian socialism to poverty eradication in terms of affirmative action for empowering the poor. For the first time, in mid-1960s, attempts were made to estimate poverty in terms of expenditures on a basket of consumer goods, thus, arriving at some minimum requirements for a basic standard of living. The Indian poor have been studied in more repetitive detail than the poor of any other developing countries even though their number and the situation may not have changed very much in recent years. As Sen pointed out 'The Indian Poor may not be accustomed to receiving much help, but he is beginning to get used to being counted'. Several researchers like Dandekar and Rath (1971), Ojha (1971), Minhas (1971), Bardhan (1974), Ahluwalia (1978), Vadyanathan (1979), Jain and Tendulkar (1989, 1998), Ravallion and Datt (1996), Dubey and Gangopadhyay (1998) etc. and institutions like World Bank, the Finance Commission and the Planning Commission have estimated the incidence of poverty in India. Dandekar and Rath (1971) have specified their poverty line as the amount of money which is necessary to purchase a low cost diet that provide 2250 calories per day. They found that 40 per cent of the rural and 50 per cent of the urban population live below the poverty line in 1960-61. They also found wide regional variations in the incidence of poverty. Ojha (1971) using calorie norm of 2250, estimated the poverty line in terms of per capita expenditure limits of Rs. 15 to 18 for the rural areas and Rs. 8 to 11 for urban in 1960-61 prices. Bardhan (1974) found that in 1978-79, about 54 per cent of the rural population and 41per cent of the urban population live below the poverty line, thus, reversing the rural/urban position. The Planning Commission figures on poverty measures during 1977-78 indicate that the incidence of poverty is higher (48 per cent) in rural areas than in urban areas (41 per cent). National Sample Survey (NSS) of India suggested that about 46 per cent of the total population was in poverty in 1973-74. Taking a longer period, 1956-74, and using his poverty line the amount of income necessary to purchase a low cost diet providing 2250 calories per person pre day, Ahluwalia found no consistent upward or downward trend of poverty figures in rural India. The percentage of poverty has declined initially from over 50 per cent in the mid-fifties to around 40 per cent in 1960-61, rising sharply through the mid-sixties, reaching a peak in 1967-68, and then declined again (Ahluwalia, 1978). His finding was confirmed by Rao, who concentrated on starvation poverty in rural India for the same period (Rao, 1981). The above analysis clearly reveals the fact that over the 1960s and in the early 1970s, there was little or no change in the proportion of the Indian population in absolute poverty and the main beneficiaries have been the better of groups due to the steady industrial and agricultural growth during this period. In fact, unregulated capitalist economic growth did not benefit the poor.

Since 1970s, India has reduced poverty substantially due to its improvement in human development indicators and rise in the growth rate. But the progress has been uneven over time and across states and the number of poor has continued to rise. From the early 1950s to mid-1970s, poverty rates fluctuated (Ravallion and Datt, 1996). Then from 1973-74 to mid-1980s, incidence of poverty has declined from 54 per cent in 1973-74 to 38 per cent in 1986-87. Poverty reduction was slow in the 1980s. Poverty incidence dropped sharply during 1990s. In 1991-92, a transitory worsening of poverty incidence occurred with the 1991 balance of payment (BoP) crisis and decline in growth and stabilisation measure.

Studies made by Tendulkar (1998), Datt and Ravallion (1998), Dubey and Gangopadhyay (1998) show that during the early 1990s the increased poverty incidence was associated with factor like poor harvests, limited agricultural imports and high food prices as well as statistical questions related to the small samples in those years and the price indices used to deflate the expenditure data. By 1993-94, the incidence of poverty had decreased to 35 per cent from 38 per cent in 1987-88.

India reduced the depth and severity of poverty even faster than it's incidence ratio. Thus, the decline of poverty was the process through which poverty being reduced improving the consumption of those far below the poverty line. Despite these successes, over 310 million people were living in poverty in 1993-94. The Planning Commission has estimated the incidence of poverty at the national and state level using the methodology of the Lakdawala Committee Report and applying it to consumption expenditure data from the large samples surveys (55$^{th}$ round, 1999-00) on consumer expenditure conducted by the NSSO. The proportion of poor in both the rural and urban areas has declined from 1973-74 to 1999-2000 and declined more sharply in the late 1990s. The incidence of poverty sharply declined from 37.3 per cent in 1993-94 to 27.1 per cent in rural areas and from 32.4 per cent in 1993-94 to 23.7 per cent in urban areas of the country. The overall poverty ratio has declined by nearly 10 per cent i.e. from 36 per cent in 1993-94 to 26.1 per cent in 1999-2000. In absolute terms, the number of poor also declined from 321 million in 1973-74 to 260 million in 1999-2000. This indicates that India has reduced poverty substantially but poverty measures have declined marginally.

Most of the analysts opine that growth is the most important factor for reduction of poverty. Understanding the causes and nature of differences in levels and growth of income and expenditure across the regions (states) is very important because even small differences in the growth rates, if cumulated over a long period of time, may have substantial impact on the standards of living of people (Barro and Sala-i-Martin, 1995) and consequently on the poverty level of the region. Rapid economic growth remains the best bet for reducing India's immense problems of poverty (Jha, 2003). Per capita income growth mostly accounted for the poverty reduction (Bhalla, 2003). It is important to note that the macro economic changes do not confirm to the changes in living condition of the poor and decline of poverty. Further, inequality in any respect gives rise to unequivocal negative effects on subsequent growth and development, and worsens economic, social, and political tension among regions leading to misallocation of resources (Chowdhury, 2003). Therefore, it is important to identify the sources of changes in growth in order to recommend appropriate policies for accelerating growth and achieving equity by raising the standards of living of people in different states. The trends and patterns of poverty at the state level is having a causal link with the patterns of both per-capita income and expenditure growth at the state level, which is shown by the growth elasticity of poverty (Kakwani,1980). Hence, it is essential to show the trends of growth at the state level and find the possible linkages between inter-state disparity in growth and poverty reduction.

The increasing inter-state disparity is evident in rural per-capita consumption expenditure. There is a strong pattern of inter-regional 'divergence' in average per capita expenditure (APCE). States that started off with higher APCE levels also had higher growth rates of APCE between 1993-94 and 1999-00. The state in low APCE growth rate had low rate of per-capita SDP and states in the high APCE growth rate had comparatively high annual growth rates of per capita SDP between 1993-94 and 1999-00. The correlation between the two is 0.45 which is significant (Angus Deaton and Jean Dreze, 2002). The responsiveness of growth to incidence of poverty varies from state to state. This responsiveness is known as Growth Elasticity of Poverty. The Growth Elasticity of Poverty (Poverty Gap) increased in India from 1973-74 to 1983-(N. Kakwani and K. Subarao, 1990).

Official estimates of incidence of poverty are by and large underestimates and thus, do not give a true picture of poverty in India. Poverty being a sensitive issue in Indian politics, economists and officials at the government level has this narrow attitude of manipulating statistics to make the achievements of the Government look impressive. The massive reduction in the incidence of poverty between 1983 and 1987-88, as reported by Planning Commission in 1990 is largely a consequence of the peculiar statistical artifacts used by it and the extent of real reduction of poverty incidence is indeed lower. There is a substantial under estimation of rural poverty using official poverty line for all states as compared to a constant calorie measure. Jones and Sen (2001) remarked in their study that the actual calorie intake at the official poverty lines are far below the norms originally proposed by the Planning Commission in 1973-74 as the minimum calorie norms.

The normal method of measuring poverty in India is by the 'poverty ratio' or 'headcount ratio'. This ratio, however, makes no distinction within the broad category of the poor depending upon their actual levels of consumption and deprivation. For instance, it gives equal weight to someone who is extremely poor and another who is just below the poverty line. As a result, the poverty ratio fails to capture the depth and severity of poverty in an adequate manner. Finally, the Planning Commission has accepted the methodology for estimation of poverty measures as recommended by Expert Group. On the basis of which the magnitude of different poverty measures like poverty ratio, poverty gap index and the squared poverty gap index estimated by the Planning Commission using NSS quinquennial rounds data is provided in Table-6.3. The number of poor is declining at a faster rate in rural areas but it is fluctuating with no such definite trend in urban areas during the period 1977-78 to 1999-00. The poverty measure like poverty ratio, poverty gap index and the squared poverty gap index had declined both in rural and urban India during the period 1973-74 to 1999-00. The magnitude of these measures indicates that poverty ratio, poverty gap index and the squared poverty gap index are higher in rural areas than urban areas of the country during the above period. The coefficients of variation of these measures reveal that the rate of decline of these measures is higher in rural areas than in urban areas. The Lorenz ratio had also declined marginally in both rural and urban India during the above period. It is also seen that the overall poverty ratio, PGI and FGT have shown a substantial decline since 1973-74. The Planning Commission predicts further significant decline of these measures to occur in near future.

**Table–6.3**

**FGT poverty measures and the Lorenz ratio over different NSSO rounds in India**

| *Year* | *Number of poor (Million)* | | | *Poverty Ratio (H)* | | | *Poverty Gap Index (PGI)* | | | *Squared Poverty Gap (SPG)* | | | *Lorenz Ratio* | |
|---|---|---|---|---|---|---|---|---|---|---|---|---|---|---|
| | *Rural* | *Urban* | *Total* | *Rural* | *Urban* | *Total* | *Rural* | *Urban* | *Total* | *Rural* | *Urban* | *Total* | *Rural* | *Urban* |
| 1973-74 | 261 | 60 | 321 | 56.4 | 49.0 | 54.9 | 16.56 | 13.64 | 15.95 | 6.18 | 5.62 | 6.48 | 0.274 | 0.301 |
| 1977-78 | 264 | 65 | 329 | 53.1 | 45.2 | 51.3 | 15.73 | 13.13 | 15.15 | 6.48 | 5.25 | 6.21 | 0.339 | 0.345 |
| 1983-84 | 252 | 71 | 323 | 45.7 | 40.8 | 44.5 | 12.32 | 10.61 | 11.96 | 4.78 | 4.07 | 4.61 | 0.297 | 0.330 |
| 1987-88 | 232 | 75 | 307 | 39.1 | 38.2 | 38.9 | 9.11 | 9.94 | 9.32 | 3.15 | 3.60 | 3.22 | 0.282 | 0.354 |
| 1993-94 | 244 | 76 | 320 | 37.3 | 32.4 | 36.0 | 8.45 | 7.88 | 8.30 | 2.78 | 2.82 | 2.79 | 0.289 | 0.339 |
| 1999-00 | 193 | 67 | 260 | 27.1 | 23.7 | 26.1 | 5.26 | 5.17 | 5.21 | 1.48 | 1.59 | 1.54 | 0.254 | 0.317 |

**Source: Planning Commission: Ninth Five Year Plan 1999-2002, pp. 34.**

But there is little doubt that while India has experienced a large reduction in its incidence of poverty in recent decades, it is possible that the rates of decline are overstated for the last half of the 1990s (Mehta and Shah, 2003). Datt and Ravallion (2004) concluded that India probably maintained a similar rate of reduction in its incidence of poverty in the 1990s and 1980s.

To ascertain the inter-state disparity in incidence, intensity, depth and severity of poverty, the measures like the head count ratio (H); poverty gap ratio (Ip); poverty gap index (PGI) and FGT indices are estimated respectively for the rural and urban areas of India and its fifteen major states. These estimates are presented in the Table-6.4. The coefficient of variation of these estimates is also computed for the rural and urban areas of these states to know the disparity in the level of poverty and its different dimensions. The three indices – H, PGI and FGT are the extensive measures of poverty in the sense that FGT measures distinguish three components for different values of its severity parameter, $\lambda$. When $\lambda = 0$, the measure reduces to the incidence ratio; for $\lambda = 1$, it reduces to poverty gap index indicating the depth of poverty; and for $\lambda=2$, it reflects the distribution of income among the poor indicating severity of poverty. The last measure is popularly known as the squared poverty gap index or FGT index. The inter-state disparity for different dimensions of poverty is carried out for the rural and urban India and its constituent major states separately for two periods - 1993-94 and 1999-00 using the NSS data of 50$^{th}$ round (1993-94) and 55$^{th}$ round (1999-00).

The poverty estimates in Table-6.4 reveals that the incidence of poverty in the rural areas of the country have decreased during the period 1993-94 to 1999-00 both in India and its constituent major states. The inter-state disparity is observed in the incidence, poverty gap ratio, poverty gap index and severity index in both the periods 1993-94 and 1999-00. The coefficient of inter-state variation of poverty reveals that the incidence and intensity have increased from 37.7 and 11.91 per cent in 1993-94 to 57.1 and 15.5 per cent in 1999-00 respectively. Similarly, the coefficient of inter-state variation in depth and severity has also increased from 89.2 and 50.4 per cent in 1993-94 to 98.8 and 74.2 per cent in 1999-00 respectively.

**Table–6.4**

**Incidence (H), intensity (Ip), depth (PGI) and severity (FGT Index) of poverty in rural and urban India and its fifteen major states: 1993-94 and 1999-2000**

| *States* | *Rural* | | | | | | | | *Urban* | | | | | | | |
|---|---|---|---|---|---|---|---|---|---|---|---|---|---|---|---|---|
| | *1993-94* | | | | *1999-00* | | | | *1993-94* | | | | *1999-2000* | | | |
| | *H* | $I_p$ | *PGI* | *FGT* | *H* | $I_p$ | *PGI* | *FGT* | *H* | $I_p$ | *PGI* | *FGT* | *H* | $I_p$ | *PGI* | *FGT* |
| A. Pradesh | 0.159 | 0.183 | 0.029 | 0.008 | 0.111 | 0.163 | 0.018 | 0.005 | 0.382 | 0.242 | 0.092 | 0.031 | 0.265 | 0.208 | 0.055 | 0.016 |
| Karnataka | 0.299 | 0.212 | 0.063 | 0.020 | 0.174 | 0.183 | 0.032 | 0.008 | 0.402 | 0.282 | 0.113 | 0.043 | 0.252 | 0.221 | 0.056 | 0.018 |
| T. Nadu | 0.326 | 0.224 | 0.073 | 0.024 | 0.205 | 0.186 | 0.038 | 0.010 | 0.398 | 0.257 | 0.102 | 0.038 | 0.222 | 0.214 | 0.048 | 0.015 |
| Kerala | 0.258 | 0.219 | 0.057 | 0.019 | 0.094 | 0.156 | 0.015 | 0.004 | 0.245 | 0.227 | 0.056 | 0.019 | 0.203 | 0.195 | 0.039 | 0.011 |
| W.Bengal | 0.408 | 0.202 | 0.082 | 0.024 | 0.318 | 0.203 | 0.065 | 0.019 | 0.224 | 0.202 | 0.045 | 0.014 | 0.149 | 0.169 | 0.025 | 0.007 |
| Bihar | 0.582 | 0.252 | 0.147 | 0.050 | 0.442 | 0.196 | 0.087 | 0.024 | 0.346 | 0.227 | 0.079 | 0.025 | 0.330 | 0.203 | 0.067 | 0.019 |
| Gujarat | 0.222 | 0.182 | 0.040 | 0.011 | 0.132 | 0.171 | 0.023 | 0.006 | 0.279 | 0.222 | 0.062 | 0.019 | 0.156 | 0.151 | 0.024 | 0.006 |
| Haryana | 0.280 | 0.198 | 0.055 | 0.017 | 0.083 | 0.150 | 0.013 | 0.004 | 0.164 | 0.180 | 0.029 | 0.008 | 0.101 | 0.211 | 0.021 | 0.008 |
| MP | 0.406 | 0.232 | 0.094 | 0.031 | 0.371 | 0.206 | 0.075 | 0.022 | 0.484 | 0.278 | 0.135 | 0.050 | 0.385 | 0.248 | 0.096 | 0.032 |
| Maharastra | 0.379 | 0.244 | 0.093 | 0.032 | 0.238 | 0.184 | 0.044 | 0.012 | 0.350 | 0.288 | 0.101 | 0.041 | 0.269 | 0.251 | 0.068 | 0.024 |
| Orissa | 0.497 | 0.240 | 0.119 | 0.039 | 0.481 | 0.244 | 0.108 | 0.035 | 0.497 | 0.276 | 0.115 | 0.043 | 0.428 | 0.256 | 0.110 | 0.038 |
| Punjab | 0.118 | 0.174 | 0.021 | 0.005 | 0.064 | 0.130 | 0.008 | 0.002 | 0.114 | 0.152 | 0.017 | 0.004 | 0.058 | 0.119 | 0.007 | 0.001 |
| Rajasthan | 0.265 | 0.196 | 0.052 | 0.015 | 0.136 | 0.150 | 0.020 | 0.005 | 0.305 | 0.229 | 0.070 | 0.022 | 0.197 | 0.177 | 0.035 | 0.009 |
| UP | 0.432 | 0.245 | 0.106 | 0.036 | 0.312 | 0.186 | 0.058 | 0.016 | 0.353 | 0.256 | 0.090 | 0.032 | 0.309 | 0.195 | 0.049 | 0.013 |
| Assam | 0.450 | 0.184 | 0.083 | 0.022 | 0.401 | 0.210 | 0.084 | 0.026 | 0.077 | 0.129 | 0.010 | 0.002 | 0.076 | 0.194 | 0.015 | 0.004 |
| India | 0.373 | 0.228 | 0.085 | 0.028 | 0.271 | 0.194 | 0.053 | 0.015 | 0.324 | 0.249 | 0.081 | 0.028 | 0.237 | 0.218 | 0.052 | 0.016 |

This clearly indicates the increase in inter-state variation of poverty with all its dimensions during the period 1993-94 to 1999-00. It is also noticed that the incidence, intensity and FGT indices is the highest in Bihar followed by Orissa and the lowest in Punjab and the second lowest in A.P. during 1993-94. But PGI is the highest in Rajastan and lowest in Punjab during the same period. In 1999-00, though the position of Punjab has remained unchanged, Orissa has taken the place of Bihar with the highest value (Bihar being the second highest) in these poverty measures.

On the other hand, the coefficient of inter-state variation in intensity has decreased and all other measures like incidence, depth and severity has marginally increased during the period 1993-94 and1999-00 in the urban areas of the fifteen major states of the country. The coefficient of variation of H, PGI, and FGT has increased from 37.5, 48.6 and 56 per cent in 1993-94 to 46.5, 59.1 and 68.2 per cent respectively in 1999-00. It clearly indicates that the increase in inter-state disparity of poverty measures in the urban areas of major constituent states of the country during the period 1993-94 to 1999-00. It is also observed that incidence, depth and severity is found to be the highest in Madhya Pradesh followed by Orissa and the lowest in Assam followed by Punjab. In 1999-00, Orissa and Punjab have taken the rank of Madhya Pradesh and Assam respectively. But the intensity of poverty is the highest in Maharastra followed Madhya Pradesh in 1993-94. In 1999-00, the intensity of poverty has increased and it is being the highest in Orissa followed by Maharastra.

The Sen Index distinguishes three components embodied in it viz., the relative number of poor indicating the incidence of poverty; the average income shortfall of the poor indicating their deprivation (intensity) and the distribution of income among the poor indicating their relative deprivation (severity). The advantage of Sen's index is that it is very useful for policy purposes. Two different measures such as M-value[5] and F-value[6] measures derived from the Sen's index have a lot of policy implications. The Sen index and its related derived measures along with the growth elasticity of poverty is presented in Table-6.5. The Sen index as an indicator of severity of poverty provides the almost same scenario of severity of poverty among the major states of the country as reflected by the FGT index.

## Table–6.5

**Sen's index, M-value and F-value of Sen's index and the growth elasticity of poverty in rural India and its fifteen major states**

| States | *Intensity Ratio* | | *Sen's Index* | | | *M-Value of Sen's Index* | | | *F-Value of Sen's Index* | | | *Growth Elasticity of poverty* | | |
|---|---|---|---|---|---|---|---|---|---|---|---|---|---|---|
| | *1993-94* | *1999-00* | *1983* | *1993-94* | *1999-00* | *1983* | *1993-94* | *1999-00* | *1983* | *1993-94* | *1999-00* | *1983* | *1993-94* | *1999-00* |
| Andhra Pradesh | 0.183 | 0.163 | 0.08 | 0.05 | 0.05 | 0.05 | 0.03 | 0.03 | 0.06 | 0.04 | 0.03 | -3.47 | -3.22 | -2.52 |
| Assam | 0.184 | 0.210 | 0.11 | 0.12 | 0.14 | 0.1 | 0.11 | 0.12 | 0.14 | 0.16 | 0.17 | -4.06 | -4.25 | -3.08 |
| Bihar | 0.252 | 0.196 | 0.26 | 0.22 | 0.15 | 0.28 | 0.22 | 0.14 | 0.51 | 0.38 | 0.19 | -2.2 | -2.62 | -3.1 |
| Gujarat | 0.182 | 0.171 | 0.08 | 0.06 | 0.04 | 0.06 | 0.04 | 0.02 | 0.07 | 0.05 | 0.03 | -3.72 | -3.99 | -3.63 |
| Haryana | 0.198 | 0.150 | 0.07 | 0.08 | 0.02 | 0.04 | 0.05 | 0.01 | 0.05 | 0.06 | 0.01 | -3.56 | -3.83 | -4.74 |
| Karnataka | 0.212 | 0.183 | 0.13 | 0.11 | 0.05 | 0.1 | 0.08 | 0.03 | 0.12 | 0.09 | 0.03 | -2.68 | -3.02 | -3.93 |
| Kerala | 0.219 | 0.156 | 0.13 | 0.08 | 0.02 | 0.1 | 0.05 | 0.01 | 0.13 | 0.06 | 0.01 | -2.92 | -3.44 | -4.67 |
| Madhya Pradesh | 0.232 | 0.206 | 0.19 | 0.16 | 0.15 | 0.16 | 0.12 | 0.12 | 0.22 | 0.16 | 0.15 | -2.55 | -2.72 | -2.61 |
| Maharashtra | 0.244 | 0.184 | 0.16 | 0.15 | 0.08 | 0.13 | 0.11 | 0.05 | 0.18 | 0.14 | 0.06 | -2.78 | -2.55 | -3.23 |
| Orissa | 0.240 | 0.244 | 0.30 | 0.19 | 0.22 | 0.33 | 0.18 | 0.2 | 0.63 | 0.26 | 0.28 | -1.96 | -2.62 | -2.11 |
| Punjab | 0.174 | 0.130 | 0.05 | 0.03 | 0.01 | 0.02 | 0.02 | 0.01 | 0.03 | 0.02 | 0.01 | -3.37 | -5.01 | -6.53 |
| Rajasthan | 0.196 | 0.150 | 0.19 | 0.08 | 0.03 | 0.14 | 0.06 | 0.02 | 0.16 | 0.06 | 0.02 | -1.82 | -3.74 | -4.76 |
| Tamil Nadu | 0.224 | 0.186 | 0.27 | 0.12 | 0.07 | 0.25 | 0.09 | 0.05 | 0.37 | 0.1 | 0.05 | -1.77 | -2.91 | -3.13 |
| Uttar Pradesh | 0.245 | 0.186 | 0.17 | 0.16 | 0.10 | 0.14 | 0.13 | 0.07 | 0.19 | 0.17 | 0.09 | -2.72 | -2.73 | -3.49 |
| West Bengal | 0.202 | 0.203 | 0.15 | 0.12 | 0.11 | 0.15 | 0.1 | 0.08 | 0.25 | 0.14 | 0.1 | -1.94 | -3.61 | -3.27 |
| All India | 0.228 | 0.194 | 0.18 | 0.13 | 0.09 | 0.15 | 0.10 | 0.07 | 0.20 | 0.13 | 0.08 | -2.47 | -2.92 | -3.16 |

The value of the index has declined in all the states except Assam during the period 1983 to 1999-00 indicating the highest severity of poverty in Orissa followed by Bihar. The severity of poverty is the lowest in Punjab. The M-values of the Sen's index has also declined in all states except Assam during the period 1983 to 1999-00. In Assam, it has marginally increased from 0.10 to 0.12 during the above period. In 1999-00, it was the highest in Orissa (0.20) followed by Bihar (0.14) and the lowest (0.01) in Haryana, Punjab and Kerala. This indicates that about 20 per cent of the state's income is necessary to bring the poor to the poverty line in Orissa whereas it is 14 per cent in Bihar and only 1 per cent in Haryana, Punjab and Kerala. On the other hand, the F-value of Sen's index has drastically declined in all states except in Assam during the period 1983 to 1999-00. In Assam, it has marginally increased from 0.14 to 0.17 during the above period. It has declined from 0.63 and 0.51 in 1983 to 0.28 and 0.19 in 1999-00 in Orissa and Bihar respectively. This percentage is again the highest in Orissa followed by Bihar in the country and the lowest in Haryana, Punjab, West Bengal and Kerala. This reveals that Orissa requires the highest transfer of income of about 28 per cent from the non-poor to the poor to reach the poverty line by suitable pro-poor policy in the state. This figure is the second highest in Bihar.

To examine how growth affects poverty, poverty elasticities with respect to the mean per capita consumption expenditure is computed with changes in inequality effect kept constant. These elasticities are referred as growth elasticities and have been derived by Kakwani (1989) for all the poverty indices. In the present study the growth elasticity of poverty has been calculated for the poverty gap index. The growth elasticity of urban India was initially higher than that of the rural India. Since then the elasticity in rural India is rising faster than urban India. Elasticity measured during 1993-94 and 1999-2000 shows that for the rural India growth elasticity of poverty is higher that than of the urban India. It shows that the rural economy is becoming a homogenous group while the urban economy is becoming more and more heterogeneous. The above figure shows that for the rural India, the 'growth elasticity of poverty'[7] is rising faster than urban India. This reveals that the rural poverty gap is reducing because of the growth in consumption expenditure in rural area. The urban poverty gap reduction is showing less response to the growth of urban consumption expenditure.

It is evident from the above description that the low per capita income states are not only having low growth rate, but also the growth they are achieving is leading to low poverty reduction. The high per capita income states are experiencing rapid income growth as well as high poverty reduction. In other wards, the developed states have performed well in growth as well as in terms of its redistribution while the poor states have failed in both fronts. Growth in income or consumption expenditure is important for poverty reduction. But uneven distribution of growth could not create much impact on poverty reduction. For the urban India responsiveness of growth is less in comparison to the rural India. The economic policy should have a higher focus on redistribution. Otherwise economic growth will divert from its objectives of social well being.

When we compare rural and urban areas of the country and its major states, both incidence and severity are more pronounced in the rural areas then the urban areas. Poverty in all its dimension has decreased over time in all the states but the changes are not uniform. There is a high inter-state disparity in poverty reduction during nineties. The reduction rate is high in the developed states. It is clear from the above analysis that the developed states like Haryana and Punjab have done pretty well in rural poverty reduction whereas backward states like Bihar and Orissa always doing far below their expected rate of poverty reduction. So the poorer states are lagging behind their richer counterparts in rural poverty reduction. Rural areas exhibit less inter-state disparities than urban areas. It is evident from the above description that the low per capita income states are not only having low growth rate, but also the growth they are achieving is leading to low poverty reduction. The high per capita income states are experiencing rapid income growth as well as high poverty reduction .In other words, the developed states have performed well in growth as well as in terms of its redistribution. While the poor states have failed in both fronts.

## 6.6 Estimation of the Poverty Lines for Various Occupation Groups in Orissa

For national/regional policy purposes, one should use a national/regional poverty line. However, for international comparisons, the so-called dollar-a-day line is commonly used. Originally, it was calculated from 1985 data on country specific poverty lines for a number of low income countries. The mean of national poverty lines for Bangladesh, India, Indonesia, Kenya, Morocco, and Tanzania was estimated at $370 per annum or $1.01 per day measured in 1985 international prices and adjusted to local currency using purchasing power parities (PPP). This was revised in 1999 using the 1993 data of ten countries, the median of poverty lines were estimated at $392.88 per annum or $1.08 per person per day measured in 1993 international prices and adjusted to local currency of 1993 purchasing power parities (PPP).[8] The rate is $1 PPP (1993) = R 7.016, as quoted in the latest World Bank publication. Thus $1.08 was equivalent to INR 7.57728 in 1993 prices. This is the PPP rate associated with private consumption within GDP, rather than the overall GDP PPP rate.

For comparison with the national poverty line, we need to convert this to a monthly figure. If the 30 days recall reflects genuine consumption over 30 days, we should multiply our rupee figure by 30 to get the monthly equivalent for genuine consumption over 30 days; we should multiply our rupee by 30 to get the monthly equivalent for comparison purposes. However, since the term '30 day' is used as a proxy for 'one month' and so prefer to multiply by 365/12 = 30.417. The rupee international poverty line in 1993 is then works out to be INR 230.48 per person per month.

Since the International Poverty Line (IPL) is derived at 1993 prices, it is required that we deflate it to prices for the year the poverty incidence is to be calculated. The recommended methodology is to inflate the IPL using the domestic consumer price index. In the case of India, it creates a problem as to which price index to be used, as a single CPI in India has not compared the relative merits and demerits of different Indian price indices. It was recommend for using Wholesale Price Index (WPI) of primary food products for updating the IPL to current prices (Dubey and Crook, 2001).

Table-6.6 reports the Official Poverty Line (OPL) for Orissa and India and the INR equivalent of dollar a day poverty line. Note that the IPL is systematically lower than both the urban poverty lines for all India and Orissa but higher than both poverty lines in case of rural areas of the state as well as the country. Other important thing to note from this table is that the OPL of Orissa relative to all India OPL. In rural sector, rural OPL of Orissa was higher than all India rural OPL in 1983 and 1987-88. However, in 1993-94 and 1999-00 it is lower. As will be shown later, it has very important implication on poverty trends in Orissa. However, urban OPL of Orissa is systematically higher than all India urban OPL.[9]

**Table–6.6**

**Poverty lines for Indian and Orissa**

*Rupees Per Person Per Month*

| *Years* | *IPL All-India* | *OPL All India: Rural* | *OPL All India: Urban* | *OPL Orissa: Rural* | *OPL Orissa: Urban* |
|---|---|---|---|---|---|
| 1983 | 96.57 | 89.50 | 115.65 | 106.28 | 124.81 |
| 1987/88 | 130.66 | 115.20 | 162.16 | 121.42 | 165.40 |
| 1993/94 | 230.48 | 205.84 | 281.35 | 194.03 | 298.22 |
| 1999/00 | 380.29 | 327.56 | 454.11 | 323.92 | 473.12 |

**Source: Dubey and Crook, 2001.**

**Note: IPL-International Poverty Line and OPL-Official Poverty Line.**

In India, the poverty is estimated using consumption expenditure distribution of the population. The National Sample Survey Organisation of the Government of India provides information on this welfare indicator and the other requirement for calculating poverty line using a suitable poverty norm.

The poverty norm used in India for calculating poverty is based on Food Energy Intake (FEI) method. This norm was suggested by the Task Force appointed by the Government of India (GOI, 1979). The Task Force recommended as per capita daily average food energy requirement of 2435 kcal for Indians living in the rural areas. For the urban area, the Task Force recommended the food energy requirement at 2095 kcal. This food energy requirement was converted to monetary equivalent at INR 49.56

for rural and INR 56.64 for urban areas respectively at 1973-74 prices at the all India level. This norm has been kept invariant since then. However, as NSSO expenditure distribution data is in current rupees, this norm is updated for price changes periodically. Given the size of the country, the prices of various commodity groups are likely to be different across space as households' consumption choices would vary depending upon locally produced food items. The all India norm is first adopted for major states in the Indian union for the price variation across states relative to all India. Then the state-wise price indices, available for rural and urban sector separately for most of the so-called major Indian states, are used to update the norm for respective states.

The NSSO has been collecting information on consumption expenditure of a fraction of Indian households since early 1950s every year. However, in early 1970s, it was decided to restrict this exercise at large scale. Starting 1973-74, the large sample survey has been conducted roughly at five years interval, called large sample surveys. Given the size of the country a representative sample has to be fairly high; during the large sample surveys, information on consumption expenditure of the households is collected for over 100,000 households covering almost entire territory of the Indian Union except some humanly inaccessible areas. For purposes of sampling, the country has been divided into 77 (now 78) relatively homogeneous agro-climatic zones, called NSS Regions. Prior to 1998, the NSSO used to publish expenditure distribution of population and other characteristics by states and place of residence of population according to a pre-defined expenditure classes, and poverty line was estimated both by the government agencies as well as researchers from the disaggregated expenditure distribution data at state-level and also from the expenditure distribution data for the country. However, since 1998 the expenditure data collected by the NSSO has been made available to researchers at the unit record level that contains information not only on consumption expenditure at the household level but also on demography characteristics of the household members, the quantity and value of consumption of various commodities and so on. Now, household level consumption expenditure data is available for four most recent rounds of quinquennial surveys on consumption expenditure, 1983, 1987-88, 1993-94 and 1999-00.

## Table–6.7

### Average normative calorie requirement in Orissa and India (1993-94 and 1999-00)

*(K. calories/person per day)*

| *Year and Sector* | *Sector* | *Methodology 1* | | *Methodology 2* | | *Methodology 3* | | *Methodology 4* | |
|---|---|---|---|---|---|---|---|---|---|
| | | *Orissa* | *All India* | *Orissa* | *All India* | *Orissa* | *All India* | *Orissa* | *All India* |
| 1993-94 | Rural | 2334 | 2396 | 2259 | 2309 | 2337 | 2401 | 2263 | 2314 |
| 1993-94 | Urban | 2071 | 2093 | 2053 | 2042 | 2134 | 2152 | 2078 | 2091 |
| 1999-00 | Rural | 2352 | 2325 | 2272 | 2252 | 2357 | 2331 | 2277 | 2258 |
| 1999-00 | Urban | 2069 | 2064 | 2014 | 2005 | 2113 | 2109 | 2056 | 2049 |

**Notes: Calorie requirement is calculated using the Task Force Methodology, 1979 as follows:**

**(i) Methodology-1: Simply the normative average calorie;**

**(ii) Methodology-2: The normative average calorie requirement after adjusting for age categories;**

**(iii) Methodology-3: The normative average calorie requirement after adjusting for occupation categories; and**

**(iv) Methodology-4: The normative average calorie requirement after adjusting for both age & occupation categories.**

**Source: Dubey and Crook, 2001.**

The availability of unit record data facilitated poverty estimation at NSS region level by several researchers (Dreze and Srinivasan, 1996 and Dubey and Gangopadhyay, 1998).[10]

The Indian poverty norm was derived using Food Energy Intake. It was estimated that on an average, the Indian living in the rural areas requires 2435 k. calories per day. The urban requirement was estimated to be 2095 k. calories. The average normative calorie requirement, the very basis of Indian poverty norm, seems to have undergone some change since it was derived. The Table-6.7 shows the average normative calories requirement for Orissa and all India in 1993-94 and 1999-00.[11]

Comparison of normative requirements at the all India level with those derived by the Task Force shows a decline; the same requirements estimated by the Task Force continue to be used today. But we find that average calorie requirements are lower by 121 calories for the rural sector in 1993-94. In 1999-00 the requirement has declined further to 2258, a fall by 177 calories that approximately by 7 per cent if the requirement is adjusted for occupational classification and for ageing population. Even if we follow the Task Force Methodology and adjust it for age distribution of the population only, there is a significant decline in normative calorie requirement. In other words, the Indian poverty line is overestimated, due to over estimation of the normative calorie requirements. Since the calorie requirements are declining as evident from Table-6.7, it could be that poverty incidence is being overestimated in India including Orissa.

In this study, we have estimated the income poverty lines for four different occupation groups of rural Orissa using the cost of calorie function suggested by Greer and Thorbecke (1986) on the basis recommended daily allowance (RDA) of 2400 calories and the per capita /per unit total consumption expenditure (which is used as the proxy variable for the income of the households) form unit record data of 600 households collected during the 55th round of NSSO. We have selected an equal number of 150 households for each occupation category for estimating the occupation-wise poverty lines. The estimated poverty line for different occupation types along with number of poor household and their percentage to total households along with updated poverty lines of major studies in India are presented in Table-6.8.

## Table–6.8

### A comparative analysis of poverty estimates for rural Orissa

| *Study reference* | *Poverty Line at constant prices in (in Rs.)* | *Col. 3 at current prices 1999-00 (Rs.)* | *Type of occupation* | *As per our study* | | | | | |
|---|---|---|---|---|---|---|---|---|---|
| | | | | *In per capita terms* | | | *In per unit terms* | | |
| | | | | *Poverty Line (in Rs.)* | *No. of poor households* | *% of households below poverty line* | *Poverty Line (in Rs.)* | *No. of poor households* | *% of households below poverty line* |
| Dandekar & Rath (1971) & Ahluwalia (1977) | 15.00 (1960-61) | 256.13 | Type-A | 294.46 | 51 | 31.9 | 338.52 | 58 | 36.3 |
| Minhas (1974) | 20.00 (1960-61) | 341.00 | Type-B | 278.67 | 73 | 45.6 | 324.85 | 83 | 51.9 |
| Sixth Plan (1978) | 58.33 (1970-71) | 362.80 | Type-C | 270.86 | 82 | 51.3 | 320.35 | 88 | 55.0 |
| IRDP Manual (1986) | 106.70 (1984-85) | 361.20 | All occupations | 276.42 | 316 | 52.7 | 322.88 | 344 | 57.3 |
| SGSRY (GOI, 1999) | 191.00 (1991-92) | 346.70 | | | | | | | |

**Note: (i) Refer Pramod Kumar (2001) and Panda, C. (2003). (ii) Estimated from 55th round NSS data.**

The poverty line estimates in terms of monthly per capita and monthly per unit indicate that the poverty line estimate for type-D occupation is the lowest (i.e. Rs. 276.42 and Rs. 322.88 respectively) and it is the highest (i.e. Rs. 194.46 and Rs. 338.52 respectively) for type-A occupation households. The poverty estimate for type-B occupation households almost coincides with the estimates for all households. It is estimated that the percentage of households below poverty line is the highest for type-D occupation and is the lowest for type-A occupation households (measured both in per capita and per unit consumption). The poverty line estimates in per unit is found to be higher than the poverty lines measured in per capita for all occupation groups (in absolute value). The percentage of households below poverty line decreases when measured in per unit instead of per capita which is really remarkable for the rural economy of Orissa. The estimated poverty line for all sample households is Rs. 276 in per capita terms and 327 in unit terms which can be compared with the all India estimates presented in Table-6.8. It is noticed that the estimated poverty line figure is much less than all estimates except Dandekar and Rath (1971) and Ahluwalia (1977).

## 6.7 Changing Scenario of Incidence of Poverty in Orissa

The rate of growth of an economy is a simple and summarized measure of how quickly the average income of the population is rising. Though the percolation effect of growth is not automatic, it has been observed that poor growth is a major cause of continuing high poverty and that strong growth in general, and strong agricultural growth in particular, has a perceptible poverty-reducing impact. The trend and variation in the magnitude and incidence of poverty across sectors, regions, social classes, and occupations in Orissa are examined in this section.

### *6.7.1 Inter-sectoral Variation in the Incidence of Poverty*

In most of the cross-sectional studies based on NSS data, consumption pattern of rural and urban sector of the country have been separately examined. These studies revealed marked differences in the consumption habits in the two sectors of the country (Gupta, 1968; 1970; Mahajan, 1970; Panda, 1996 and Sarangi, 2004). In fact, several items appear to be luxuries in the rural sector happens to be the necessity items in the urban sector. The factors responsible for such differences seem to be numerous. The principal ones being the variation in the standard of living across region/sector , occupational pattern of the population, relative prices of commodities, and extent of manetisation prevailing in the two sectors, and so on.

As per the recommendations of the Expert Group on the methodology of estimating poverty (1993), the Planning Commission of India also estimated state specific poverty measures using the date of NSS quinquennial rounds (27th round, 1973-74 to 55th round, 1999-00). The estimates of the Planning Commission on different poverty measures for the rural and urban Orissa during the period 1973-74 to 1999-00 are presented in Table-6.9. In addition to this, some other measures like Sen's index, M-value and F-value of Sen's index, growth elasticity of poverty and Lorenz ratio for the rural and urban Orissa during the period 1983 to 1999-00 is also given in the above table. The magnitude of the absolute number of poor figures. reveals that the number of poor first increased during 1973-74 to 1983 then decreased till 1999-00 in rural Orissa. But the magnitude of the absolute number of poor increased throughout in urban Orissa during the above period. The poverty ratio has also declined in both rural and urban Orissa during the last three decades.

The overall poverty ratio also followed the same pattern in the state. This ratio in rural areas is much higher than urban areas of the state. Further, the inter-sectoral coefficient of variation indicates that poverty ratio had declined at a faster rate in rural areas than the urban areas of the state during 1973-74 to 1999-00. The poverty gap index and the squared poverty gap index had also declined in both the sector of the state during the last three decades. The poverty gap indices are higher in rural areas than urban areas and the reverse is the case with squared poverty gap indices in the state during the above period. The inter-sectoral coefficient of variation indicates that both the poverty gap indices and squared poverty gap indices had declined at a faster rate in rural areas than urban areas of the state. This clearly indicates that these poverty measures almost follow the All-India pattern. But the rate of decline of these measures in the state is much lower than All-India rates.

## Table–6.9

**FGT and Sen's poverty measures and the Lorenz ratio over different NSS rounds in Orissa**

| Year | Number of poor (lakhs) | | | Poverty Ratio | | | Poverty Gap Index (PGI) | | | FGT Index (or SPG) | | |
|---|---|---|---|---|---|---|---|---|---|---|---|---|
| | Rural | Urban | Total | Rural | Urban | Total | Rural | Urban | Total | Rural | Urban | Total |
| 1973-74 | 146.3 | 14.2 | 160.5 | 0.673 | 0.556 | 0.662 | 0.176 | 0.187 | 0.189 | 0.071 | 0.064 | 0.067 |
| 1977-78 | 152.5 | 14.9 | 167.4 | 0.724 | 0.509 | 0.701 | 0.185 | 0.198 | 0.211 | 0.089 | 0.076 | 0.082 |
| 1983 | 157.3 | 15.3 | 172.6 | 0.684 | 0.497 | 0.663 | 0.169 | 0.176 | 0.154 | 0.072 | 0.068 | 0.069 |
| 1987-88 | 148.0 | 17.8 | 165.8 | 0.584 | 0.426 | 0.557 | 0.117 | 0.122 | 0.119 | 0.038 | 0.045 | 0.042 |
| 1993-94 | 140.9 | 19.7 | 160.6 | 0.498 | 0.407 | 0.486 | 0.119 | 0.115 | 0.117 | 0.039 | 0.043 | 0.041 |
| 1999-00 | 143.7 | 25.4 | 169.1 | 0.481 | 0.435 | 0.474 | 0.108 | 0.110 | 0.109 | 0.035 | 0.038 | 0.037 |

| Year | Sen Index ($P_S$) | M-value of $P_S$ | F-value of $P_S$ | Sen Index ($P_S$) | M-value of $P_S$ | F-value of $P_S$ | $\eta_{pr}$ (India) | $\eta_{pu}$ (India) | $\eta_{pr}$ (Orissa) | $\eta_{pu}$ (Orissa) | Lorenz Ratio | |
|---|---|---|---|---|---|---|---|---|---|---|---|---|
| | Rural | | | Urban | | | Rural | Urban | Rural | Urban | Rural | Urban |
| 1983 | 0.254 | 0.47 | 0.13 | 0.215 | 0.39 | 0.18 | -2.47 | -2.57 | -1.96 | -2.24 | 0.272 | 0.278 |
| 1987-88 | 0.190 | 0.38 | 0.14 | 0.186 | 0.42 | 0.15 | -2.71 | -2.62 | -2.44 | -2.32 | 0.267 | 0.254 |
| 1993-94 | 0.160 | 0.26 | 0.11 | 0.153 | 0.34 | 0.13 | -2.92 | -2.58 | -2.62 | -2.28 | 0.258 | 0.315 |
| 1999-00 | 0.155 | 0.28 | 0.05 | 0.146 | 0.27 | 0.09 | -3.16 | -2.73 | -2.11 | -2.13 | 0.280 | 0.313 |

**Note:** $\eta_{pr}$ and $\eta_{pu}$ are the growth elasticity of poverty in rural and urban areas respectively;

**SPG-** Squared poverty gap.

The Sen's index, on the other hand, reflected the same pattern of decline in both rural and urban Orissa indicating reduction of severity of poverty in the state during the last two decades. The M-value and F-value associated with Sen's index had also declined in both the sectors of Orissa during 1983 to 1999-00. The value of Sen's index is little higher in rural than urban areas but both the M and F-values are much higher in Urban areas than in rural areas of the state during the above period. The inter-sectoral coefficient of variation indicates that the Sen's index and its associated measures (M and F-values) had declined at a faster rate in rural areas than in urban areas of the state during the above period. The higher values of M-value measures reveal that the percentage of state income necessary to bring the poor to the poverty line is higher in urban areas than in rural areas of the state. On the other hand, the higher values of F-value measures indicates that the percentage of transfer of income from the non-poor to the poor necessary to bring the poor to the poverty line is higher in the urban areas than in the rural areas of the state. The favourable indication provided by the growth elasticity of poverty is that it is rising in both sectors of the state till 1993-94. These elasticities are higher in rural areas with higher inter-sectoral coefficient of variation indicating that the poverty ratio is declining at a faster rate in rural areas than urban areas of the state. On the other hand, the Lorenz ratio provided a different picture in both rural and urban Orissa. Though poverty ratio declined over the period of analysis (1983 to 1999-00), the inequality in the distribution of income rose in urban areas but first declined and then rose in rural areas indicate widening the gap between the rich and poor especially more in urban areas of the sate.

### *6.7.2 Trends of Poverty Measures in Rural Orissa*

Here, the focus is confined to the long-term trends in the incidence and other measures of rural poverty in Orissa. It is found that there has been a steady decline in the poverty ratio in Orissa between 1977-78 and 1993-94. In the second half of the 1990s, poverty ratio has remained almost satisfactory. This is quite unlike the experience of other low-income states and all India, and is perhaps due to the poor agricultural growth performance of Orissa. However, there is an immediate and straightforward explanation for the stagnation of rural poverty ratio during the second half of the 1990s. This has to do with the regional trends in poverty ratio. The poverty ratio in southern and northern regions of Orissa has in fact increased between 1993-94 and 1999-00, unlike the earlier period (1987-88 to 1993-94), and since almost 75 per cent of the state's poor belong to these regions, this has influenced the overall poverty ratio.

The long-term fluctuation in the number of poor persons, percentage of households below poverty line and the various other poverty measures like incidence, poverty gap index and the squared poverty gap index for rural Orissa during the period from 1957-58 to 1999-00 are presented in Table-6.10. The number of poor persons as reflected in the table indicates that initially it was first increasing and then decreasing. The overall linear trend shows that it is increasing at a constant rate 1.15 millions per annum (with t-ratio-5.245, *F*-32.74, $R^2$-0.05). It was the highest 9167.77 million in 1970-71 and the lowest (108.54 million) in 1958-59. We compare the coefficient of variation in two different period 1957-58 to 1969-70 and 1970-71 to 1999-00, it is found that the coefficient variation value are very close to each other indicating that the coefficient of variation in the number of poor persons almost same in the two periods. On the other hand, the household poverty ratio figures reflect a different picture. It is highly fluctuating over the entire period of analysis (1958-59 to 1999-00). But the overall linear trend indicates that poverty ratio figures in different year are declined at a constant rate of 0.99 per cent per annum. It is the highest (78.6 per cent) in 1970-71 and the lowest (38.4 per cent) in 1999-00. The coefficient of variation of the poverty ratio in the two period are diverging indicating that fluctuations are less during the period 1957-58 to 1969-70 and it is much more during the period 1969-70 to 1999-00. On the other hand, the poverty measures like poverty ratio, poverty gap index and squared poverty gaps reflects almost similar picture with different rates of decline. The poverty ratio, the poverty gap index and the squared poverty gap index have very low values of coefficient of variation in the first period (1957-58 to 1969-70) and high value in the second period (1970-71 to 1999-00) indicating the fluctuations of these measure are less in the first period and much higher in the second period. But the overall trend reveals that these measures are declining over the period of analysis. The incidence was the highest (79.84 per cent) in 1961-62 and lowest (48.13 per cent) in 1999-00. But both poverty gap index and the squared poverty gap index were the highest in 1957-58 and the lowest in 1989-90. The overall linear trend of incidence of poverty indicates that it is decreasing at a constant significant rate of 1.03 per cent per annum (t = -4.73, *F*=22.42 and $R^2$ =0.512). Similar is the case with poverty gap index and squared poverty gap ratio. Poverty gap index has been decreasing at a constant significant ratio of 0.50 per cent (t = -4.11, *F*=16.93 and $R^2$ =0.492) whereas the squared poverty gap index has been decreasing at a significant constant rate of 0.27 per cent per annum (t = -4.11, *F*=16.96 and $R^2$ =0.435).

Like the poverty ratio, the poverty gap index, FGT and Sen Indices (Sen index for 1973-74 and 1977-78 not estimated) are found to be higher in rural areas than urban areas over the quinquennial rounds. This provides a clear picture of higher level of depth and severity of poverty in rural areas than urban areas of the state during the period 1973-74 to 1999-00.

The above analysis focuses on the incidence of poverty in rural and urban Orissa. The poverty estimates of the Planning Commission reveals that Orissa continues to be the poorest among all the major states of the country surpassing Bihar which was still the poorest till 1993-94 (GoI, 2001). The incidence of poverty in the state has declined over time but the rate of decline is sluggish. The incidence of rural poverty has declined from 67.28 per cent to 48.01 per cent; the urban poverty from 55.62 per cent to 42.83 per cent and the combined rural-urban poverty from 66.18 per cent to 47.15 per cent during the last three decades from 1973-74 to 1999-00. But it is significant to note that poverty ratio was stagnated at 48 per cent to 49 per cent during the period 1993-94 to 1999-00 unlike the case of other states in general and low income states in particular. However, the aggregate poverty ratio hides significant regional and social class differences in the poverty ratio.

**Table–6.10**

**Trend of poverty measures in rural Orissa**

| *NSSO Survey period* | *NSS Rounds* | *Poverty lines (in Rs.)* | *Number of poor persons (in lakhs)* | *Percentage of households below PL* | *Incidence of poverty (in %)* | *Poverty Gap Index (in %)* | *Squared poverty Gap (in %)* |
|---|---|---|---|---|---|---|---|
| 1 | 2 | 3 | 4 | 5 | 6 | 7 | 8 |
| 1957-58 | 13 | 16.12 | 109.78 | 64.70 | 73.18 | 23.180 | 11.129 |
| 1958-59 | 14 | 16.29 | 108.54 | 67.21 | 71.88 | 18.967 | 8.474 |
| 1959-60 | 15 | 16.45 | 115.56 | 67.06 | 69.65 | 19.494 | 7.723 |
| 1960-61 | 16 | 16.62 | 129.68 | 70.61 | 72.61 | 20.129 | 8.287 |
| 1961-62 | 17 | 19.95 | 118.64 | 57.33 | 79.84 | 13.909 | 5.912 |
| 1963-64 | 18 | 21.94 | 120.09 | 66.14 | 59.35 | 17.954 | 7.468 |
| 1964-65 | 19 | 23.77 | 130.78 | 65.55 | 69.18 | 18.528 | 7.548 |
| 1965-66 | 20 | 26.93 | 130.96 | 68.34 | 73.74 | 18.280 | 7.806 |
| 1966-67 | 21 | 31.75 | 138.07 | 71.76 | 72.31 | 19.001 | 7.963 |
| 1967-68 | 22 | 34.74 | 140.32 | 70.61 | 74.70 | 19.980 | 8.449 |
| 1968-69 | 23 | 36.23 | 151.87 | 74.62 | 74.43 | 24.308 | 11.070 |
| 1969-70 | 24 | 35.40 | 145.08 | 70.67 | 79.03 | 22.902 | 10.637 |

*(Contd...)*

*(Table 6.10 Contd...)*

| *1* | 2 | 3 | 4 | 5 | 6 | 7 | 8 |
|---|---|---|---|---|---|---|---|
| 1970-71 | 25 | 35.24 | 167.77 | 78.60 | 74.12 | 22.173 | 10.162 |
| 1972-73 | 26 | 41.00 | 146.29 | 73.31 | 67.28 | 23.693 | 10.952 |
| 1973-74 | 27 | 46.87 | 142.24 | 65.48 | 71.05 | 17.662 | 7.108 |
| 1977-78 | 28 | 58.89 | 152.50 | 68.80 | 72.38 | 20.443 | 8.955 |
| 1983 | 32 | 106.28 | 157.43 | 63.31 | 68.43 | 16.962 | 7.126 |
| 1986-87 | 42 | 116.38 | 156.44 | 59.07 | 67.53 | 11.950 | 4.462 |
| 1987-88 | 43 | 121.42 | 148.02 | 51.95 | 58.42 | 11.699 | 3.840 |
| 1989-90 | 44 | 125.65 | 135.12 | 47.28 | 57.64 | 8.454 | 2.403 |
| 1990-91 | 45 | 133.13 | 123.36 | 43.65 | 51.79 | 5.376 | 1.532 |
| 1992-93 | 46 | 142.94 | 118.41 | 40.77 | 46.39 | 8.195 | 2.530 |
| 1993-94 | 50 | 194.03 | 140.90 | 41.36 | 49.80 | 11.93 | 3.96 |
| 1999-00 | 55 | 323.92 | 143.69 | 38.04 | 48.13 | 10.77 | 3.45 |

**Source:** **(i) The World Bank (1997), India: Achievements and Challenges in Reducing Poverty, Washington DC.**

**(ii) NSS Reports of different rounds**

### *6.7.3 Regional Variation in the Incidence of Poverty*

Apart from the broad inter-sectoral differences in household consumption and poverty, considerable inter-regional differences in consumption and poverty also exist within each sector. Natural resource endowments, physical and climatic conditions, economic factors like opportunities for employment and income; demographic factors like household size and it's composition; degree of urbanisation; cultural factors and sociological factors vary wide across sectors also across regions resulting in a considerable variation in the level of consumption and poverty.

The climate and geography have significant influence on economic and social activities of the people living in a region. The state of Orissa can be divided into various regions on the basis of distribution of forms and minerals, soil and rainfall, concentration of tribal population, development of industry etc. However, the National Sample Survey Organisation (NSSO) divides the state into three distinct regions viz. Coastal, Southern and Northern. The Coastal region constitutes 11 districts viz. Balasore, Cuttack, Ganjam, Puri, Nayagarh, Khurda, Bhadrak, Jajpur, Kendrapara, Jagatsinghpur and Gajapati. The Southern region constitutes 8 districts namely, Kandhamal, Nawapara, Nawarangpur, Malkangiri, Rayagarh, Kalahandi, Koraput and Boudh. The Northern region constitutes 11 districts viz. Sambalpur, Sundargarh, Keonjhar, Mayurbhanj, Dhenkanal, Jharsuguda, Bolangir, Bargarh, Angul, Sonepur and Deogarh. The Coastal region has plain areas with good cultivatable land but some district like Cuttack and Kendrapara suffers from the ravages of high flood and some other coastal districts also periodically lashed by violent cyclones. This region is relatively developed with high concentration of general population. In this region agriculture is the main occupation of the people. Besides, many people are engaged in white-collar and blue-collar jobs. The Southern region is relatively backward and is dominated mainly by tribal population. The people of this region live in small villages where the households are scattered in various hilltops. Most of them are practicing shifting and jhoom cultivation. Some of them live in plain areas are engaged in settled agriculture. Besides cultivation, tribals mainly depend on collection of minor forest products for their livelihood. Many of them live in sub-human conditions. On the other hand, the Northern region is rich in minerals with comparatively balanced distribution of tribal and non-tribal population. This region is rich in mineral resources and considered as the industrial belt of the state. In this region also agriculture is the prime occupation of the people. Besides, many people engaged in blue-collar jobs like production process, mining, quarrying etc. These variations in regional characteristic will definitely reflect inter-regional or spatial variations in the consumption pattern vis-a-vis the incidence, depth and severity of poverty in the state.

The region-wise estimates of the incidence poverty over different NSS rounds are presented in Table-6.11. The poverty estimates reveal that the incidence of poverty in the Coastal Orissa had declined from 58 per cent to 31.8 per cent in the rural areas and from 56.5 per cent to 33.6 per cent in the rural and urban combine but fluctuating in between 47.2 to 41.8 in urban areas during the period from 1983 to 1999-2000. But the incidence of poverty scenario is different in the Northern and Southern region of the state. In Northern Orissa, the incidence of poverty had declined till 1993-94 and then rose in 1999-00 in both the rural and urban areas and also for rural–urban combine. It is the highest (54.3 per cent) in 1983 and the lowest (45.8 per cent) in 1993-94 in the rural areas. But in Southern Orissa, it was fluctuating during the period from 1983 to 1999-2000. It is also noticed that the incidence poverty in the region was the highest (87.1 per cent) during 1999-2000 and the lowest (68.8 per cent) in 1993-94 in the rural areas; and the highest (52.9 per cent) during 1987-88 and lowest (49.1 per cent) during 1993-94 in urban areas. But the overall rural and urban poverty in the Coastal region had declined during the period 1983 to 1999-00 with no such definite pattern is noticed in Northern and Southern region of the state during this period.

The estimates of incidence of poverty presented in Table-6.11 reveals that in the Coastal and Northern region, the incidence of poverty is the highest among the ST households followed by SC then 'Other' households in the rural and urban areas during 1999-00. The pattern is little different in the Southern region where the incidence of poverty is again the highest among ST households followed by SC then 'Other' households in the rural and it is the highest among the SC households followed by ST then 'Other' households in the urban areas of the state.

**Table–6.11**

**Region-wise trends in the incidence of poverty in Orissa (1983 to 1999-00)**

| *Region* | *Rural* | | | | *Urban* | | | | *All* | | | |
|---|---|---|---|---|---|---|---|---|---|---|---|---|
| | 1983 | 1987-1988 | 1993-1994 | 1999-2000 | 1983 | 1987-1988 | 1993-1994 | 1999-2000 | 1983 | 1987-1988 | 1993-1994 | 1999-2000 |
| Coastal | 58.0 | 48.4 | 45.3 | 31.8 | 46.2 | 42.1 | 47.2 | 41.8 | 56.5 | 47.7 | 45.6 | 33.6 |
| Northern | 75.2 | 61.0 | 45.8 | 49.8 | 54.3 | 39.9 | 32.5 | 43.9 | 72.3 | 58.2 | 43.9 | 49.1 |
| Southern | 80.8 | 83.0 | 68.8 | 87.1 | 45.5 | 52.9 | 41.9 | 46.1 | 79.1 | 80.3 | 66.1 | 81.9 |
| All Orissa | 68.43 | 58.62 | 49.80 | 48.13 | 49.66 | 42.58 | 40.68 | 43.54 | 66.24 | 56.75 | 48.64 | 47.37 |

It is also found that the Southern region is the poorest in state having more than 80 per cent rural people below the poverty line, whereas this proportion is around 51 per cent for Northern region and only 29.3 per cent for the coastal region in 1999-2000. It is remarkable to note that in Coastal Orissa rural poverty has declined at a similar pace with the All-India average. These estimates suggest dramatically regional divergence of poverty in Orissa. Much of this divergence can be attributed to the concentration of tribal population. Even in northern region Keonjhar and Mayurbhanj with higher proportion of tribals appear to be the poorest having 61.92 per cent and 68.42 per cent rural poverty respectively.

One factor that may partly explain the persistence of a very high incidence of poverty in the southern region of Orissa is the pattern of distribution of the poor and non-poor around the poverty line. It is noticed from Table-6.12 that a little more than 40 per cent of the poor belong to the category of very poor i.e. those who are below three-fourth of the poverty line. Among the non-poor 54.5 per cent is lowest non-poor i.e. one and half times above the poverty line.

**Table-6.12**

**Region-wise pattern of distribution (as per cent of rural population) of rural poor and non-poor (relative to the poverty line 1993-94)**

| *Region* | *Very Poor* | *Poor* | *Total Poor* | *Lowest Non-Poor* | *Non-Poor* | *Total Non-poor* |
|---|---|---|---|---|---|---|
| Coastal | 19.03 | 26.33 | 45.36 | 36.56 | 18.08 | 54.64 |
| Southern | 34.08 | 34.94 | 69.02 | 24.10 | 6.87 | 30.97 |
| Northern | 18.99 | 26.65 | 45.64 | 33.42 | 20.94 | 54.36 |
| Orissa | 15.26<br>(40.08) | 21.97<br>(59.02) | 37.23<br>(100.00) | 34.19<br>(54.48) | 28.57<br>(45.52) | 62.76<br>(100.00) |

**Source: Human Development Report, 2004.**

### *6.7.4 Social Class Variation in the Incidence of Poverty*

Poverty patterns are also related to social differentiation. Orissa has a very high share of ST population, i.e. 22.13 per cent in 2001 as compared to only 8.01 per cent in India, while the proportion of SC population is around the All-India average (i.e. 16.53 in Orissa and 16.33 in India). Table-6.13 depicts the trend of poverty among different social groups in Orissa and all India during 1987–88 to 1999-2000. It also compares the plight of socially deprived groups in Orissa with their counterparts in the rest of the country. The trend depicts the decline in the incidence of the poverty among all the social groups in both rural and urban areas of the state as well as in the country during the period 1983 to 1999-2000. At all India level among the social groups, the reduction of poverty of SCs is marginally better by over 22 per cent than the other two social groups which are about 9 per cent. The decline in the incidence of poverty is about 20 per cent for SCs, 14 per cent for STs and 23 per cent for others. The incidence of poverty among social classes in the state has also declined over time but the rate of decline is sluggish. In urban areas the picture is completely different.

Table-6.13 depicts the estimates of rural and urban poverty among social groups which reveals that the incidence of poverty among the ST and SC population stood at 73.8 and 52.3 per cent in rural areas and 59.38 and 72.03 per cent in the urban areas respectively as against state average of 48.04 per cent and 43.59 per cent in these areas (Haan and Dubey, 2003). The incidence of rural poverty for ST has marginally declined from 87.08 per cent in 1983 to 73.08 per cent in 1999-00. The decline in rural poverty is significant in case of other category and SC population. All-India ST and SC population have fared better where incidence of poverty is 44.35 per cent and 35.44 per cent respectively. This result indicates the plight of socially deprived and vulnerable section, STs and downtrodden and weaker section of the society, SCs are still worse off in the state which gives a clear signal to planners of Orissa to make special and dedicated effort for tribal development. But the problem is a thorny problem and the task ahead is really a difficult one.

## Table–6.13

**Trends in the incidence of poverty of social classes of Orissa and all India (1983 to 1999-00)**

| *Social Group* | *Rural* | | | | *Urban* | | | | *Total* | | | |
|---|---|---|---|---|---|---|---|---|---|---|---|---|
| | *1983* | *1987-88* | *1993-94* | *1999-2000* | *1983* | *1987-88* | *1993-94* | *1999-2000* | *1983* | *1987-88* | *1993-94* | *1999-2000* |
| **Orissa** | | | | | | | | | | | | |
| ST | 87.08 | 83.82 | 71.31 | 73.08 | 73.73 | 61.37 | 62.81 | 59.38 | 86.22 | 82.34 | 70.76 | 72.08 |
| SC | 75.99 | 65.75 | 49.79 | 52.30 | 69.53 | 59.52 | 45.46 | 72.03 | 75.38 | 65.35 | 49.39 | 55.08 |
| Others | 58.52 | 47.31 | 40.79 | 33.29 | 41.86 | 37.87 | 36.32 | 34.18 | 56.16 | 45.92 | 39.55 | 33.48 |
| All | 68.43 | 58.42 | 49.80 | 48.13 | 49.66 | 42.58 | 40.68 | 43.51 | 66.24 | 56.75 | 48.64 | 47.37 |
| All India | | | | | | | | | | | | |
| ST | 63.89 | 56.31 | 47.05 | 44.35 | 55.30 | 52.26 | 35.67 | 37.42 | 63.27 | 55.93 | 46.29 | 43.67 |
| SC | 58.96 | 50.79 | 48.27 | 35.44 | 56.12 | 54.65 | 49.08 | 39.13 | 58.50 | 51.38 | 48.42 | 36.14 |
| Others | 40.90 | 33.80 | 31.20 | 21.14 | 39.94 | 36.44 | 28.67 | 20.78 | 40.66 | 34.48 | 30.46 | 21.04 |
| All | 46.51 | 39.36 | 37.28 | 26.50 | 42.32 | 39.16 | 31.70 | 23.98 | 45.57 | 39.31 | 35.95 | 25.87 |

**Source: Director of Economics and statistics, Orissa, Bhubaneswar.**

Orissa has been one of the poorest states in India with highest incidence of rural poverty. The overall poverty level in Orissa has been relatively high during 1990s and incidence of poverty is not uniform across all regions and among the social groups. While there was sharp decline in poverty in coastal area over period its regional share in the state poverty has been shifted to southern and northern areas between 1993-94 and 1999-00. In other words, southern region shared disproportionately higher burden of poor during late 1990s. In fact poverty ratio has been increased in other two regions, more pronouncedly in southern region. However, these two regions constitute about 70 per cent of the total tribal population of the state and about 79 per cent in northern and 85 per cent in southern regions are extremely poor.

## 6.8 Empirical Analysis

Among the socio-economic factors which influence the household consumption, occupation is an important factor which effects household consumption vis-a-vis the magnitude and incidence of poverty. For computing household daily requirement of calorie and nutrients, the allowances recommended by Nutrition Experts Group of the Indian Council of Medical Research (ICMR, 1968) vary over different age-sex groups also across different occupation groups. Information on work activities of adults in the household is not available. However, the NSS provides information about some broad categories of means of livelihood classes which depends on the household occupation. In case the members of a household have pursued more than one occupation, the broad categories (i.e. means of livelihood) have been determined on the basis of major source of income during the last 365 days. It would be reasonable to assume that the work activities of the adult males in the family correspond to that of household occupation. Different occupations involve different degrees of human labour. Even within an occupation, different operations may involve human labour in different degrees. In this study, we have classified household occupation into 4 categories:

(i) salaried and regular wage earner household (type-A occupation);

(ii) small business and trader households (type-B);

(iii) cultivator households (type-C);

(iv) agriculture and other labour households (type-D) on the basis of means of livelihood of a household.

The classification of work activities of the households is based on the National Classification of Occupation (NCO) 1986 with little modification. The salary and wage earner households (type-A occupation) include (a) professional, technical and related workers (b) administrative, executive and managerial workers and (c) clerical and related workers. The small business and trader households (type-B occupation) include shopkeepers, traders and hawkers; the cultivator households (type-C occupation) include cultivators owning land more than 2.5 hectares; and finally, agricultural and other labour households (type-D occupation) include small farmers owning land less than or equal to 2.5 hectares; fisherman, hunter, logger related workers; service workers, production and related workers; transport equipment operators; and all other workers. The modifications are made in occupation type-D by including small cultivators with fisherman, hunter, logger and related workers since all these activities involve strenuous work.[12]

In this study, both the traditional and sophisticated poverty ratios and indices are estimated to measure the magnitude and incidence of poverty in the rural sector of Orissa. For convenience, we have classified the poverty measures into three broad categories:

Traditional measures;

Modern measures; and

Recent measures.

The traditional measures include basically the ratios and indices like (i) head count ratio (poverty incidence ratio) (ii) poverty gap or intensity ratio (iii) normalised deficit ratio or poverty gap index and (iv) the squared poverty gap index. The modern measures include some important indices like Sen index (or poverty-deprivation index), Takayama index and FGT index. Finally, the recent measures include some popular normative or ethical measure of poverty like Atkinson Index, Clark, Hemming and Ulph (CHU) index and the Pyatt index.

### *6.8.1 Occupational Variation in the Incidence, Depth and Severity of Poverty*

The average income both in per capita and per unit reflects the living standard of a household. The average per unit income is a better measure of the standard of living of a household than the average per capita income because the average in per capita income ignores the household composition. The occupation-wise average household income, income of the poor households and the traditional measures of poverty are presented in Table-6.14. The average per capita income is the highest (Rs. 382.87) for type-A occupation households followed by type-B occupation households. It is the lowest (Rs. 237.56) for type-D occupation households. The same pattern of expenditure distribution is observed in per unit terms. The overall average per capita and per unit expenditure is Rs. 321.65 and Rs. 338.52 respectively. This clearly reveals that the standard of living of type-A occupation households are much better than other occupation households and type-D occupation households have a very poor living standard. Further, the mean per capita/unit expenditure and truncated the mean per capita/unit expenditure of the poor households in different occupation groups provides a different picture of poverty scenario in the state. Both the mean per capita/unit income/truncated income is again the highest for the type-A occupation households and the lowest for the type-D occupation households in the state. This indicates that the type-D occupation households are closer to the poverty line and the type-A occupation households are far away from the poverty line.

The popular traditional measures generally include the head count ratio (H), the poverty intensity ratio ($I_p$) and the poverty gap index ($I_w$). The head count ratio measures the incidence poverty and the normalised average poverty gap measures the intensity of poverty. It is also called the 'income gap ratio' (Sen, 1976) or the 'poverty gap ratio' (Clark, Hemming and Ulph, 1981). Another traditional measure is called poverty gap index (PGI) proposed by Watt (1968) which measures both the incidence and intensity of poverty which is otherwise known as depth (incidence + intensity) of poverty. From Table-6.14, it is evident that the incidence of poverty is the highest i.e. 63 per cent and 65 per cent for the type-D occupation households and it is the lowest i.e. 29 per cent and 32 per cent in terms of per capita and per unit respectively for the type-A occupation households.

## Table–6.14

### Occupation-wise traditional poverty measures for Orissa

| *Occupation of the household* | *Mean income* | *Mean income of the poor* | *Truncated mean income of the poor* | *Mean poverty gap* | *Normalised poverty ratio* | *Head count ratio* | *Income gap ratio* | *Poverty gap index* |
|---|---|---|---|---|---|---|---|---|
| | $\mu$ | $\mu_p$ | $\mu_p^{\bullet}$ | $\bar{g}$ | $I_n$ | H | $I_p$ | $I_w$ |
| In per capita terms | | | | | | | | |
| Type-A | 382.87 | 197.16 | 236.13 | 54.836 | 2.394 | 0.289 | 0.218 | 0.063 |
| Type-B | 300.19 | 174.57 | 224.90 | 77.431 | 4.302 | 0.351 | 0.221 | 0.108 |
| Type-C | 261.39 | 194.11 | 219.75 | 57.891 | 8.961 | 0.557 | 0.229 | 0.128 |
| Type-D | 237.56 | 169.70 | 212.56 | 62.296 | 21.754 | 0.633 | 0.247 | 0.157 |
| All Occup. | 321.65 | 230.77 | 260.96 | 63.292 | 32.257 | 0.523 | 0.245 | 0.123 |
| In per unit terms | | | | | | | | |
| Type-A | 395.56 | 245.06 | 278.55 | 48.996 | 1.997 | 0.316 | 0.137 | 0.053 |
| Type-B | 342.47 | 249.73 | 272.97 | 44.321 | 2.861 | 0.475 | 0.151 | 0.072 |
| Type-C | 335.67 | 248.05 | 275.62 | 45.985 | 4.376 | 0.401 | 0.156 | 0.095 |
| Type-D | 276.88 | 219.62 | 245.30 | 74.467 | 23.023 | 0.654 | 0.253 | 0.166 |
| All Occup. | 338.52 | 230.78 | 272.05 | 63.292 | 32.257 | 0.548 | 0.215 | 0.097 |

**Note: Estimated from NSS 55th round (1999-00) data.**

The overall incidence is 52 per cent and 55 per cent in term of per capita and per unit respectively. The poverty intensity ratio is very high for the type-D occupation households and it is little less for the type-A occupation households. The poverty gap index which reflects the depth of poverty is also the highest for the type-D occupation households and lowest for the type-A occupation households both in term of per capita and per unit.

The above analysis distinctly reveals that the incidence, intensity and depth of poverty are the highest among small farmer, agricultural labour and non-farm labour households and relatively much lower on salaried and regular wage earning households. When we compare the other two occupation groups namely small business and trader households and cultivator households, the former category of households are relatively better off than later category of households as the incidence, intensity and depth of poverty is relatively less on these households in the state.

The modern non-ethical measures of poverty include a number of poverty indices. We have examined here some of the most popular and widely used measures like Sen's measures (1976), Foster, Greer and Thorbecke (1984) or FGT measures and the Takayama index in this study. Sen derived the severity measures of poverty by combining the head count ratio, the poverty intensity ratio and the Gini coefficient of inequality among the poor (as a measure of severity of poverty). This index provides the overall composite picture of poverty (incidence, intensity and severity). On the other hand, the FGT measures have incorporated the coefficient of variation as a measure of severity of poverty and derived an alternate measure of poverty popularly known as the FGT measures. This index is also a composite index of poverty which measures the incidence, depth and severity of poverty. All the indicators in the two indices would, however, yield different estimates since they capture different dimension of poverty. The advantage of FGT index is that it is additively decomposable but the Sen index is not decomposable. The Sen index is a normalised index whereas FGT index is not normalised and its value varies between 0 to n. The third popular modern measure is the Takayama index which is also a composite index based on the truncated income distribution of both poor and non-poor while the income distribution of non-poor was ignored by the other two earlier measures.

The relevant results of Sen, FGT and Takayama measures are presented in Table-6.15. The figures in the table indicates that the severity of poverty is found to be the highest for the type-D occupation households and the lowest for the type-A occupation households both in terms of per capita and per unit. It provides a conflicting picture for type-B and type-C occupation households. In per capita terms, the severity of poverty for type-C occupation households is relatively higher than type-B occupation households. But it is reversed when measured in per unit terms. The Gini coefficient of inequality ($G_p$) which reflects the income distribution of the poor is the highest for type-A occupation households, and the lowest for type-B occupation households in terms of per capita and for type-D occupation households in term of per unit. It is due to high degree of heterogeneity in the income distribution of type-A occupation households because this occupation category includes of household members with white colour and blue colour job and other regular wage earners. These households have stable and regular flow of income. On the hand, the FGT measures reflect almost the same scenario of poverty among the four categories of households. The Sen index reflects highest intensity of poverty for type-D occupation households and the lowest intensity for type-B occupation households whereas the FGT index indicates highest depth of poverty for type-D occupation households and the lowest depth of poverty for type-B occupation households. The difference in these two measures lies in their absolute value but the ranking of occupation on the basis of severity is same. In order to accommodate deprivation relative to individuals above the poverty line Takayama (1979) defines the censored income distribution as one where all incomes above the poverty line are set equal to the poverty line, and the uses the Gini index of the censored distribution as an index of poverty. This Gini index of the censored distribution is known Takayama index. It provides the same scenario on the severity of poverty like Sen and FGT indices. The severity of poverty as per this index is again the highest for type-D occupation households and the lowest for type-A occupation households which are already inferred from Sen and FGT indices. So it is revealed that all the three measures reflect the same scenario of poverty. The ranking occupation groups according to Sen and FGT severity indices can be seen similar to that of the head count ratio. The ranking by Takayama index is more of less identical to Sen and FGT severity indices even though their absolute values are different.

### Table–6.15

### Occupation-wise positive poverty measures in Orissa

| *Occupation of the household* | *Sen's measure (Ps)* | | | *Takayama Index* ($P_T$) | *FGT measure* ($P_{FGT}$) | | |
|---|---|---|---|---|---|---|---|
| | *Ip* | *Gp* | *Ps* | | $\alpha = 0$ | $\alpha = 1$ | $\alpha = 2$ |
| **In per capita terms** | | | | | | | |
| Type-A | 0.218 | 0.649 | 0.092 | 0.057 | 0.289 | 0.063 | 0.026 |
| Type-B | 0.221 | 0.474 | 0.135 | 0.089 | 0.350 | 0.108 | 0.041 |
| Type-C | 0.229 | 0.607 | 0.175 | 0.095 | 0.467 | 0.128 | 0.043 |
| Type-D | 0.247 | 0.561 | 0.212 | 0.110 | 0.633 | 0.157 | 0.054 |
| All Occup. | 0.245 | 0.557 | 0.178 | 0.099 | 0.529 | 0.123 | 0.045 |
| **In per unit terms** | | | | | | | |
| Type-A | 0.137 | 0.812 | 0.066 | 0.043 | 0.316 | 0.053 | 0.011 |
| Type-B | 0.151 | 0.773 | 0.107 | 0.060 | 0.475 | 0.072 | 0.024 |
| Type-C | 0.156 | 0.768 | 0.125 | 0.051 | 0.491 | 0.095 | 0.016 |
| Type-D | 0.253 | 0.655 | 0.201 | 0.112 | 0.654 | 0.166 | 0.056 |
| All Occup. | 0.215 | 0.624 | 0.156 | 0.086 | 0.523 | 0.112 | 0.036 |

The recent development in poverty measures is the ethical indices of poverty based on the normative approach to poverty. The most popular ethical measure of poverty is the Clark, Hemming and Ulph (CHU) and Pyatt indices. CHU (1981) index is based on the Atkinson's normality measure of inequality index for the distribution of income among the poor. It measures the proportionate loss in welfare of the individuals/households with income below 'the equally distributed equivalent income' with respect to poverty line. The value of this index depends on the poverty aversion parameter, 'β'. The index is relatively sensitive to large poverty gaps. On the other hand, Pyatt (1987) exploited the idea of censored income proposed by Takayáma (1979) in the context of poverty measurement. The way of deriving his poverty measure is novel. He decomposed the income of each unit into two parts, viz. (i) basic income and (ii) affluence. Finally, he derived the index which is almost similar with the rank ordering index derived by Sen (1976). The results of these measures are described in Table-6.16. The figures in the table reveal that both the CHU and Pyatt indices also provide the same pattern of intensity and severity of poverty among the different occupation groups like Sen, FGT and Takayama indices even though their absolute value differs. But here severity is measured in terms of welfare losses. Although as the inequality aversion parameter is reduced the variation in severity among the occupation groups would be somewhat greater. Both the CHU and Pyatt's measure also provide the same ranking of different occupation households as that of Sen, FGT and Takayama indices.

## 6.9 Conclusion

The conclusions drawn on the basis of the above analysis are as follows:

The international incidence of poverty in developing economies has varied across the regions. Poverty has declined in the regions of fast Asia, Latin America, Middle-East, North Africa, South Asia and sub-Saharan Africa. Wide variation in poverty across countries within each region and also observed. In most of the East Asian countries poverty has risen as a result of the financial crisis of the rate 1990s while most of the African countries have experienced an increase in the incidence of poverty. Poverty is rampant in the less developed countries of Africa and Asia. However, the African LDCs are more poverty ridden than the Asian LDCS. The situation in developing countries like India, China etc. is much better than the less developed countries of the world. The incidence of poverty is very high in all these countries particularly on $2-a-day norm. Incidence and gap of poverty on the basis of $1-a-day norm is not much either for Affrican LDCs or for Asian LDCs. After a decade of liberal trade poverty has not been reduced in those countries.

**Table–6.16**

**Occupation-wise ethical poverty measures in Orissa**

| *Occupation of the hhs* | *Atkinson Index ($P_A$)* | | | | | *CHU Index ($P_{CHU}$)* | | | *Pyatt Index ($P_P$)* |
|---|---|---|---|---|---|---|---|---|---|
| | $\varepsilon = 0.5$ | $\varepsilon = 1.0$ | $\varepsilon = 1.5$ | $\varepsilon = 2.0$ | $\varepsilon = 2.5$ | $(\beta = -0.5)$ | $(\beta = 0.5)$ | $(\beta = 1.0)$ | |
| **In per capita terms** | | | | | | | | | |
| Type-A | 0.032 | 0.031 | 0.029 | 0.028 | 0.027 | 0.071 | 0.078 | 0.082 | 0.115 |
| Type-B | 0.062 | 0.061 | 0.060 | 0.059 | 0.058 | 0.117 | 0.132 | 0.138 | 0.186 |
| Type-C | 0.094 | 0.093 | 0.092 | 0.090 | 0.088 | 0.137 | 0.145 | 0.149 | 0.211 |
| Type-D | 0.124 | 0.122 | 0.121 | 0.119 | 0.117 | 0.166 | 0.174 | 0.179 | 0.249 |
| All Occup. | 0.090 | 0.089 | 0.088 | 0.086 | 0.085 | 0.140 | 0.149 | 0.154 | 0.217 |
| **In per unit terms** | | | | | | | | | |
| Type-A | 0.037 | 0.037 | 0.037 | 0.036 | 0.036 | 0.055 | 0.058 | 0.060 | 0.092 |
| Type-B | 0.040 | 0.039 | 0.040 | 0.039 | 0.039 | 0.066 | 0.070 | 0.071 | 0.110 |
| Type-C | 0.052 | 0.051 | 0.049 | 0.048 | 0.047 | 0.078 | 0.082 | 0.084 | 0.126 |
| Type-D | 0.130 | 0.128 | 0.127 | 0.126 | 0.124 | 0.018 | 0.184 | 0.188 | 0.258 |
| All Occup. | 0.080 | 0.079 | 0.078 | 0.077 | 0.076 | 0.121 | 0.127 | 0.130 | 0.189 |

The present study examines poverty in the dimensions of incidence, intensity, depth and severity in India and its constituent major states during 1983 to 1999-00. Though the extent of poverty has decreased over time in all the states, uniformity in such reduction is not observed in the states. A wide inter-state disparity is observed in the depth and severity of poverty and relative deprivation both in rural and urban areas. Rural areas exhibit relatively more inter-state variation in the incidence of poverty.

Relative deprivation has also declined overtime in almost all the states and such a decline is attributed to the fact that the decline in inequality has been more pronounced than the rise in per capita consumption expenditure especially in rural areas. Reduction in absolute poverty as well as relative deprivation has been presumably the outcome of massive anti-poverty programmes implemented in both rural and urban areas. Interstate variation in severity of poverty and relative deprivation are explained by the factors like distributional inequality and state of development. Absolute poverty and relative deprivation co-jointly persists in the states. Selective and effective intervention of the Government is necessary to bring about changes in the distributional structure of income and the development perspectives.

We have also estimated the income poverty lines for four different occupation groups of rural Orissa using the cost of calorie function suggested by Greer and Thorbecke (1986) on the basis recommended daily allowance (RDA) of 2400/2700 calories and the per capita/per unit total consumption expenditure. The estimated poverty line for different occupation types are compared with the updated poverty lines of major studies in India. The poverty line estimates in terms of monthly per capita and monthly per unit indicate that the poverty line for type-D occupation is the lowest (i.e. Rs. 276.42 and Rs. 322.88 respectively) and it is the highest (i.e. Rs. 194.46 and Rs. 338.52 respectively) for type-A occupation households. The poverty line for type-B occupation households almost coincides with the estimates for all households. It is estimated that the percentage of households below poverty line is the highest for type-D occupation and is the lowest for type-A occupation households (measured both in per capita and per unit consumption). The poverty line estimates in per unit is found to be higher than the poverty lines measured in per capita for all occupation groups (in absolute value). The percentage of households below poverty line decreases when measured in per unit instead of per capita which is really remarkable for the rural economy of Orissa. The estimated poverty line for all sample households is Rs. 276 in per capita terms and Rs. 327 in per unit terms.

The aggregate poverty ratio hides significant differences in the poverty ratio among social classes (ST, SC and 'Other') as well as across different regions of the state. The trend of poverty ratio in the state is also influenced significantly due to wide variation in the trend of poverty ratio among the social classes and also in the trend of poverty ratio across the three regions of the state. One possible important reason for the persistence of high incidence of poverty in the state might be the percentage of very poor people between the ST and SC population and backward Southern region of the state which is dominated by the ST and SC population. The above analysis also clearly reveals that the incidence, depth, severity and intensity of poverty are the highest among the ST households, followed by SC households then by 'other' households. A broad based and sustained growth of agriculture along public intervention in the areas of health care, basic education, nutritional support, public distribution system etc. can make sustained dent on poverty and food security in the State like Orissa where social indicators especially for ST and SC population are highly unfavourable.

The relevant results of Sen, FGT and Takayama measures indicates that the severity of poverty is found to be the highest for the type-D occupation households and the lowest for the type-A occupation households both in terms of per capita and per unit. It provides a conflicting picture for type-B and type-C occupation households. In per capita terms, the severity of poverty for type-C occupation households is relatively higher than type-B occupation households. But it is reversed when measured in per unit terms.

There is consistence evidence of continuing poverty decline in the nineties in term of head count ratio. The extent of the decline, however, remains somewhat uncertain. The main argument of using the head count ratio is that it has good 'communicative value', is so far as it is relatively easier to understand and interpret. However, this transparency is to some extent deceptive, and much caution is required in interpreting poverty trends on the basis of head count ratio. Sometimes the head count ratio turns out to be no less informative than the poverty gap index and other measure of poverty. So it is important to calculate the poverty gap index, squared poverty gap index, and FGT index etc., to discover what refinements these measures provide us.

## REFERENCES

1. We are Using these Two Terms—energy and Calorie Synonymously in this chapter.
2. It May be Noted that Rowntree (1901) has used the 'Primary Poverty'.
3. The HDI is Based on Three Indicators: Longevity—measured by Life Expectancy at Birth; Education Attainment—measured by a Combination of Adult Literacy (Two-Third Weight) and Enrollment Ratio (One-Third Weight); and the Standard of Living as Measured by real GDP per capita (for Detail see HDR, 1997, UNDP).
4. The HPI Concentrates on Deprivation in Three Essential Elements of Human Life-longevity Knowledge and a Decent Standard of Living. The First Deprivation Relates to Survival i.e. Vulnerability to Death at a Relatively Early Age. The Second Deprivation Relates to Knowledge i.e. being Excluded from the World of Reading and Communication. The Third Deprivation Relates to a Decent living Standard in Terms of Economic Provisioning (for detail see HDR, 1997, UNDP).
5. M-Value measure:

   The Advantage of Sen's Index is that it is very Useful for Policy Purposes. Two Different Measures such as M-value and F-value Measures Derived from the Sen's Index have a Lot of Policy Implications. The M-value Measure is Defined as:

   $M_s = P_s (z/\mu_p)$

   Where 'z' is the Poverty Line, $\mu_p$ is the Mean Income of the Poor and $P_s$ is the Sen's Index. M-Value Measures the Percentage of the State's Income to be Spent for the Poor to Bring them to the Poverty Line (i.e. the People Living Below the Poverty Line will be having the Consumption Expenditure which will be Equivalent to the Poverty Line Consumption Expenditure).

6. F-Value measure:

   Another Measure Related with Sen Index is the F-value Measure which is Defined as

   $F_s = P_s\,[z/(\mu - H\mu_p)]$

   F-value Measures the Percentage of the Transfer (of Income) from the Non-poor to the Poor without Changing the State's Income so that they (the Poor) can come to the Poverty Line.

7. Growth Elasticity of Poverty:

   The Growth Elasticity of Poverty Measures the Response of the Level of Poverty due the Growth of Consumption Expenditure over Time. It is Defined as the Ratio of Mean Expenditure of the Poor and the Poverty Gap which is given by

   $\varepsilon_p = -\,\mu_p/(z - \mu_p)$

   The 'Growth Elasticity of Poverty' is Negative Indicating an Inverse Relationship Between Growth of Consumption Expenditure and the Poverty Gap $(z - \mu_p)$. Elasticity Varies Between Zero and Infinity. When All the People Below Poverty Line have Zero Income which Means $\mu_p = 0$, the Elasticity will be zero ($\varepsilon_p = 0$). When All the People Below Poverty Line will Come to the Poverty Line then $\mu_p = z$ and the Denominator will be Zero which Implies $\varepsilon_p = \infty$.

8. The Details of its Derivation and Other Related Issues see Mac Donald, L and Bradford Smith, K: Purchasing Power Parity and the International Development Targets, DFID Internal Paper, 2001.

9. Dubey and Crook (2001) have Looked at much more Details on This Issue and its Implications on Poverty Incidence Across the States.

10. For Details on NSS Sampling Design see GoI (1983), GoI (1987), GoI (1993) and GoI (1999) and Dubey and Gangopadhyay (1998).

11. See Also Dubey, 2002.

12. (a). Specific $i^{th}$ Food item Groups are: (i=1, 2, ...7), Cereals –1, Pulses & its Products-2, Milk & Milk Products-3, Edible Oil-4, Meat, Fish and Egg-5, Vegetables & Fruits-6, Sugar and Gur-7.

    (b) Occupation Groups (k=1, 2 ..., 4) are: Type-A=1, Type-B=2 & Type-C=3 & Type-D=4

    (c) Household Size ($n_k$) of the $k^{th}$ Group (k=1, 2,..., 4): $n_1 = n_2 = n_3 = n_4 = 160$.

# 7

# SUMMARY OF THE FINDINGS

Poverty is a phenomenon which is complex in its origin as well as in its manifestations. It is a great moral and social challenge. It is not a recent phenomenon in India. Ample evidence of its abject incidence among the masses is found in the literary and descriptive accounts of pre-colonial and colonial times. Poverty is such a situation where a section of the society could not meet even the minimum requirements of living. In India, it is found that the problem of poverty is an enormous one—about one-fourth of the population is below poverty line and it is also observed that largest number of poor live here. Since independence, each plan document has been making big pronouncement for the removal of poverty. Yet after 50 years, India is still struggling with poverty. Though the incidence of poverty has declined from 45 to 26 per cent during 1950-2000, but the population growth has led to doubling of the number of poor in the same period from 164 million to 320 million. The poverty is still a challenge and has become a controversial issue because the process of growth is accompanied with increasing intensity of poverty. The fruits of growth do not seem to be percolated to the poor. So the planners and policymakers suggest alternative paths for the eradication of poverty. Recently, along with the economic poverty, social poverty is also observed which is the result of economic poverty and reflects itself in high infant mortality rate, high maternal mortality rate, high illiteracy rate, and high level of unemployment rate. It is being thought in these days that the problem of poverty is complex in context, texture, characteristics, impact and implications as such it cannot be characterised adequately in terms of income, expenditure or consumption pattern alone. It has also been realised by the social scientists and social activists that poverty in countries like India has to be studied in a wider framework of reference, which should be more empirical and less abstract, more micro-social and micro-economic and less macro-social and macro-economic. Thus, the focus should be on human degradation resulting from poverty and not on the number only. Now what is required is a multidimensional concept of poverty inclusive of environment, access to services and social and psychological supports.

The study is based on more than one source of data, yet the main data source for the study is the NSS data on consumption expenditure collected by the National Sample Survey Organisation (NSSO) during its different rounds (27$^{th}$ to 55$^{th}$) from 1972-73 to 1999-00 and National Accounts Statistics of India, 1950-51 to 2000-01 collected by the Central Statistical Organisation (CSO), Government of India. We do so primarily because for delineating temporal changes in the NSS data. It is, thus, the time profile of the NSS data used in this study that can take up as far back as 1983 and brings us as close to the present time as 1999-2000. Further, the period from 1983 to 1993-94 surrogates the pre-reform period while the period from 1993-94 to 1999-00 is expected to capture the changes brought about by the economic reforms resulting a drastic change in the poverty and inequality scenario in the country. The data set for 1987-88 has little importance in the study because weather condition was not good and the year was not a normal year. This may, likely throw up distortions in the rural consumption patterns many times more than the urban areas. Further, the purpose of using data of Quinquennial Surveys is that these surveys are based on thick sample. Though, annual surveys on consumption expenditure selecting thin samples have been conducted by the NSSO in recent rounds, most of the analysis and debates on consumption, inequality and poverty based on the Quinquennial Surveys. The sixth quinquennial survey includes 71,355 rural households and 48,924 urban households. The study is also based on validated NSS unit record data of 600 rural households collected during the sixth quinquennial survey uniformly distributed over different parts of the state to examine some specific aspects of household consumption, disparities in living standards and incidence of poverty.

We have reviewed critically the major issues that have emerged from the numerous studies on the estimates of poverty and effectiveness of poverty alleviation scheme in India during the past five decades. The success that has been achieved must be viewed in the context of the enormity of the problem that still remains. Deprivations of social and economic indicators spread across different regions and states, infrastructural bottlenecks and other growth constraints, distributional inequalities compounded by ill targeting and wrong incentive signals, inefficiency of management and the challenges to grow and survive in a world of globalisation and market integration yet to make people to live a better life, have all eluded our early efforts during the fifty years of the country's economic development.

Poverty trends in India have been a matter of extensive controversy and confusion still reminds about the extent to which poverty has declined during the nineties. The incidence of poverty is declined at a rate of 1 per cent per year. However, the performance is uneven among the states. Some states are doing better than other states. Widening of regional disparities and limited growth in backward areas have made the overall growth process less pro-poor overtime. As a result, even if poverty is reported to have declined in the country, the rural poverty ratio continues to be high. It is high in the states like Orissa, Bihar, Madhya Pradesh and North-Eastern states. It is also true that higher growth rates may not be sustainable if they are not accompanied by wide dispersion of purchasing power with higher levels of employment. Agricultural development along with the development of agro-industries must be viewed as a core area in this dimension. Recent evident indicates that inequality in India have been rising since the initiation of economic reforms (1991).

There is no single source from which one can directly get consistent data for India regarding incomes distribution over a period of time so that one can draw inference about relative poverty or income disparities and its pattern over time, which is of almost importance for policy formulation. Despite this drawback, we are able to track the pattern of changes in relative poverty and compared it with the movements in per capita income and absolute poverty. Our analysis is indeed useful to verify two widely held viewpoints, especially at a time when empirical evidence have began to accumulate against them and require further support in their favour in order to convincingly contradict both the widely held view points (i) poverty is more a direct reflection of low levels of per capita income rather than skewed income distribution and (ii) relative poverty and income disparities increased initially with the increase in real per capita income but subsequently it diminishes as per capita income grows further (Prof. Kuznet's famous inverted-U hypothesis). The broad conclusions and policy implications that have emerged from our analysis are as follows.

It is clearly demonstrated during the course of our analysis that mere increase in per capita income is not enough to reduce poverty rather redistribution of per capita income and rate of change in the prices of cereals are crucial variable, which govern the level of absolute poverty in India. This also contradicts the general belief that poverty is more a direct reflection of low levels of per capita income rather than skewed income distribution.

The available evidence from rural and urban areas of the Indian economy does not support Prof. Kuznets inverted-U hypothesis regarding real per capita income and relative poverty. Our inference is not the only one, but there are many other evidences like, the one provided by Deininger and Squire (1996), which has been accumulated over the years again the inverted-U hypothesis. This has serious implications for future growth since conventional wisdom that higher inequality promotes growth finds no clinching evidences in its favour during the recent past. Rather Smith (2001) has effectively demonstrated that high initial income inequality is an impediment for a higher economic growth. The need in India is to design policies, which must lessen relative poverty or income inequalities.

The estimates of consumption expenditure provided by National Account Statistics are much higher than those given by the National Sample Survey Organization. The substantial under estimation of consumption expenditure on the part of NSSO has occurred because of a fairly low estimate of miscellaneous items in the category of non-food expenditure. There is an urgent need on the part of NSSO to amend it since it significantly affects relative disparities in non-food consumption expenditure, which has serious policy implications.

It is observed that during 1993-94 to 1999-00 the real per capita NDP growth rate has been maximum both in rural and urban areas, but relative disparities in food consumption expenditure too have increased. Moreover, household saving-income ratio has expanded further which is mainly on account of enhanced savings, especially by those whose monthly per capita expenditure is the highest. It is reflected by the fact that one of the important sources of income is through interest and divided. This compiled with substantial under reporting of non-food consumption expenditure of households in the higher expenditure classes leave little room for doubt about income distribution becoming more skewed since liberalization. This has raised serious apprehension about the official claim of a significant reduction of absolute poverty both in rural and urban areas. Our apprehensions are well supported by the evidences about poverty reduction, based on other information like employment and unemployment surveys and the preceding official surveys on consumption expenditure based on these samples. No rational policy framework can be designed in developing countries especially where reliable and correct poverty estimates are not available. Time has come when higher authorities should properly monitor the entire survey, rather than taking it as a routine work. They must comprehend the significance of their exercise as future course of policy depends a lot on their estimates.

The international inequality scenario reveals that public policy aimed for reducing inequality such as socialism or welfarism or combination of the two has significant influence in reducing income inequality. Market or state-mediated policies aimed at enhancing economic growth including promotion of the education, health and economic freedom may not help to reduce income inequality. There is no convincing evidence that economic growth per se could lower income inequalities. In the South-Asian economies in general and India in particular, there are wide variety of subsidies right from education, health to rail and road transport. In addition, trade unions are powerful in the organized sector.

Despite all this, the overall impact of these measures is found to be negligible and hence, income inequality is relatively high in those countries. Given the extent to which global forces are putting downward pressure on lower income groups and upward pressure at the top, it is unlikely that income inequality will decline significantly in the near future.

In the absence of clear evidence of rising intra-rural inequality within the states, we find strong indications of a pervasive increase in economic inequality in the nineties. There has been strong 'divergence' of per capita expenditure across states; with the better of states (particularly in the southern and western region) are growing more rapidly than the poorer states thereby widening the regional inequality. The rural-urban disparities of per capita expenditure have also risen in most of the states. Inequality has increased within the urban areas of most of the states. The combined effects of these different forms of rising inequality are quite large. In the rural areas of some of the poorest states, there has been virtually no increase in per capita expenditure in the nineties. The compounding of the inter-state divergence and the rising rural-urban disparities produces sharp constructs in APC growth between the rural sector of the slow growing states and the urban sector of first growing states. This has further compounded the intra-urban inequality which is itself quite substantial especially during mid- and late-nineties.

The international incidence of poverty in developing economies has varied across the regions. Poverty has declined in the regions of Asia, Latin America, Middle-East, North Africa, South Asia and sub-Saharan Africa. Wide variations in poverty across countries within each region are also observed. In most of the East Asian countries poverty has risen as a result of the financial crisis of the late 1990s while most of the African countries have experienced an increase in the incidence of poverty. Poverty is rampant in the less developed countries of Africa and Asia. However, the African LDCs are more poverty ridden than the Asian LDCs. The situation in developing countries like India, China etc. is much better than the less developed countries of the world. The incidence of poverty is very high in all these countries particularly on $2-a-day norm. The incidence and poverty gap on the basis of $1-a-day norm is not much either for African LDCs or for Asian LDCs. After a decade of liberal trade, poverty has not been reduced in those countries.

The present study examines poverty in the dimensions of incidence, intensity, depth and severity in India and its constituent major states during 1983 to 1999-2000. Though the extent of poverty has decreased over time in all the states, uniformity in such reduction is not observed in the states. A wide inter-state disparity is observed in the depth and severity of poverty and relative poverty both in rural and urban areas. Rural areas exhibit relatively more inter-state variation in the incidence of poverty.

Relative deprivation has also declined overtime in almost all the states and such a decline is attributed to the fact that the decline in inequality has been more pronounced than the rise in per capita consumption expenditure especially in rural areas. Reduction in absolute poverty as well as relative poverty has been presumably the outcome of massive anti-poverty programmes implemented in both rural and urban areas. Interstate variation in severity of poverty and relative deprivation are explained by the factors like distributional inequality and state of development. Absolute poverty and relative deprivation co-jointly persists in the states. Selective and effective intervention of the Government is necessary to bring about changes in the distributional structure of income and the development perspectives.

The climate and geography have significant influence on economic and social activities of the people living in a region. Myrdal (1968) is of the opinion that natural factors like climate, topography, etc. can not be neglected while explaining economic conditions of a region or a country. The state of Orissa can be divided into various zone or regions on the basis of distribution of forests, mineral, soil, rainfall, concentration of tribal population, development of industries etc. The climate and geography have significant influence on economic and social activities of the people living in a region.

Orissa is the costal state with a large coastline of about 400 kms and area of 155,860 sq. km. Geographically, Orissa represents an extensive plateau sloping gently into coastal plain along the

Bay of Bengal. There are four physical regions namely, the northern plateau which is an extension of the mineral bearing zone of Chhotanagpur plateau; the Eastern Ghats representing the hill ranges, the coastal plains and the river basins of the central table land. Cultivators and agricultural labour taken together constitute 60.2 per cent of the main workers in the state, whereas this segment accounts for 44.5 of the total rural workforce. All other workers in the rural areas consists 18.2 per cent main workers out of which 3.4 per cent are in household industry and the remaining are other workers. Most of workers under the category of 'other workers' are engaged in some sort trade, services, construction etc. hand-based productive work being the most predominant activities for the bulk of the rural population in the state, the size distribution of land, intensity and pattern of land use and productivity, largely determine their economic conditions. The size distribution of landed assets among rural population has important bearing on the state's economy.

The NSS division of Orissa into three distinct regions viz., Southern, Coastal and Northern is noteworthy. It is interesting to note that the southern region is relatively backward and dominated by tribal population. The people of this region live in small villages where households are scattered in various hilltops. Most of them practise shifting cultivation. Some of them who live in plain areas are engaged in settled cultivation. They are adversely affected by scanty and erratic rainfall. Besides cultivation, tribals mainly depend for their livelihood on the collection of minor forest products. Many of them live in subhuman conditions. Poverty is rampart in this region. The coastal region consists of plain areas with good amount of cultivable land but some of the districts (Cuttack and Balasore) suffers from the ravages of high flood and some part of the costal districts are prone to cyclones. The tribal population also lives in small pockets of this region. Agriculture is the main occupation of the people of this region. Besides this, many people are engaged in white color and blue color jobs. The northern region is rich in mineral with comparatively balanced distribution of industry and mines. Agriculture is the prime occupation of the people. Besides this, many people engaged in blue color jobs like production process, mining and quarrying etc.

In view of the above, we have selected the sample households which are evenly distributed over the three NSS ranges to get balanced and representative sample households that can provide a clear picture of the magnitude and incidence of poverty of the state. The study basically deals with two interlinked areas—consumption and poverty. For the analysis of consumption behaviour we have used both grouped and ungrouped (600 households) NSS data of 55$^{th}$ round (June, 1999-July 2000) the sixth quinquennial survey on consumption expenditure. But for the estimation of poverty line we have used validated unit record NSS data of 600 households scattered over the three NSS regions of the state. We have selected 200 households from each region which are again scattered over different stratums of the NSS region.

The economic profile of Orissa reflects certain peculiarities. The density of population varies from district to district. The coastal districts are thickly populated. Majority of them remain in rural areas banking on agriculture only. Three-fourth of the population are cultivators and agricultural labourers. Unemployment and underemployment are rampant and they are more acute in the rural areas. Infrastructure required for the economy is poorly developed. It ranks 14$^{th}$ among the 16 major states in the availability of infrastructure. About 48 per cent of the total population of Orissa remains below the poverty line. One of the main causes of poverty is the sluggish growth of agriculture production with marginal diversification in cropping pattern and absence of significant industrial expansion. The socio-economic indicators of the state indicate the distress fact of continued backwardness.

Orissa has the highest proportion of people living below the poverty line among the Indian states. The proportion of the urban poor is also not less. The urban poverty is an offshoot of rural poverty since rural poor migrate to urban areas to seek employment and income. The poor constitutes mostly landless agricultural labourers and small cultivators. The highest portion of the poor is seen in hilly infertile areas with tribal concentration. The social and ethnic characteristic of the poor are exhibited with the downtrodden section of the society such as SC and ST and some sections of Muslims and Christians. The SC and ST communities are mostly poor. They are lacking human capital. Their quality of life is very poor. They have not gained much access to social services like health and education. They have a low health profile and a low level of educational achievements. The proportion of people below poverty line is found to be more than 60 per cent up to the period 1983-84 estimated by a number of researchers (Mahendra Dev et.al. 1985, M.S. Ahluwalia, 1978, Minhas, Jain and Tendulkar, 1991 and Government of India, 1993 etc.). The estimates of Mahendra Dev et al. (1992) and the planning commission of India reveals that during the period 1961-62 to1986-87 about 65 per cent of rural population were below the poverty line in the state. As per the estimates of Export Group (1993), the percentage of rural people below the poverty line in Orissa was about 69 per cent during the period from 1973-74 to 1983-84. This percentage declined to 61.5 per cent during year 1987- 88. As per the estimates of the Export Group (1993) the absolute number of the rural poor in Orissa witnessed a rising trend during the period 1973-74 to 1983-84. The number of poor was increased from 14.438 million in 1973-74 to 16.93 million in 1983-84 and then marginally declined to 16.09 million 1987-88. In the year 1973-74, the number of poor (both rural and urban) for all Orissa was 75.58 million which was declined to 17.56 million in 1987-88.

The Export Group (1993) on estimation of poverty line has suggested micro level and regional level studies on poverty estimation and its level and incidence which can throw more light on the exact magnitude and severity of poverty in the regions/ states. Such studies from time to time will helpful to capture the importance of antipoverty programmes on the living standards of the people of a region or state. The study is an attempt to estimate poverty line for the states and also to investigate the levels of incidence and severity of poverty for helping planners to re-orient or re-cast the developmental policy in desired direction on the basis of the results of this regional level study.

In Chapter-III, we have estimated the specific and income adult equivalent scale for nine broad food item and five broad non-food item groups for the rural sector of Orissa using the iterative procedure of Singh and Nagar (1973) which is an extensive and modified approach of the well known Prais and Houthakker's iterative procedure (1955). These specific and unit adult equivalent consumer scales are used to estimate the poverty line in per unit terms for the state. The estimated results of adult equivalent unit consumer scales reveal that the adult equivalent scales for adult males are the highest for most of the food items except milk and milk products, salt and spices, fuel and light and clothing are the scale of which are found to be the highest for adult females except type-D occupation households. For milk and milk products, the scales are highest and for other items the scale are lowest for children (0-4 years). No such definite pattern is observed in the scales for other items of consumption among the six age-sex groups in each type of occupation households.

Chapter-IV, indicate that Engel ratios and Engel elasticities are estimated for different food and non-food items (including consumer durables) from eleven formulations of Engel functions to know the household consumption pattern separately for the rural and urban sector of the state. Engel analysis is carried out using the Dummy Variable Interaction Model (DVIM) to investigate the inter-sectoral and inter-occupational variation in the consumption pattern of the state.

In the empirical analysis on Engel curves, we have experimented with six two parameters and five three parameters Engel functions for various food and non-food items separately for the rural and urban sector of the state. It is observed from chapter-IV that no unique Engel function suffices for the complete range of consumption items and also for a particular consumption item in the two sectors of the state. The different best-fit Engel functions for the same item of consumption in the two sectors is a clear indication of inter-sectoral variation in the consumption pattern of different durable and non-durable goods. This is because different Engel functions have different assumptions and yielding different marginal propensity to consume, Engel elasticities, saturation levels and threshold income mentioned section-4.5 of chapter-IV (Table-4.10 and 4.11).

The cross-sectional analysis of household consumption analysed above reveals the presence of inter-sectoral variation in household consumption in the state. The time-series analysis on household consumption of food and non-food items from 27th round (1972-73) to 55th round (1999-2000) also reveal the same picture of significant inter-sectoral variation in the household consumption behaviour in the state. The expenditure on food items is found to be much higher than non-food items during the last 17 years. But the percentage of food expenditure to total expenditure has declined from 75 per cent in 1972-73 to 64 per cent in 1999-2000 in the rural areas and from 72 per cent in 1972-73 to 57 per cent in 1999-2000 in the urban areas. On the other hand, the percentage of expenditure on non-food items to total expenditure increased from 24.94 per cent in 1972-73 to 35.88 per cent in 1999-2000 in the rural sector and from 21.58 per cent in 1972-73 to 43.05 per cent in urban sector. The diversification of expenditure from food consumption to non-food consumption is a clear indication of improvement in the standard of living of the people in both sectors of the state.

In chapter-V, the inequality figures conform that rural economy in most of the states are moving towards a homogeneous unit unlike the urban economy during the post-reform period, the urban attracts more private investment than the rural areas. That is why growth remains concentrated in urban areas of most of the states. Urban areas are viewed as the growth pole of the economy. But the fruits of growth reach a small section of population in the urban areas of most of the states.

In chapter-VI, we have applied Greer and Thorbecke Cost of Calories Function (CCF) method to estimate poverty line on the basis of monthly per capita expenditure (MPCE) and monthly per unit expenditure (MPUE) separately for the households of four occupation groups and for all households of rural Orissa. The poverty line estimated for different occupation types reveals that it is the lowest both in MPCE (Rs. 262) and in MPUE (Rs. 323) for type-D occupation households and is the highest both in MPCE (Rs. 294) and MPUE (Rs. 339) for type-A occupation households. If we imagine a poverty line scale, type-D occupation households tops the list followed by type-C, then by type-B and finally, type-A occupation households both in term of MPCE and MPUE.

In this study, both the traditional and sophisticated poverty ratios and indices are estimated to measure the magnitude and incidence of poverty in the rural sector of Orissa. For convenience, we have classified the poverty measures into three broad categories viz. traditional measures, modern measures and recent measures. The traditional measures include basically the ratios and indices like (i) head count ratio (poverty incidence ratio) (ii) poverty gap or intensity ratio (iii) normalised deficit ratio or poverty gap index and (iv) the squared poverty gap index. The modern measures include some important indices like Sen index (or poverty-deprivation index), Takayama index and FGT index. Finally, the recent measures include some popular normative or ethical measure of poverty like Atkinson Index, Clark, Hemming and Ulph (CHU) index and the Pyatt index. It is distinctly reveals that the incidence, intensity and depth of poverty are the highest among small farmer, agricultural labour and non-farm labour households and relatively much lower on salaried and regular wage earning households. When we compare the other two occupation groups namely small business and trader households and cultivator households, the former category of households are relatively better off than later category of households as the incidence, intensity and depth of poverty is relatively less on these households in the state.

It is also concluded that the calorie contribution of cereals is the highest followed by vegetables to the calorie intake of the households of each type of occupation and also for all households. But the calorie contribution of other food item like milk and its products; pulses and its products; sugar and gur; edible oil; meat, fish and egg and salt and spice is meager to the calorie intake of households of different occupation group. It is also concluded that the Engel ratio for food and non-food items indicate the standard of living of a household which in turn reflects the level and severity of poverty.

## 7.1 Testing of Hypothesis

A number of hypotheses have been formulated in Chapter-I based on the review of past studies. These hypotheses are tested here taking into account the empirical analysis of the study.

We have selected durable-log Engel function (DL) for cereals, edible oil, vegetables, all food items, and fuel and light; the exponential Engel function (EX) only for durables, the linear Engel function (L) for meat, fish and egg; pan, tobacco and intoxicants and all non-food items (including durable) and finally, the parabolic Engel function (P) for pulses and its product; milk and its product and clothing. While selecting the functional form of a Engel function for each consumption item, the plausibility of Engel elasticities are taken into account. It is noticed that the Engel elasticities obtained from the same functional form for each item are different across the sectors. The inter-sectoral variation in household consumption is bound to appear because it depends on the level of mean specific item expenditure and the mean total expenditure, which are different across the sectors. Apart from this, inter-sectoral variation may also arise because of certain basic differences such as income, household size and its composition, level of education, occupational structure, social class, physical and climatic conditions, opportunities for employment, habits and customs, cultural factors etc. across the rural and urban sector of the state. It is also observed from Table-4.3 that both the Engel ratios and elasticities estimated from the same functional form for each type of occupation are found to be different. Generally, urban Engel elasticities are lower than the rural elasticities for food items and reverse is the case for non-food items. From the sectoral analysis, it is evident that rural elasticities are greater than urban elasticities for the food items like cereals; pulses and its products; edible oil; meat, fish and egg also food item taken as whole and the reverse in the case for other food items like milk and milk products and vegetable. But for the non-food items like clothing, durables, fuel and light and pan, tobacco and intoxicants urban elasticities are greater than rural elasticities, which confirm hypothesis-1.

In chapter-IV, it is noticed that the Engel elasticities are less than unity for cereals, pulses and its products; edible oil; vegetables; all food items; pan, tobacco and intoxicants, all food items in both rural and urban sectors of the state indicating that these items are necessities in both sectors. But the elasticity for milk and milk products is less than unity in the rural areas and greater than unity in the urban areas. On the other hand, the elasticity for meat, fish and egg is greater than unity in the rural areas and less than unity in urban areas. But the elasticities are greater than unity for clothing, durables and all non-food items in both the sectors of the state. It clearly indicates that milk and milk products is a necessity item in the rural sector and it is luxury item in the urban sector and the reverses in the case for meat, fish and egg in these two sectors. But clothing and durables are the luxury items in both the sectors of the state. It also noticed from Table-4.10 and 4.11 that the Engle ratios and elasticities for most of the food items like cereals, pulses and its product, edible oil are less than unity and for most of the non-food items like durables, clothing and miscellaneous items, these ratios and elasticities are greater than unity for each type of occupation households and for all households. Hence, hypothesis-2 is partially accepted.

For empirical verification of the inter-sector variation in household consumption, the Dummy Variable Interaction Model used also confirm the existence of significant inter-sector variation in the consumption of various food and non-food items except pan, tobacco and intoxicants in the state. The overall inter-sectoral variation in the consumption of milk and milk products, pulses and its producers, meat, fish and egg and all food items, fuel and light, clothing, durables (both all minor and major) and all non-food items is due to significant change in the average expenditure and marginal propensity to consume of the households in both the sectors of the state. On the other hand, the inter-sectoral variation in the consumption of cereals, edible oil and vegetables is due to significant change in the average income of the household but the variation in the consumption pattern of pulses and its products is due to significant change in marginal propensity to consume of the households in both sectors of the state. But there is no significant change in the inter-sectoral variation in consumption of pan, tobacco and intoxicants. This may be due to the facts that of under reporting of socially unacceptable consumption items like liquor, brown sugar, charas etc.

The occupational variation in the consumption pattern of rural households reveals that the expenditure on all food and non-food items except meat, fish and egg; beverages and fuel and light has shown both slope and intercept homogeneity across different occupations. The overall occupational heterogeneity in the consumption pattern for cereals, beverages and fuel and light is due to variation in intercept but for meat, fish is due to slope. It implies that the overall heterogeneity in the consumption pattern of all items except cereals, meat, fish and egg, beverages and fuel and light across different occupations is due to the variation in marginal propensity to consume and mean level of expenditure per capita. But the overall heterogeneity in the consumption pattern of meat, fish and egg over the occupations is due to variation in the marginal propensity to consume. Finally, the overall heterogeneity in the consumption of cereals, beverages and fuel and light over the occupations is due to the variation in the mean level of expenditure only. This confirms hypothesis-3 (except for pan, tobacco and intoxicants).

It is noticed that adult equivalent scales for cereals is the highest for adult females in all type of occupations except type-B occupation. These scales for pulses and its product and edible oil is found to be highest for adult females except type-B occupation household. This clearly reveals that specific and income adult equivalent consumer scales for different items of consumption vary across households of different occupation groups. The specific and income equivalent scales are the highest for adult males for the items like meat, fish and egg, vegetable, sugar and gur, beverages, pan, tobacco and intoxicants and miscellaneous items in all types of occupation households. On the other hand, for other items like fuel and light and clothing these scales are found to the highest for adults females. But for milk and milk products, these scales are the lowest for each type of occupation households. For cereals; pulses and its product and edible oil, no such definite pattern is observed in ranking adult equivalent scales for all occupation groups. Among adolescence boys and adolescence girls, these scales are generally higher for adolescence boys for most of the items of consumption in all occupation groups and also for all households. This clearly indicates that for some items, the adult equivalent scales are the height for adult males and for some other items these scales are highest for adult females and for all items except milk and milk products, these scales are the lowest for the children (0-14 years). One interesting feature of the income adult equivalent scales are that these scales are the highest for adult males followed by adult females then by adolescent boys, and girls (13-18 years) then by boys and girls (5-12 years) and finally by children. So, these scales are arranged in a descending order from adult male to children except in occupation type-B where this scale is the highest for adult females. This clearly reveals that hypothesis-4 is partially accepted.

In chapter-V, the summary information and the inequality estimates reveals that the inequality in the distribution of household total consumption expenditure is the highest for type-A occupation households (Gini = 0.3862) and the second highest among the type-C occupation households. The Lorenz curve for type-B and type-C occupations almost coincide both on the lower and upper side of the distribution with slightly bulging out from the Lorenz curve of the type-B occupation households. Hence, there is no ambiguity in ranking the occupation distribution. The Gini coefficient is the lowest for type-D occupation households. All other measures of inequality provide the same ranking to the occupational distribution of MPCE. The estimates of the measures like Theils measure (both entropy and second measure), squared coefficient of variation, relative mean deviation, Kondor inequality indices also provides highest values for type-A occupation households, the second highest value to type-C occupation which is then followed by type-B and the lowest value to type-D occupation households. This is also evident from the Lorenz curves of the four occupational distributions. The estimate of Theils entropy and second measures are very close to each other. The relative mean deviation (RMD) and Kondor index provides the same ranking of inequality to these four occupation distributions. The Atkinson's inequality indices for different value of the inequality aversion parameter also provide the same ranking of inequality among the four occupation categories. This clearly confirms hypothesis-5.

The distribution of per capita consumption expenditure overstates the degree of inequality among individuals in all occupation categories except type-A occupation households. When households are taken as the relevant units, the distribution of per capita consumption expenditure is found to overstate the degree of inequality only in type-D occupation households. It, thus, follows that the distribution of household consumption expenditure, if not adjusted for household size and consumption effect, is likely to over/under estimate the extent of true inequalities among households. The bias could be on either side. The contribution of occupational factor to per equivalent adult consumption expenditure inequality among adults is about 22 per cent in the rural sector. The distribution of household consumption expenditure which do not take into account for effects of household composition are likely to provide biased estimates of the contribution of occupational factors to overall inequality. The empirical findings on the ranking of households by per equivalent adult consumption expenditure (MPUE) are differing significantly from the ranking by monthly per capita consumption expenditure (MPCE) in each occupation group. This implies that many households classified as poor according to the criterion of MPCE will not be so classified by the criterion of MPUE. Hence, the estimates of absolute poverty based on monthly per capita consumption expenditure distribution would be erroneous. Hence, hypothesis-6 is rejected.

An occupation-wise analysis of poverty measures indicates that the incidence of poverty is the highest i.e. 63 per cent and 65 per cent for the type-D occupation households and it is the lowest i.e. 29 per cent and 32 per cent in terms of per capita and per unit respectively for the type-A occupation households. The overall incidence is 52 per cent and 55 per cent in term of per capita and per unit respectively. The poverty intensity ratio is very high for the type-D occupation households and it is little less for the type-A occupation households. The poverty gap index which reflects the depth of poverty is also the highest for the type-D occupation households and lowest for the type-A occupation households both in term of per capita and per unit. The relevant results of Sen, FGT and Takayama measures are presented in Table-6.15. The figures in the table indicates that the severity of poverty is found to be the highest for the type-D occupation households and the lowest for the type-A occupation households both in terms of per capita and per unit. It provides a conflicting picture for type-B and type-C occupation households. In per capita terms, the severity of poverty for type-C occupation households is relatively higher than type-B occupation households. But it is reversed when measured in per unit terms. The Gini coefficient of inequality (Gp) which reflects the income distribution of the poor is the highest for type-A occupation households, and the lowest for type-B occupation households in terms of per capita and for type-D occupation households in term of per unit. Hence, Hypothesis-7 is accepted.

The relevant results of Sen and FGT measures indicates that the severity of poverty is found to be the highest for the type-D occupation households and the lowest for the type-A occupation households both in terms of per capita and per unit. It provides a conflicting picture for type-B and type-C occupation households. In per capita terms, the severity of poverty for type-C occupation households is relatively higher than type-B occupation households. But it is reversed when measured in per unit terms. Hypothesis-8 is accepted as per FGT measures (Table-6.8) and rejected as per other recent measures. Since the FGT measures are better and popular measures of poverty we accept this hypothesis.

# BIBLIOGRAPHY

Ahluwalia, M.S., (1978): 'Rural Poverty and Agricultural Performance in India', *Journal of Development Studies*, Vol. 14.

Ahluwalia, M.S., N. G. Carter and H.B. Cherery (1979): 'Growth and Poverty in Developing Countries', *Journal of Development Economics*, Vol. 6.

Ahluwalia, Monteks (1986): 'Rural Poverty, Agricultural Production and Prices: A re-examination', *Agricultural Change and Rural Poverty* (eds.), John W. Mellor and Gunvart M. Desai, Oxford University Press, New Delhi, pp. 59-75.

Ahluwalia, M.S., (1976), Inequality, Poverty and Development, *Journal of Development Economics*, Vol. 13.

Anand, S and Kanbur, S.M.R. (1993a): 'The Kuznets Process and the Inequality-development Relationship', *Journal of Development Economics*, Vol. 40.

Atkinson, A.B., (1987): 'On the Measurement of Poverty', *Econometrica*, Vol. 55, pp. 749-64.

Balakrishna, S., (1981): 'Incidence of Rural Poverty in Recent Years', *Behavioural Science and Economic Development*, Vol. 3, No. 1.

Bardhan, P., (1971): 'On the Minimum Level of Living and the Rural Poor: A Further Note', *Indian Economic Review*, Vol. 6.

Bardhan, P.K, (1970): 'On the Minimum Level of Living and the Rural Poor', *Indian Economic Review,* Vol. 5.

Bardhan, P.K., (1973): 'On the Incidence of Rural Poverty in Rural India in the Sixties', *Economic and Political Weekly* (Annual Number), February.

Barten, A.P., (1968): 'Estimating Demand Equations', *Econometrica,* Vol. 36, No. 2, pp. 213-51.

Batchelder, A.B., (1971): *The Economics of Poverty,* Wiley, New York.

Benus, J.J., Kmenta, and H. Shapiro (1976): The Dynamics of Household Budget Allocation to Food Expenditurers, *Indian Economic Review,* and Statistics, vol. LVIII, No. 2.

Berg, A. D., (1968): 'Malnutrition and National Development', *American Economic Review,* Vol. 12, No. 2, pp. 27-38.

Bhalla, Surjit S., (2003): 'Recounting the Poor: Poverty in India, 1983-99', *Economic and Political Weekly,* Vol. XXXVIII, No. 4, January.

Bhatia, B. M., (1967): *Famines in India: A Study of Some Aspects of the Economic History of India (1960-1965),* Asia Publishing House, London.

Bhatt, Anil (1990): *Poverty, Tribals and Developments: A Rehabilitation Approach,* Monohar Publication, New Delhi.

Bhattacharya, N., (1963): 'On Some Variable Elasticity Engel Curve Forms', *Sankhya Series,* Vol. B26, pp. 1-16

Bhatty, I.Z., (1974): 'Inequality and Poverty in Rural India', Vaidyanathan, A., (1974): Some Aspects of Inequalities in Living Standards in Rural India, in *Poverty and Income Distribution in India,* in T.N. Srinivasan and P.K. Bardhan (ed.), Statistical Publishing Society, Calcutta, pp. 291-336.

Brahmamurty, M.R. and Mitra, Anup (2003): *'Economic Growth, Poverty and Reforms in India'*, A Decomposition Analysis Based on State Level Data, Final Report of SANEI Round (VI), Sponsored project, March 2005.

Blackorby, C. and D. Davidson (1980): 'Ethical Indices for the Measurement of Poverty', *Econometrica,* Vol. 48.

Blaylock, J. R. and D. M. Smallwood (1982): 'Analysis of Income and Food Expenditure Distribution: A Flexible Approach', *Review of Economic Statistics,* Vol. 64, No. 1, pp. 104-109.

Blundell, R. W., (1980): 'Estimating Continuous Consumer Equivalence Scales in an Expenditure Model with Labour Supply', *European Economic Review,* Vol. 14, pp. 145-57.

Brown, J. A. C., (1954): 'Consumption of Food in Relation to Household Composition and Income', *Econometrica,* Vol. 22, pp. 444-60.

Brown, M. G. and S.R. Johnson (1984): 'Equivalent Scales and Scale Economics and Food Stamp Allotments: Estimation from the Nation-wide Food Consumption Survey, 1977-78', *American Journal of Agricultural Economics,* Vol. 66, No. 3, pp. 286-93.

Buse, R.C. and L. E Salathe (1978): 'Adult Equivalent Scales: An Alternative Approach', *American Journal of Agricultural Economics,* Vol. 60, pp. 460-68.

Chandra, A. K., (1977): *'Challenges of Tribal Poverty—A Case Study of Rural Indebteness and Credit Institution'*, Quarterly Journal of Lal Bahadur Sastri National Academy of Administration, Government of India, Vol. XXII, No. 1.

Chatterjee, G.S., Sankar, D., and Paul, G., (1963): *'A Preliminary Study on the Dietary Levels of Households in Rural India'*, Working Paper (mimeo), Indian Statistical Institute.

Clerk, S. R. Hemming and D. Ulph (1981): 'On Indices for the Measurement of Poverty', *Economic Journal,* Vol. 91.

Coondoo, D., (1969); 'The Effect of Relative Prices on Engel Elasticity of Cereals in India', *Anthaniti,* Vol. 12.

Dandekar, V. M. and N. Rath (1971): *'Poverty in India'*, Indian School of Political Economy, Poona.

Dandekar, V. M., (1981): 'On Measurement of Poverty', *Economic and Political Weekly,* Vol. 25.

Das, S.K. and Baura, A. (1996): 'Regional Inequality, Economic Growth and Liberalisation: A Study of the Indian Economy', *Journal of Development Studies,* Vol. 32, No. 3, pp. 364-390.

Deaton, A. (2003): 'Prices and Poverty in India, 1987-2000', *Economic and Political Weekly,* Vol. XXXVIII, No. 4, January.

Deaton, A. S. and Anne Case (1987): 'Analysis of Household Expenditure, Living Standards Measurements Study', Working Paper No. 28, The World Bank, Washington D.C., USA.

Deaton, A., (2003): 'Adjusted Indian Poverty Estimates for 1999-2000', *Economic and Political Weekly,* Vol. XXXVIII, No. 4, January.

Deepaklal, (1976): 'Agricultural Growth, Real Wages and Rural Poor in India', *Economic and Political Weekly,* June 26, pp. A47-A61.

Daeton, A. and Dreze, J. (2002): 'Poverty and Inequality in India: A Re-examination', *Economic and Political Weekly,* September 7.

Dreze, J and A. Sen (1990): *The Political Economy of Hunger,* (3 Vols.), Oxford Clarendor Press.

Dutt, G., Kozel, V., and Ravallian, M., (2003): 'A Model-based Assessment of India's Progress in Reducing Poverty in the 1990s', *Economic and Political Weekly,* Vol. XXXVIII, No. 4, January.

Dutta Roy, Choudhury, U. (1993): *'Inter-state Variations in Economic Development and Standard of Living'*, National Institute of Public Finance and Policies, New Delhi.

Dutta, B.C., (1980): 'Inter-sectoral Disparties and Income Distribution in India: 1960-61 to 1973-74', *Indian Economic Review,* Vol. 15.

Dutta, B.C. (1994): 'Poverty in India: Trends, Determinants and Policy Issues', Discussion Paper No. 94-16, Indian Statistical Institute, New Delhi.

EPW Research Foundation (1997): *National Accounts Statistics of India,* 1950-51 to 1995-96, Revised Edition, Mumbai.

Foster, J. and A. F. Shorrocks (1991): 'Sub-group Consistent Poverty Indices', *Econometrica,* Vol. 59.

Foster, J., (1984): 'On Economic Poverty: A Survey of Aggregate Measures', *Advances in Econometrics,* Vol. 3.

Foster, J., J. Greer and E. Thorbecke (1981): '*A Class of Decomposable Poverty Measures*', Working Paper No. 243, Department of Economics, Cornell University.

Foster, J., J. Greer and E. Thorbecke (1984): 'On the Class of Decomposable Poverty Measures', *Econometrica,* Vol. 52, pp. 761-766.

Gadgil, D.R., (1945): Poona: *A Socio-economic Survey, Part-1,* Gokhale Institute of Political and Economics Publication No. 12.

Gopalan, C., Rama Sastri, B.V., and Balasubramanian (1971): *The Nutritive Value of Indian Foods,* Indian Council of Medical Research, Hyderabad.

Gopalan, C., Rama Sastri, B.V., and Balasubramanian (1980): *Nutritive Value of Indian foods,* National Institute of Nutrition, Indian Council of Medical Research, Hyderabad, p. 29.

Government of India (1973): Draft Fifth Five Year plan, 1974-79, Part I, Planning Commission, New Delhi.

Government of India (1974): Perspective of Development: 1961-76, Implications of Planning for Minimum Level of Living, in Srinivasn T.N. and Bardhan, P.K. (eds), *Poverty and Income Distribution in India,* Statistical Publishing Society, Clacutta.

Government of India (1981a): *A Technical Note on the Sixth Five Year Plan of India,* Planning Commission, New Delhi.

Government of India (1982): *Report of the Expert Group on Programmes for Alleviation of Poverty,* Planning Commission, New Delhi.

Government of India (1983): *National Nutrition Monitoring Bureau (1983)*: ICDS: An Assessment, Hyderabad.

Government of India (1986): *The Study Group on the Concepts and Estimation of Poverty Line,* Planning Commission, New Delhi.

Government of India (1993): *Report of the Expert Group on Estimation of Proportion and Number of the Poor*, Planning Commission, New Delhi.

Government of India, National Nutrition Monitoring Bureau (1983): ICDS: An Assessment, Hyderabad, 1983.

Government of India (1985): Report of the Working Group of Evolving an Acceptable Methodology for Identification of the Poor, Ministry of Planning, C.S.O., New Delhi, December.

Hagenaars, A., (1987): 'A Class of Poverty Indices', *International Economic Review*, Vol. 28.

Houthakkar, H. S., (1957): 'An International Comparison of Household Expenditure Patterns, Commemorating the Centenary of Engel's Law', *Econometrica*, Vol. 25, pp. 244-97.

Iyengar, N.S., Jain, L.R. and Srinivasan, T.N. (1968): 'Economics of Scale in Household Consumption: A Case Study', *Indian Economic Journal*, (Econometric Annual), Vol. 15, pp. 465-77.

Jain, L. R. K.. Sundaram and S. Tendulkar (1989): 'Levels of Living and Incidence of Poverty in Rural India: A Cross Section Analysis', *Journal of Quantative Economics*, Vol. 5.

Jodha, N.S. (1986): 'Common Property Resources and Rural Poor', *Economic and Political Weekly*, Vol. 21, 5th June.

Kakwani, N. and Pernia, E. (2000): 'What is Pro-poor Growth', *Asian Development Review*, Vol. 18, No. 1.

Kakwani, N. C. and K. Subbarao (1990): 'Rural Poverty and its Alleviation in India', *Economic and Political Weekly*, Vol. 25.

Kakwani, N. C., (1980a): *Income Inequality and Poverty: Methods of Estimation and Policy Applications*, Oxford University Press, New York.

Kakwani, N. C., (1980b): 'On a Class of Poverty Measures', *Econometrica*, Vol. 48, pp. 437-46.

Kakwani, N. C., (1984): 'Issues in Measuring Poverty', *Advances in Econometrics,* Vol. 3.

Kakwani, N. C., (1993): 'Performances of Living Standards: An Internal Comparison', *Journal of Development Economics,* Vol. 41.

Kakwani, N.C. (1977): 'Measurement of Poverty and the Negative Income Tax', *Australian Economic Papers,* Vol. 16, pp. 237-48.

Kravis, I. B. (1960): 'International Differences in the Distributions of Income', *Review of Economics and Statistics,* November.

Krishnamurty, K. S., (1990): *Poverty and Income Distribution,* Oxford University Press (ed.), Bombay.

Kundu, A. (1981): 'Measurement of poverty – Some Conceptual issues', *Anvesak,* Vol. 11, pp. 80-96.

Kundu, A. and T. E. Smith (1983): 'An Impossibility Theorem on Poverty Indices', *International Economic Review,* Vol. 24.

Kuznets, Simon (1955): 'Economic Growth and Income Inequality', *American Economic Review,* March, p. 18.

Lamm, R.M. Jr. (1982): 'A System of Demonic Demand Functions for Food', *Applied Economics,* Vol. 14, No. 4, pp. 375-89.

Lewis, G.W. and D.T. Ulph (1988): 'Poverty, Inequality and Welfare', *Economic Journal,* Vol. 98.

Lipton, M. and M. Ravallion (1993): 'Poverty and Policy', Working Paper Series, No. 1130, World Bank Washington, D.C.,.

Liviatan, N. (1961): 'Errors in Variables and Engel Curve Analysis', *Econometrica,* Vol. 29, pp. 336-62.

Lydall, H.F. (1960): 'The Inequality of Indian Incomes', *Economic and Political Weekly,* Special Number, June, pp. 873-874.

Madalgi, S.S., (1971): 'Poverty in India- A Comment', *Economic and Political Weekly,* February 20.

Mahendra, Dev. S. (1988): 'Regional Disparities in Agricultural Labour Productivity and Rural Poverty in India', *The Indian Economic Review,* Vol. 23, No. 2 (July – Sept. 1988), pp. 167-205.

Mahendra, Dev. S (1992): 'Rural Poverty of India: Incidence, Issues and Policies', *Asian Development Review,* Vol. 10, No. 1.

Majumdar, R.C., Roychoudhury, B.C., and Dutta, K., (1967): *An Advanced History of India,* Macmillan Publisher, London.

Mehta, A.K. and Shah, A (2003): 'Chronic Poverty in India: Incidence, Causes and Policies', *World Development,* Vol. 31, No. 3, pp. 491-511.

Minhas, B.S. (1971): 'Rural Poverty and the Minimum Level of Living', *Indian Economic Review,* Vol. 6.

Minhas, B.S., (1970): 'Rural Poverty, Land Redistribution and Development', *Indian Economic Review,* Vol. V, No. 1, April; Reprinted in Sankhya, Series C, Vol. 36, 1974, pp. 252-263.

Mohalannobis, P.C. (1960): 'A Method of Futile Graphical Analysis', *Econometrica,* Vol. 28, pp. 325-351.

Morris, M.D. (1979): *Measuring the Condition of the World's Poor: The Physical Quality of Life Index,* Pergamon Press, Oxford.

Muellbauer, J. (1980): 'The Estimation of the Prais – Houthakker Model of Equivalence Scales', *Econometrica,* Vol. 48, No. I, pp. 153-76.

Mukharjee, M., (1969): *National Income of India, Trends and Structure,* Statistical Publishing Society, Calcutta, p. 83.

Mukherjee, M, N. Bhattacharya and G.S. Chatterjee (1972): 'Poverty in India: Measurement and Amelioration', *Commerce,* Vol. 125.

Mukherjee, M.M. and Ghosh, A.K. (1951): 'The Pattern of Income and Expenditure in the Indian Union—A Tentative Study', Bulletin of the International Statistical Institute, Vol. XXXII, Part-II, International Statistical Conference, India.

Mukherjee, M., (1969): 'Size and Aerial Distribution of the Levels of Living in India', *Sankhya Series B,* Vol. 31, Parts 3 and 4., pp. 459-478.

Mukhopadhya, R. (1987): 'A Study of Regional Patterns on Consumer Patterns in Rural India', *Journal of Quantative Economics,* Vol. 3, No. 1, pp. 117-36.

Nicholson, R.J., (1967): The Distribution of Personal Income, *Lloyds Bank Review*, January, London.

Ojha, P.D. (1970): 'A configuration of Indian Poverty, Inequality and Levels of Living', *Reserve Bank of India Bulletin*, January.

Ojha, P.D. (1970): 'A Configuration of Indian Poverty: Inequality and Levels of Living', *Reserve Bank of India Bulletin*, January.

Oshima, Harry T., (1962): 'The International Comparison of Size Distribution of Family Incomes, with Special Reference to Asia', *Review of Economics and Statistics*, November, pp. 39-445.

Osmani, S.R. (ed.) (1992): *Nutrition and Poverty*, Clarendon Press, Oxford.

Pal, Satya (1989): *Inequality, Poverty and Consumption*, Common Publishers, New Delhi.

Panda, B.K. (1996): 'Consumption Pattern in Orissa: An Econometric Analysis', (Unpublished Ph.D. Thesis), Department of Economics, Berhampur University, Bhanjabihar, Orissa.

Panda, B.K., and Sarangi, P., (2004): 'Incidence of Poverty Among the Tribals in Orissa: An Empirical Analysis', *Studies in History and Culture*, Vol. 9, No. 2, September.

Panikar, P.G.K., (1972): 'Economics of Nutrition', *Economic and Political Weekly*, Annual number, February, pp. 413-430.

Paul, S. (1985): 'On the Estimation of Continuous Equivalent Scales', *Indian Economic Review*, Vol. 620, No. 1, pp. 117-42.

Pradhan, A.K. (2003): 'Socio-economic Development of Juanga of Keonjhar District in Orissa', (Unpublished Ph.D. Thesis) Submitted to Department of Economics, Berhampur University, Bhanjabihar, Orissa.

Pradhan, N.B. (1979): 'Economic Backwardness and Development of Orissa', (Ph.D. Thesis Unpublished), Submitted to Department of Economics, Berhampur University, Orissa.

Pradhan, N.B., Panda, B.K. and Sarangi, P., (2005): Dynamics of Poverty and Underdevelopment in Orissa, *Vision*, Vol. XXV, No. 1-2, July-September.

Pyatt, G. (1987): 'Measuring Welfare, Poverty and Inequality', *Economic Journal*, Vol. 97.

Radha Krishna, R. and Misra, G.K. (1970): 'A Regional Approach to the Consumption Pattern in India', *Arthvijnon*, Vol. 12, pp. 523-63.

Radhakrishna, R. and Sharma, Atul (1976): 'Inflation and Disparities in Level of Living', *Indian Economic Journal*, April-July, pp. 364-373.

Rajaraman, Indira, (1975): 'Poverty, Inequality and Economic Growth: Rural Punjab 1960-61 to 1970-71', *Journal of Development Studies*, Vol. II, No. 4, July, pp. 278-289.

Rao, B. Sarveswara and V.N. Deshpande. (1982): *Poverty: An Interdisciplinary Approach*, Published for Madras Institute of Development Studies, Madras by Somaiya Publications Pvt. Ltd., Madras.

Rao, V.K.R.V., (1973): *An Essay in India's National Income*, George Allen and Unwin Ltd., London, 1938, p. 22.

Ravallion, M. (1988): 'Expected Poverty Under Risk-induced Welfare Variability', *Economic Journal*, Vol. 98, pp. 1171-82.

Ravallion, M. (1992): 'Poverty Comparison – A Guide to Concepts and Methods, Living Standard Measurement', Study of Working Paper No. 88, World Bank, Washington D.C.

Rowntree, S. (1901): *Poverty: A Study of Town Life*, Macmillan Publication, London.

Roy, J. and Dhar, S.K. (1960): 'A Study on the Pattern of Consumer Expenditure in Rural and Urban India', *Studies on Consumer Behaviour*, A. Ganguly (ed.), Asian Publishing House, Bombay.

Rudra, A. (1974): '*Minimum Levels of Living – A Statistical Examination*', in Srinivasan and Bardhan (eds).

Sarangi, P. (2004): *Consumption and Poverty in Orissa: An Econometric Analysis,* M.Phil (unpublished) Dissertation Submitted to Berhampur University, Orissa.

Sastry, S.A.R. (1980): 'A Study of Literature on Poverty, Income Distribution and Development', *Antha Vijnane,* March, Vol. 22, No. 1.

Sen, A. (1973): 'Poverty, Inequality and Unemployment: Some Conceptual Issues in Measurement', *Economic and Political Weekly,* Special Number, August.

Sen, A. (1979): 'Issues in the Measurement of Poverty', Scandinavian *Journal of Economics,* Vol. 81, pp. 285-307.

Sen, A.K. (1981): *Poverty and Famines: An Essay on Entitlement and Deprivation,* Clarendon Press, Oxford.

Sen, A.K. (1984): 'Family and Food: Sex Bios in Poverty', in A.K. Sen (ed.), *Resources, Values and Development,* Black Well, Oxford.

Sen, A.K., J. Muellbaner, R. Kanbar, K. Hart and B. Willaims (1987): *The Standard of Living,* Cambridge University Press.

Sharma, B.D. (1987): 'Measuring Poverty and Equalitarian Trends', *Journal of Social Sciences and Humanities,* Vol. 1, North Eastern Hill University.

Singh, B. (1972): 'On the Determination of Economics of Scale in Household Consumption', *International Economic Review,* Vol. 13, No. 2, pp. 257-270.

Soltwo, Lee (1965): *Towards Income Equality in Norway,* University of Wisconsin Press, Madison.

Srinivasan, T.N. and P.K. Bardhan (1974): *Poverty and Income Distribution in India.* (eds.) Statistical Publishing Society, Calcutta.

Srinivasan, T.N., P.K. Bardhan and Srinivasan, (1988): *Rural Poverty in South Asia,* Columbia University Press, New York.

Subramanian, S. (1989): 'Poverty Minimization in the Light of-Life Boat Ethics', *Journal of Quantative Economics,* Vol. 5.

Subramanian, S. (1997): *Measurement of Inequality and Poverty,* (ed.), Oxford University Press, New Delhi.

Sukhatme, P.V. and S. Margen (1980): 'Relationship Between Under Nutrition and Poverty', *Indian Economic Review,* Vol. 16.

Sukhetme, P.V., (1965): *Feeding India's Growing Millions,* Asia Publising House, Bombay.

Sundaram, K. and S.D. Tendulkar (1985): 'Anti Poverty Programmes in India: An Assessment', in S. Mukhapadhyay (ed.) *The Poor in Asia: Productivity – Raising Programmes and Strategies,* Asian and Pacific Development Centre, Kuala Lumpur.

Suryanarayana, M.H. (1995): 'Growth, Poverty and Levels of Living: Hypothesis, Methods and Policies', *Journal of the Indian School of Political Economy,* Vol. 7.

Swamy, S. (1967): 'Structural Changes and the Distributions of Income by Size: The Case of India', *Review of Income and Wealth,* Series 13, pp.155-174.

Takayama, N. (1979): 'Poverty, Income Inequality and Their Measures: Professor Sen's Axiomatic Approach Reconsidered', *Econometrica,* Vol. 47.

Tedford, J.R., Capps, O.Jr., Havlicek, J. Jr. (1986): 'Adult Equivalent Scales Once More- a Developmental Approach', *American Journal of Agricultural Economics,* Vol. 67, No. 4, pp. 322-331.

Tendulkar, S.D. and L.R. Jain (1995): 'Economic Reforms and Poverty', *Economic and Political Weekly,* Vol. 30.

Thakur, D.S., (1985): 'A Survey of Literature on Rural Poverty in India', *Margin,* April,. NCAER, New Delhi.

Thon, D. (1979): 'On Measuring Poverty', *Review of Income and Wealth,* Vol. 25.

Townsend, P. (1985): 'A Sociological Approach to the Measurement of Poverty: A Rejoinder to Prof. Amartya Sen', Oxford Economic Papers, Vol. 37.

Vaidyanathan, A., (1974): 'Some Aspects of Inequalities in Living Standards in Rural India', *Poverty and Income Distribution in India,* Statistical Publishing Society, Calcutta, pp. 215-241.

Vyas, V.S., (1972): Internation Change, Agricultural Production and Rural Poverty, *Commerce,* Vol. 19, August.

Watts, H. (1968): 'An Economic Defination of Poverty', in D.P. Moyrihan (ed.), *On Understanding Poverty,* Basic Books, New York.

Wells, J., (1974): 'Distribution of Earning, Growth and Structures of Demand in Brazil During 1960's', *World Development,* No. 1, January, pp. 9-24.

Wilkinson, R.G., (1992): 'Income Distribution and Life Expectancy', *BMJ,* Vol. 304, pp.165-168.

Wood, G.D. (2003): 'Staying Secure, Staying Poor: The Faustian Bargain', *World Development,* Vol. 31, No. 3, pp. 455-471.

World Bank (1986): *Poverty and Hunger: Issues and Options for Food Security in Developing Countries,* D.C. World Bank, Washington.

World Bank (2000). *World Development Report 2000/2001: Attaking Poverty.* Oxford University Press, Oxford.

Zubrigg, S. (1983): 'Ideology and the Poverty Line Debates', *Economic and Political Weekly,* Vol. 18.

# INDEX

## N



## O



## P